CARFREE CITIES

Venice, 1997

CARFREE CITIES

J.H. CRAWFORD

FOREWORD
JAMES HOWARD KUNSTLER

GRAPHICS
ARIN VERNER

UTRECHT

INTERNATIONAL BOOKS

2002

Dedication
I dedicate this book to my parents
Ann and Vance Crawford

Colophon
Book design & typography by J.H. Crawford
Drawings & photo retouch by Arin Verner
Cover by Karel Oosting
Body text: Monotype Bembo
Marginalia: Helvetica Light
Printed in the Netherlands by
Drukkerij Giethoorn Ten Brink

J.H. Crawford
http://www.carfree.com/
mailbox@carfree.com

Permissions
Drawings and quotations taken from
A Pattern Language by Christopher Alexander,
copyright ©1977 by Christopher Alexander.
Used by permission of Oxford University Press.

Notices
Published by International Books
Alexander Numankade 17
3572 KP Utrecht
The Netherlands
+31 30 273 1840
fax +31 30 273 3614
E-mail: i-books@antenna.nl
First hardcover edition March 2000
2004 2003 2002   ISBN 90 5727 042 0   2 3 4 5 6 7 8

CONTENTS

Foreword 7

Preface 17

Introduction 21

PART I
ON CITIES

Yardsticks for Cities 37

Cities & Transport 53

Wicked Cars 69

Better Public Transport 85

Sustainable Cities 109

PART II
CARFREE CITIES

Design Parameters 125

City Topology 131

City Districts 143

City Blocks 153

Buildings 161

Passenger Transport 173

Freight Delivery 195

PART III
GOING CARFREE

Support for Carfree Cities 225

Planning Carfree Cities 247

Some Modest Proposals 279

Afterword 287

APPENDICES

Resources at Carfree.com   291
The Bicycle City   293
The Auto-Centric Carfree City   295
Bibliography   297
Illustrations   305
Index   309
Conversion Tables   323
The Author   324

FOREWORD

James Howard Kunstler

Something momentous and rather sinister happened in the United States in the second half of the 20th century: we transformed our lovely New World landscape, and virtually all our townscapes, into an immense, uniform automobile slum, from sea to shining sea. In the process, we created an everyday environment that is ecologically catastrophic, economically futureless, socially poisonous, and spiritually degrading. We Americans like to think of ourselves as the avatars of progress. Fittingly, we have demonstrated that the national automobile slum is a failed experiment in human ecology, and now we must move on to create a better living arrangement.

We didn't mean it to work out this way—but then the law of unintended consequences is always cruelest to the well-intentioned. We meant to construct an automobile utopia—a drive-in civilization of perfect comfort and ease—and it became instead "the fiasco of suburbia," in Léon Krier's apt phrase, a disaggregated wasteland of shrieking signage, throwaway architecture, and impoverished public space. Americans also have short attention spans, and so it is bitterly ironic that this enormous fiasco was inaugurated in the wake of the "City Beautiful" movement (roughly 1890-1918), a great patriotic effort to pull together the architecture and civic design of our nation in order to make our towns and cities worthy of what had suddenly, by the 1890s, become a great and powerful nation. The brief, bright era of the City Beautiful movement (sometimes called "American Renaissance") gave us our most beloved public places—from the Copley Square library in Boston to the San Francisco Civic

Center. But at the height of this era, Henry Ford perfected his Model T in a greasy Detroit workshop, and as soon as the terrible bother of World War One was concluded, America dropped the City Beautiful cold and embarked, with all our stupendous wealth, energy, and ingenuity, on a new campaign to retrofit every town, big and small, and all the countryside in between, for the accommodation of cars. By the eve of World War Two, we had accomplished the astounding feat of making all our cities look like the inventory yard of Henry Ford's greasy workshop.

After World War Two, we resumed this operation with mad glee and an inflated sense of entitlement on account of having won such a decisive victory against the forces of manifest wickedness. We built the colossal Interstate highway system—including freeways through most city centers—and laid the armature for the ghastly explosion of suburban tract housing, shopping centers, franchise food sheds, and other accessories of the vaunted "world's highest standard of living" that ensued. And here we are, stuck with it all, at a time when ominous currents of world economic and political change suggest that we cannot possibly continue this mode of living.

Now, a few points must be emphasized if anyone—particularly a non-American—might understand why we undertook this foolish campaign. One is that, the City Beautiful movement aside, American cities were never very nice. They were products of the industrial age, which was itself an economic and cultural experiment—something that the world had never seen before. American cities rapidly achieved a monstrous scale, and life within them assumed the flavor of an industrial nightmare. In fact, as soon as the railroad—the very herald of industrialism—came along in the 1850s, we got the first modern suburbs. They symbolized the impulse to flee the industrial city for its supposed antidote: country life. And indeed, for a few decades this kind of romantic railroad suburb composed of "picturesque villas," as they were advertised, probably was a lovely place to live for the fortunate few who could manage it. But city life itself in America just kept getting steadily worse, more de-natured, more oppressive in scale, more dominated by machines, noisier, smellier, more crowded, while it less and less embodied a setting for civilized human relations. The City Beautiful movement had been an organized attempt to correct all that, and, despite its signal achievements, must be considered a failure in the long run. Americans' disdain for cities persisted through the 20th century. Indeed, it only became more severe.

The automobile democratized suburbia and, from 1918 on, escaping the dreariness of the cities became the goal of the broad middle class. The business activity generated by this wish drove the boom of the 1920s. But following the Great Depression and World War Two, American cities reached a really singular apogee of horribleness, and then everybody who could get out did get out. All classes except the most improvident, oppressed, and inept vacated the city. The suburban house received its iconic designation as the "American Dream." Unfortunately, in the very process of democratizing suburbia, and of scattering the components of everyday life across every cornfield and cow-pasture, the suburbs lost the very bucolic qualities that they were created for in the first place. They steadily mutated into a cartoon of life in the country, a ridiculous abstraction of a place to live, a new wilderness of joyless vistas and free parking: the national automobile slum.

Which brings us up-to-date to the current American pre-dicament at the turn of the 21st century. We have created too many places that are not worth caring about and not worth living in, and before long (if not already) they will add up to a civilization that is not worth carrying on.

That the rest of the world, Europe in particular, has not wholeheartedly aped our behavior and trashed their cities is a fortunate thing, because we are going to need alternate models for assembling a human ecology that is worth living in, and Europe still has many excellent examples we can learn from. Personally, I feel that the future is going to require us to live differently, whether we like automobile-centered living or not, and that economic, political, and ecological forces are already underway that will compel us to change our behavior. I believe these forces will prompt us to recondense everyday life into the ecological community known as the town or city, a place that offers real spiritual rewards to its inhabitants, as well as a sound economic and social framework. There is no question that the role of the automobile will have to be reduced, perhaps even eliminated, within the organism of the city.

I have a vivid memory of living for a few years in just such a place in America. It was called a college campus integrated within a classic Main Street town. While it represents a special type of community, it had the form and capacity to provide physical places to work, sleep, eat, shop, and socialize that an ideal human ecology calls for, and it was possible to live there very pleasantly without a car. It was cognitively legible, fine-grained in scale, and possible to know intimately. Its chief axes—Main Street and the transecting spine of the campus—provided reassuring orientation. One went about on foot in places that were deliberately scaled to pedestrians. One might walk miles in a day without ever leaving the campus.

For many Americans, the college campus may be the

closest they will ever come to experiencing the living organism of a real town. I say living organism because an authentic town, like a body, adds up to more than the sum of its parts—the extra part being expressed as the spark of life. Also like a body, a living town contains the organs that sustain life: the commercial organs (shops and businesses), the cultural organs (school, library, theaters, etc.), the domestic organs (houses), and the civic organs (town hall, police station). In Europe, it is always astonishing for an American to discover that even small provincial cities like Perugia in Italy or Toulouse in France possess more civic vitality and cultural amenity than Cleveland, Detroit, Nashville, and St. Louis combined. The explanation is simple: even small European cities maintain healthy organs, while in all American towns the organs have become disaggregated and sclerotic.

I have a hunch about life in the 21st century—assuming that we survive potential cataclysms such as nuclear terrorism, global climate change, and drug-resistant epidemics, or perhaps because of them! I believe it will be the era of staying in place. I mean that literally: that the need for travel may decrease dramatically because we will do such a better job of creating towns and cities that our needs will be satisfied within the boundary of where we dwell. I'm not suggesting that people ought not to go anywhere. Even under ideal circumstances that would be ridiculous. But the rate of travel in America today is itself ridiculous. Outside my office window, on the main street of a small upstate New York town at two-thirty in the afternoon, there is a crush of cars and trucks (including many 18-wheelers) that would look to someone from our great-grandfathers' generation like a mass evacuation in wartime, and it is like this every day! Where are they all going? Well, most of the motorists (one to each car) are shopping, driving to the asteroid belt of highway strip malls and enclosed malls and national chain "power centers" and other such provisional, opportunistic agents of the corporate colonialism that has taken over in recent years and put to death the local merchants and their businesses.

For one thing, I am convinced that this way of doing business has poor long-term prospects. The global forces I alluded to earlier will have the more generalized effect of making us reduce the scale of virtually all our activities. Systems like national chain store retail, which have reached absurd economies of scale in recent decades (due to the abnormal stability of global oil prices and supplies), will not have the agility to adapt to the coming era of instability. Likewise, the system of large-scale central schools in America is demonstrably failing and already faces drastic reform. I believe that the scale of most everything will necessarily be reduced in the decades ahead.

The gigantic industrial city may also be a thing of the past. I am not proposing the end of cities, just that they, too, will be necessarily subject to the general downscaling of things in the years ahead. Personally, I believe that even cities like New York and London will benefit from downscaling. Certainly small cities and towns will benefit hugely, as their size makes them suitable again for normal life. I believe that a major element of this process of downscaling the cities, and what goes on inside them, will be the decreased volume of transport. Some of this may be ecologically driven. For instance, the prospects for continuing giant-scale industrialized agriculture in America are not good. If nothing else, we are ruining our farmland with irrigation and chemicals. It may not be possible fifty years from now to truck the components of every Caesar salad an average of 1800 miles, as we do today. There may be no such thing as highway chain restaurants or even supermarkets in the years ahead. More likely than not, the entire system will be have to be reorganized in ways that may surprise us. Local farming and value-added production may have to become more localized in an era of expensive oil and climate change. In any case, all of these changes would reduce the scale and volume of long-haul trucking.

A similar case could be made for ordinary merchandising. In America over the past fifty years, citizens have been shanghaied into becoming their own wholesale delivery system for companies that maintain colossal "stores" that are really just dressed-up warehouses. This has been a terrific boon to the retailers. The citizens are tricked into believing that they've bought at a discount, without figuring in the time and psychological abuse that the system costs them. The mere task of schlepping around between one and another of these Big Boxes has become such a grotesque ordeal for the average person navigating the eight-lane "collector" avenues of suburbia that there is not enough Prozac in the universe to ease their collective depression and anxiety. The Internet and catalog shopping are already providing relief. Just order the damn thing and let them deliver it. What an idea! It may be true that the customer likes to finger the merchandise, but in the coming world of a pedestrian-scaled city, the customer may be able to walk to the store, touch everything he pleases, and take delivery at home later.

Now a reader might make the inference that the streets would still be clogged with vehicles making deliveries. Not so, I maintain from my own experience. I grew up on the east side of Manhattan, in a neighborhood of fifteen to thirty story apartment buildings, about as dense as it gets in the urban western world. Everybody who lived there needed groceries and the overwhelming majority depended on small grocers, butchers, and bakers who distributed their stuff by means of bicycles with large cargo bins. For all this tremendous volume of business, there was never any sense of the street being overwhelmed by delivery bikes. Far from it, they just blended into the background of the normal streetscape. I think this is the kind of thing we might expect of the city in the future, and we will be happier people when it becomes the general rule.

No reasonable, reflective person who has looked a little bit into the issue can doubt that world oil production presents a gloomy picture in the long term. Virtually all the credible authorities say that peak world production will be reached in the first decade of the next century. This means the end of the cheap oil era and the beginning of the expensive oil era. It means that of all the oil under the earth's crust, we've extracted the easy half, and the remainder is either difficult or too costly to get. It is generally assumed, however, that when oil becomes a problem, "they" will "come up with" a replacement for it, say, the hydrogen fuel cell. It may be so, but I would propose that it also may not be so, or perhaps not in a way that is exactly the equivalent of what we've been running on. If these alternate fuels are not absolutely as cheap as petroleum, then there will be a new and larger class of people who will not be able to drive everywhere—and unless motoring remains utterly democratic, then mass car ownership and mass motoring will not be a feature of everyday life in the future. A politics of resentment will place the massive subsidies in jeopardy, and then motoring will go out the way it came in: as a luxury only for the very well off.

Rather than feel that something has been taken away from us, we would be wiser to see that something may be given back to us: a place to live and work in that we really love and care about and want to be in, and want to stay in, and don't feel compelled to flee from. Whatever happens to cars, or the system for deploying them, I'm confident that we will be able to get around when we have to. But I'm much more excited about living in a place at least as rewarding as my college campus was thirty-five years ago: a compact community full of cultural and social amenity, well-connected to real countryside, economically sane and sustainable, and vested with a true sense of having a future.

This is the subject of J.H. Crawford's brave treatise on Carfree Cities. Today the idea will probably be greeted with ridicule. Tomorrow, the forces of the status quo will fight against it bitterly. The day after tomorrow it will be accepted by the public as self-evidently the sanest path we could possibly choose.

I first met Mr. Crawford in Amsterdam, Holland, in the late 1990s. Both of us were, well, obsessed with these matters of the contemporary human habitat. I had published a couple of books criticizing the existing situation in America, and he was composing the first of many drafts of *Carfree Cities* from the perspective of an American in Europe. I was associated with the New Urbanist movement in America, and he was arriving at many of the same basic conclusions in his work on the future of cities, for instance, the idea that city life is indispensable to civilization in the first place. Amsterdam could not have been a better place for him to work on this— a city of surpassing charm and loveliness, which had done as much as any place on earth to take back the public realm from the car and return it to us humans.

Carfree cities is as epochal a proposition as the idea put forward by Louis Napoleon in 1851 that cities could be made sanitary and safe for public health. We should all be impressed by the need for urgency. A great idea is at hand: that human beings deserve to live in a better place than the universal car slum. The sooner we embark on this program, the sooner we will be able to say that our culture has a future.

James Howard Kunstler is the author of many books, among them: *The City in Mind: Notes on the Urban Condition; The Geography of Nowhere: The Rise and Decline of America's Man-Made Landscape;* and *Home From Nowhere: Remaking Our Everyday World for the Twenty-First Century,* all from Simon & Schuster.

Venice, 1997

Venice from the Campanile on a foggy day in 1997

PREFACE

I have been fascinated by transport in all forms ever since I was a small child, but it was years before I understood that transport systems exert a powerful influence on the quality of our daily lives. The conviction that urban cars and trucks are wrecking global ecosystems and destroying our communities finally drove me to develop a design for carfree cities and then to write this book.

It was in 1987 that I first asked: are carfree cities possible? I began to explore a variety of design concepts. Several trips to Venice introduced me to the delights of carfree city life, and this further stimulated my thinking. This book answers my question: yes, carfree cities are indeed possible and offer an approach to building cities and urban transport systems that better serve human needs. I have developed what I believe to be a coherent strategy for making a large improvement in the quality of urban life: many of the changes I propose have effects that extend beyond transport alone.

TECHNOLOGY RUNS AMOK

For far too long, we have permitted narrow commercial interests to determine when and how new technology will be applied. Society must now take control of technology and bend it to human ends. The automobile is the most extreme example of a useful technology that has been inappropriately applied. Cars have caused severe environmental problems that will continue to worsen for decades to come, no matter what we do. This is no excuse for inaction, however: the sooner we begin to act responsibly towards the environment, the better we will be able to limit the ultimate damage. If we fail to take up the stewardship of planet Earth, we face the ruin of the only home we have ever known. While many people do not yet accept the seriousness of our plight, I believe that events in the next decade will convince even skeptics that damage to global ecosystems is a clear and present danger.

Cars and trucks make truly wretched neighbors. Among the world's cities, only carfree Venice has escaped the damage cars have done to the quality of urban life. Paradoxically, the car has actually reduced mobility in cities while at the same time saddling us with a host of dilemmas we had never anticipated. I believe that the only real solution to the vexing problems of urban automobiles lies in completely car- and truck-free cities, such as proposed in Part II of this book. Carfree cities offer a more sustainable, healthier, and happier future than any plan to "improve" the car or ameliorate its impacts. I do not doubt that cars will become more efficient, cleaner, and safer (at least for their occupants), but none of these improvements can ever restore the function of streets as social spaces. The damage of cars to community forms the foundation of my argument: urban cars are anti-human.

Village near Avignon, France, 1965
Biking along a quiet country lane is one of life's great pleasures. While I still own a bicycle, I rarely ride in Amsterdam's heavy traffic. The stoic Dutch bike all winter, but I find it unpleasant in freezing weather. Bikes play a secondary role in the design for carfree cities, but there is ample room for them.

Carfree Venice draws 12 million tourists a year, by far the most of any Italian city.
"Italy's Endangered Art"
National Geographic, August 1999

The Campo, Siena, Italy, 1998

Notes for the Reader

Citations are given in the margins, as close as possible to the material being cited. Works are cited by the author's name, with the date also given in cases where multiple works by the same author are listed in the bibliography. When reference is made to specific pages, the page range concludes the entry.

See also the supplemental information available at Carfree.com, including the City Design sub-site, extensive links, and the bimonthly *Carfree Times*, which reports on progress towards carfree cities. The site is at: http://www.carfree.com/

Besakih Temple, Bali, 1985
The most important temple in Bali, Besakih is a brilliant example of the unity of Balinese design. The temple compound itself is of course carfree, but the remote site on the flanks of towering Gunung Agung can only be reached by driving or walking long distances: cars are needed in rural areas.

Part I, "On Cities," briefly summarizes a large body of knowledge about cities, their transport systems, and sustainable urban development. I have given sources in both the bibliography and marginal notes; the serious student will need to consult many of these works.

References to *A Pattern Language*

The patterns developed by Christopher Alexander *et al.* are brilliantly described and illustrated in their book, *A Pattern Language*. The patterns are numbered from 1 to 253, and it is these numbers and the corresponding pattern names that are cited throughout this book. *A Pattern Language* is a useful adjunct to this book.

Towns and Rural Areas

This book is about cities. I have given no consideration to the problems of improving life and taming the car in small towns and rural areas. While alternatives to cars may exist in towns, I expect that they will look rather different from the solutions I propose for cities. I see no alternative to continued car use in genuinely rural areas.

Conservative Solutions

In this work, I have shied away from unproven technologies. I have proposed conservative solutions that I am confident will work, even if they might be more expensive than strictly necessary. Significant cost reductions might be attained without seriously compromising the design. For example, a tram system would probably provide adequate capacity for a city of a million people, but I have favored the metro, which definitely *does* have the necessary capacity and is faster and safer. Only careful design and engineering will reveal where savings can be made. In any case, the infrastructure for carfree cities should cost less than that needed by suburban sprawl.

Pronouns

English still lacks a comfortable gender-neutral usage. I have used the male gender to denote both sexes generally.

BEAUTY MATTERS

I believe that beauty makes our lives better. I am tired of revolting public spaces and abominable buildings. I strove to make this book a thing of beauty, because I believe that beauty serves not only its own ends but also inspires people to action. I hope, therefore, that you will find beauty in both this book and the ideas it presents.

THANKS

Writing this book has taught me that genesis of a book is a cooperative effort. I offer my thanks to all who contributed to the making of this book, and in particular to: Jan van Arkel, Jim Bannon, the Bassett/Barnes/Cowan clan, Eric Britton, Ann & Vance Crawford, Marti Frank, Joseph Geraci, Piper Hollier, Marc Allen & Lynne Kocen, James Howard Kunstler, Richard Register, Jack Risemberg, Richard Risemberg, Nikos A. Salingaros, Paul Jacques Schwartzman, Arin Verner, Brenden Verner, Zenobia Verner, Charlene M. Woodcock, and Roel Zaal. Without their help, I would never have finished this book.

J.H. Crawford
Amsterdam
6 July 2002

Certaldo Alto, Italy, 1998
I laid up here one night when I was exhausted. These peaceful, exquisite surroundings were by themselves worth half a day of rest.

Summer afternoon, Amsterdam, 1998
The dubious honor of being my host during the writing of this book goes to Amsterdam. I am at times harshly critical of conditions in this city. I would have been at least as critical of any other city and made as liberal use of local bad examples.

Piazza San Marco, Venice, 1997
The main text of this book is set in a typeface called Bembo, first cut in Venice by Francesco Griffo in 1495. Griffo was employed by Aldus Manutius, a classicist who established the Aldine Press in Venice. The books of this press helped spark the Renaissance.   Lawson, 74-77

See especially *Cities and the Wealth of Nations*

INTRODUCTION

Mankind first settled in cities about 7000 years ago, and cities have served as the cradle of civilization ever since. I believe that the future of cities is assured. Culture is hosted by cities because only cities can support great libraries, symphony orchestras, extensive theater districts, major-league sports teams, and vast museums. Cities also provide the principal setting for economic activity. Jane Jacobs believes that the wealth of nations is generated mainly by innovators located in urban areas with the broad infrastructure base needed to support the establishment of new enterprises. Innovators need a vast range of goods and services close at hand, plus, of course, good transport and communications. Only cities can provide such depth of resources.

Cities ought to be places where great buildings and lively outdoor spaces are found, which was usual until modern times. The European capitals still provide many wonderful examples of good urban spaces. Piazza San Marco is perhaps the greatest of them all, peaceful yet vibrant. Most Italian cities have gorgeous squares, a few of which have been protected from cars. New York, Boston, and San Francisco still have great districts, as did most US cities until cars and suburban sprawl bled their hearts dry.

When thinking about cities, we must remember that suburbs are an urban, not rural, form. This reality clashes with the suburban leitmotif: fleeing the city to live in the countryside. However, few US suburbs still offer even the illusion of country life, and they depend on central cities for work, health care, and culture. The "national automobile slum" is thus the worst of both worlds: vast areas of forest and farmland are turned into low-density residential neighborhoods organized around automobile transport. Inhabitants of these auto-centric areas must drive great distances through repulsive surroundings to reach virtually every activity.

Rural areas supplied the people, food, and resources to fuel the urban engine that produced the bulk of our technical advances. Although some of these advances turned out to have a dark side, there can be little doubt that technology has generally improved our lives, and we have our cities to thank for this.

Predictions abound that virtual reality will reduce the need for physical presence and thereby the need for cities. While virtual reality will provide an alternative to face-to-face meetings for some task-focused groups, I believe that most people will find it an unsatisfactory substitute for personal contact. I am no technical reprobate: I have computers in my home, make extensive use the Internet, and enjoy playing computer games. But for me, no form of virtual reality will ever replace a pleasant evening stroll among the neighbors. I believe this is true for most people. For as long as people continue to want to meet in person, the future of cities is assured.

Auto-centric cities are those based on transport by private automobile. Infrequent buses offer indifferent public transport. Car ownership is nearly essential, even for the poor. Los Angeles is the archetype, although the city has recently accepted the need to increase its density and improve public transport.

Hanging out, Amsterdam, 1999

CITIES & COMMUNITY

Human scale, Siena, Italy, 1998
This small square is built to a human scale. The stone pavers are about the length of a human foot. The windows are smaller than the human form, and the door is, of course, somewhat larger. In the narrow streets just beyond, you can touch both walls with outstretched hands.

In late 1999, many activists gathered in Seattle to protest secret negotiations being conducted by the World Trade Organization. Police mishandled the demonstrators, almost all of whom were practicing nonviolence. The confrontation has become known in some quarters as the "Battle of Seattle."

City streets are the host for community, and community is central to the maintenance of a civilized society, which depends on a certain level of shared experiences and expectations. It is in the streets that the chance encounters essential to the sustenance of community occur. One indicator of the importance of this function is the degree to which its disappearance is now recognized and lamented in the USA. As classic "main street" towns have disappeared, the social space they once provided has been replaced mainly by shopping malls, a tepid substitute indeed. Not all social encounters on the streets of a well-functioning city are pleasant, but the friction that sometimes arises does serve an important function: it helps people to learn how to tolerate and get along with one another.

In the New World, quite a few social groups have been so marginalized that they no longer have a true place in society. At the same time, some of the richest members of society have in essence completely withdrawn from public life. They live in gated communities, to which the poor are only invited to wash the floors, clean the pools, and tend the gardens. Some rich people only venture into the outer world when isolated in their cars, and then often to travel to members-only venues.

The French Revolution showed how dangerous it is for a privileged aristocracy to isolate itself from the population. No one who could say "let them eat cake" could possibly have had any understanding of what life was like for nearly all her subjects. I fear that a divide is arising in modern Western societies as the degree of segregation and alienation rises. As the "Battle of Seattle" showed in 1999, leaders must maintain some sort of common ground with the rank-and-file or risk unexpected and unpleasant confrontations with those who feel that they have been disenfranchised.

The splendid isolation in which most leaders live surely does not increase their sensitivity to the plight of their constituents. Most leaders are surrounded entirely by people like themselves: rich, powerful, well-educated, and assured of a place at the table. This is true not only among national leaders but also at much lower levels of government. Almost all leaders travel by car and rarely rub elbows with those who elected them. The restoration of streets as public spaces used by everyone will help to assure that citizens from every part of society maintain at least a modicum of contact with one another and to promote conditions under which civilized societies can flourish.

Zermatt, Switzerland, 1998
A carfree place for kids to hang out. But it's not bus-free: a small, slow electric bus can be seen in the background. Kids play safely in the streets here.

CITIES & TRANSPORT

Transport is vital to cities: no city can function without its passenger and freight transport systems. As large cities based on car and truck transport approach gridlock, it has become apparent to almost everyone that a better solution is needed. So far, however, only half-hearted solutions have been proposed. While many of these proposals might somewhat improve the livability of our cities, most of them cause adverse effects, some of which are roughly as serious as the problems they are intended to cure. We must examine the prevailing assumption that continued automobile use is inescapable, and that examination is a major theme of this book.

The amount of space that an urban transport system absorbs has a critical effect on urban form. Cars are the most space-intensive form of urban transport ever devised and have forced cities to expand into rural areas. In many cities, attempts to accommodate cars required the construction of urban highways that severely damaged the neighborhoods through which they were driven. Other means would have provided better transport at far lower costs.

Rapid improvements in urban and intercity rail systems during the period 1850–1935 offered mankind the best transport that had ever been seen, but in the USA, cars began as early as 1915 to erode the quality of public spaces and to impede public transport vehicles operating on the streets. So began a long downward spiral in the quality of life in US cities.

The delivery of freight in cities has been problematic since Roman times. The chapter on freight delivery proposes a means to deliver freight in our cities simply by extending the use of standardized shipping containers. Such containers are now routinely moved by the thousand around the globe aboard ships, barges, trains, and trucks. The means I propose merely extend existing, proven technology, much of it fully automated.

The automobile industry has become such a large segment of the world economy that many fear any change that might threaten the continued production of tens of millions of cars each year. Any large decline in urban car usage will certainly cause major economic dislocations, so the change to carfree cities will require careful economic planning and implementation in phases (which is, in any case, almost essential). The auto industry will continue to sell millions of cars a year to those living in rural areas, for whom it is difficult to imagine any other practical means of transport.

Suburban neighborhood, Los Angeles, 1999

CARFREE URBAN AREAS

Some will scoff at the viability of life in carfree cities, but remember that every city was carfree until about 100 years ago.

Venice clearly demonstrates that carfree cities can at the very least continue to function in modern times. It is risky, however, to use Venice as the sole proof of the feasibility of carfree cities. Many regard Venice as a dying city and note the dramatic decline in population since 1945, from about 200,000 to around 75,000 in just 50 years. Venice is, in fact, a victim of its own success. The combination of the delightful carfree environment, together with a large helping of the world's art and architectural treasures, has made Venice one of the world's most popular tourist destinations. Rich people bought up many houses in Venice, and many of these buildings are vacant for most of the year. Other buildings have been converted to hotels to shelter the visiting hordes. Housing prices rose so much that many Venetians were forced to move to Mestre on the mainland, leading at least in part to the dramatic decline in population. Even in winter, however, Venice does not seem like a dead city: it feels like the bustling, good-humored small city that it is.

San Marco, Venice, 1997

Most large industry in Venice has relocated to nearby Mestre. Smaller industries, however, still continue to thrive. Murano, an island just north of the two main islands of Venice, has been a leading producer of fine glassware since 1291. Dozens of small glass factories still operate here, so it is evident that small industries with moderate freight requirements can survive despite the problematic freight system.

Most difficulties that beset Venice are intrinsic to its location in the middle of a shallow lagoon or related to its unique place in history. When building new carfree cities or converting existing cities to the carfree model, we will usually be able to design around constraints of this kind. Venice serves us best when we regard it simply as evidence of the high quality of life that is possible in medieval cities: four-story buildings, crooked narrow streets, and relatively high density

A reference design is a benchmark, used as a point of departure. Normally, a reference design is not actually built, although it should in principle be employable in some real situation. The reference design for carfree cities could be built without appreciable modification in several Dutch polders and other flat, sparsely-settled tracts. Local conditions will usually dictate substantial deviations.

Freiburg, Germany, 1998
A very few cars are still permitted to enter the downtown area, but it is effectively carfree. Trams provide a convenient alternative.

are in themselves no barrier to a high quality of life, so long as cars are not permitted to terrorize the streets. I would argue, in fact, that it is precisely these qualities of Venice that make it so successful, and many aspects of the "reference design" for carfree cities are indeed based on the Venetian model. To be sure, other models are also feasible: all that is necessary for the basic carfree design to work is to achieve a sufficiently high population density to support excellent public transport. This can be achieved in many different ways. At one end of the scale are the towering Modernist skyscrapers of Hong Kong and Manhattan. At the other end are low-rise, high-density urban areas like Burano (a small island near Venice) and the old lilong neighborhoods of Shanghai. (Most of the lilong areas have been demolished in favor of high-rise buildings, but when I was in Shanghai, the locals spoke longingly of the warm social environment that had characterized the narrow streets of these carfree areas.)

Further evidence of the workability of carfree cities can be seen in Europe, where many cities have made parts of downtown carfree. In a few cases, such as Freiburg, most of downtown has been made largely or entirely carfree. These areas have been popular with residents and tourists alike, and the initial opposition of merchants has generally changed to strong support within a year or two: most merchants saw their business improve once the cars were gone.

Some cities in the USA have also experimented with carfree areas, although usually on a more modest scale. Some of these experiments have been deemed unsuccessful and reversed, but it appears that most of the unsuccessful trials were in fact "transit malls," which is really another name for an outdoor bus station. Removing cars in order to replace them with diesel buses does little to improve the street in question.

Finally, we must keep firmly in mind that carfree cities

demand excellent public transport. Some existing examples of top-quality public transport will be cited later. The only barriers to achieving first-class service for all transit users are political: no technical problems remain to be solved, so long as the necessary population density is achieved. All that is lacking is the will to make the needed service improvements.

A FAILED EXPERIMENT

The USA is nearing the end of an experiment begun a century ago, an experiment also conducted in lesser degrees by the rest of the world. The experimental hypothesis is simply stated: private automobiles offer everyone the best possible urban transport. The conduct of this experiment required the demolition of streets, houses, stores, and factories and their reconstruction in new locations. It scattered populations across the countryside, devastated city centers, damaged social systems, and battered the planetary ecosystem. Rich, detailed, human-scale neighborhoods were replaced by hideous, gigantic areas scaled to the needs of cars.

A smoggy day in sprawling Los Angeles, 1999

The few good urban environments that still exist in the USA were built before the needs of cars subsumed centuries of urban planning craft. These areas are almost invariably the most beautiful parts of the city (usually also the oldest parts of town), and typically see the heaviest use. In fact, the desire for housing in these deeply-satisfying areas overwhelms the supply and drives up real estate prices. This pattern can also be seen in Europe.

The experiment was supported by the most costly civil works program in history: the construction of the US Interstate highway system. Without fast highways connecting the center city to rural areas, the exodus to the suburbs could never have proceeded so far or so fast.

Strip mall, Los Angeles, 1999

See Donald Appleyard's work for a thorough examination of the effects of cars on communities.

For more on life in contemporary US cities, see Jackson, Kay, and Kunstler. See also this book's foreword.

Even if sufficient resources can be found to sustain the experiment indefinitely, there remain many reasons to remove cars from our cities: cars are wasting our time, wrecking our lives, and destroying our societies. In the 20th century, cars have done more to damage our cities than wars, terrible as they have been. No city except Venice has been immune to the ravages of cars. Urban automobile usage amounts to an undeclared war between drivers and everybody else. Just as in a real war, there is a lot of "collateral damage." We see it around us every day in the form of the awful environments built since the needs of cars and their drivers came to dominate every aspect of urban planning.

These ugly environments seem inseparable from auto-centric development and have had a devastating effect on the civic and social functions of the public realm. These dreadful environments discourage people from spending time in public places and broadcast the message: this mess is so awful, nobody cares what you do here. It leads to isolation, cynicism, hopelessness, and antisocial behavior.

While many problems with cars are of a technical nature and therefore susceptible to engineering solutions, the most serious problems are intrinsic and cannot be solved by any application of technology. I regard the damage that cars do to social systems as the most serious problem they cause in cities. No technical improvement to cars can restore the vital function of streets as the host for community: as long as anything as dangerous and intrusive as cars and trucks rule our streets, civic life will vanish from the street.

At a deep level, Americans are finally beginning to understand that something is missing in their lives. The sudden emergence of suburban sprawl as a topic of national discussion indicates that many have realized that something was lost when sprawling suburbs replaced walkable, human-scale cities. This discussion is perhaps less evident in Europe, which was slower to adopt widespread car usage and where cars were never permitted to do as much harm to cities. (We shall see later that Le Corbusier proposed to demolish most of Paris in order to build highways and tower blocks. Fortunately, wiser heads prevailed.)

As evidence of the seriousness of our design errors, I offer the passion we now exhibit for the preservation and restoration of old urban neighborhoods. Today in the industrialized nations, almost any proposal that would damage these artifacts of civility is instantly shouted down.

Rialto Market, Venice, 1997

We have recently seen a spate of books proposing solutions to the urban transport crisis and the problem of suburban sprawl. While this marks the dawning of awareness that automobile usage in cities causes many intractable problems, the solutions so far proposed are only palliatives. This book proposes a solution that is at once radical and reactionary: radical because it proposes major changes to our cities, and reactionary because many of these changes are actually a reversion to urban patterns still widely applied just a century ago.

A Solution

"Traffic management" is not really a solution to anything. Only when kids can play ball in the street without worrying about cars has a sufficient improvement been achieved. While some traffic management schemes do improve conditions for some people, most strategies carry less-obvious drawbacks that make life worse for others. While speed bumps do slow cars down for a moment, the net result is a small decrease in average speed coupled with a significant increase in noise and exhaust emissions, a situation arguably worse than before the bumps were installed.

A woonerf is a residential street to which cars are only admitted on the condition that they proceed at dead slow. Street furniture creates a winding path that effectively enforces this condition; high speeds are impossible, and most streets are dead ends.

Rokin, Amsterdam, c.1900

Rokin, Amsterdam, 1999
From the same point as the photograph above. The canal was filled in to make a parking lot. Amsterdam resolved years ago never to repeat this mistake.

The Dutch woonerf really does improve the quality of life for residents, based as it is on the presumption that cars are admitted so long as they proceed at a walking pace and do not disrupt other activities. However, the woonerf approach is not extensible beyond local neighborhoods because cars require reasonably high-speed streets in order to provide quick transport. The woonerf solution may also simply displace traffic from one street to another, such as happened in Berkeley, California, where some residential areas were turned into a maze of dead-end streets. Traffic that had used the local streets was simply displaced to the main arteries.

A real solution to the problem of the urban automobile can only be achieved by moving cars entirely out of the city. Only by this means can we restore true peace in our streets and provide a safe environment where people are invited to linger, without fear of traffic.

If we replace auto-centric urban transport with rail-based systems, we can retain and even improve our current levels of mobility at a cost both we and the environment can bear. A carfree city designed around rail transport would greatly reduce the resources currently consumed by urban transport while providing a fast, comfortable alternative to cars.

In order to make effective use of rail systems, carfree cities will require a considerably denser pattern of living than the suburbs, but denser, carfree living can help restore community to our neighborhoods. The design for carfree cities provides a way to establish nearby parks and open space, regain peace and quiet in our homes and offices, and begin the reconstruction of social systems damaged when the automobile drove life off the street. The required density increases are by no means extreme: densities that are still common in European city centers are entirely sufficient. Even sprawling Los Angeles has a few neighborhoods that are more densely populated than the districts proposed for carfree cities.

The changes I propose are far-reaching indeed: the complete removal of cars and trucks from city streets is as sweeping a change as I can imagine. While many compromises with this radical approach are possible and probably quite workable, I think that we should adopt a policy of completely removing motorized traffic from city streets. Only in this way do we obtain the full benefits of carfree cities. However, Part III does consider design compromises that permit some level of continued urban car usage while still yielding streets that are entirely carfree.

The reference design proposes a return to traditional forms of city building, because these forms have shown their worth through the ages and because people still seem to value these areas the most. However, many architects (and a few others) continue to believe that Modernism is mankind's salvation. Modernism could be accommodated in its own district, as Léon Krier has proposed. The rest of us would be free to live elsewhere, in districts based on older, more comfortable patterns, such as those identified by Christopher Alexander.

Begijnhof, Amsterdam, 1997

One element of the reference design in particular has aroused considerable opposition: my proposal to adopt Alexander's pattern limiting building heights to four stories is strongly opposed by some, including a few people whose views I otherwise largely accept. While tall buildings are not essential to a successful city, there is no reason why a district could not be reserved for skyscrapers. In fact, the division of carfree cities into districts makes it easy to provide locations to accommodate a wide range of preferences.

The message of this book is simple: Get the cars out of the cities. The rest is simply a proposal for how to achieve this. Other methods besides those I propose would probably also work, although some might require technically-advanced transport systems whose practicality has yet to be demonstrated. Any promising method should be tested. The more carfree areas that are developed in the coming decade, the better. Some efforts will doubtless work better than others, but even the attempts that do not achieve complete success will provide interesting environments and useful lessons. I believe that nothing will sell the idea of carfree cities better than the experience of carfree areas, and Venice is certainly the best advertisement for carfree cities that I have ever seen.

Carfree cities can offer rich human experience, great beauty, and true peace. They can greatly reduce the damage we are doing to the biosphere. They permit the construction of beautiful districts in the manner of European city centers, with parks but a short walk away. Carfree cities are a practical alternative, available now. They can be built using existing technology at a price we can afford. They offer a real future for our children.

Brig, Switzerland, 1998

ORGANIZATION OF THE BOOK

The book is divided into three Parts, each beginning with an enumeration of its chapters and summaries of their contents. Part I considers cities in general and transport in particular. Part II presents the reference design for carfree cities as well as some variations on the reference design. Part III examines ways of implementing carfree cities in the real world.

Venice, 1997

PART I

ON CITIES

YARDSTICKS FOR CITIES
Presents some measuring tools useful in comparing cities and then uses them to compare Venice and Los Angeles.

CITIES & TRANSPORT
Considers the importance of transport to cities and how various transport modes affect urban form.

Los Angeles, 1999

WICKED CARS
Reviews the ravages of cars and makes a case that nothing can stop this damage in cities short of removing the cars.

BETTER PUBLIC TRANSPORT
Looks at why most people avoid public transport and how its limitations can be overcome.

SUSTAINABLE CITIES
Considers the importance of sustainable development and the role of carfree cities in achieving it.

Conversion of Units

Length

$$1 \text{ meter (m)} = 3.281 \text{ feet (ft)}$$
$$1 \text{ kilometer (km)} = 0.6214 \text{ miles (mi)}$$

Area

$$1 \text{ m}^2 = 10.76 \text{ ft}^2$$
$$1 \text{ hectare (ha)} = 2.471 \text{ acres}$$
$$1 \text{ km}^2 = 0.3861 \text{ mi}^2$$

Weight

$$1 \text{ kilogram (kg)} = 2.205 \text{ pounds}$$
$$1 \text{ tonne (t)} = 1.102 \text{ short tons}$$

Acceleration of Gravity (G)

$$980.1 \text{ cm/sec}^2 = 32.17 \text{ ft/sec}^2$$

Adult Walking Speed

$$76 \text{ m/min.} = 250 \text{ ft/min.}$$

Miscellaneous

$$1 \text{ liter (l)} = 0.2642 \text{ gallon}$$
$$1 \text{ km/l} = 2.352 \text{ mi/gallon}$$
$$1 \text{ US horsepower (hp)} = 746 \text{ watts (w)}$$

The US system of counting floors is used: the ground floor is the first floor (most Europeans count the ground floor as floor zero). The US number system is used: 10,000.00 is ten thousand. Currency is expressed in 1999 US dollars.

Approximate conversions from metric to Customary Units are given in the tables on page 323.

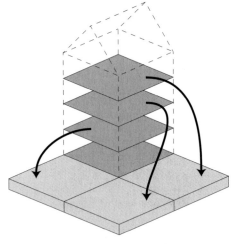

Floor Area Ratio (FAR)

This book makes frequent reference to FAR, which is simply a measure of the building density of a given site. To calculate FAR, first determine the site's Plot Ratio (PR). In the example above, the building covers 25% of the site, so PR = 0.25. The FAR equals PR times the number of stories. The building above has 4 stories, so its FAR = 0.25 x 4 = 1.

Human density is simply the number of residents and employees living and working on one hectare.

Urban forms are compared below, using data from Fouchier (1996), page 10 (Venice and carfree city by author).

District	FAR	PR	Stories	Avg Human Density
Hong Kong	3.73	.33	11.2	2205
Paris-Montholon (IX)	3.20	.55	5.9	753
Central Venice	2.69	.67	4.0	unk.
Carfree design	1.50	.38	4.0	550
French public housing	0.63	.15	4.3	186
Single-family housing	0.23	.19	1.2	39

We begin with techniques of measurement. Here at the naval shipyard in Venice, the meter and the *passo Veneto* have been cast in bronze and bolted to the wall for ready reference.

YARDSTICKS FOR CITIES

Throughout this book, we will be discussing urban form. In order to make meaningful comparisons of various urban forms, we will need some measuring tools to assist us in comparing cities and their success at meeting human needs. Transport systems exert a large influence on urban form and the quality of urban life, and urban form in turn exercises considerable influence on transport systems. Because the relationship between transport systems and quality of life is so important, many of the measures assess the performance of transport systems or the resources they consume.

The first part of this chapter defines a number of measures that indicate how well a city performs its function as the host for civilization. The second part applies these measures to two extreme urban forms: auto-centric Los Angeles and carfree Venice.

QUALITY-OF-LIFE MEASURES

Quality of life, as distinct from standard of living, cannot be measured directly, but several numerical measures are useful:
- Frequency of days with poor air quality
- Infant mortality rate
- Poverty index
- Unemployment rate
- Literacy rate
- Incarceration rate
- Incidence of mental illness

Fine public amenities, Zermatt, Switzerland, 1998

Except for air pollution, the range of variation on these measures will be relatively small among cities in rich nations.

To these statistical measures of quality of life, we must add one quality that is difficult to quantify: the prevalence of neighborhoods built on a human scale to serve human needs. Such neighborhoods are usually characterized by the following attributes:

- Priority for pedestrians
- Buildings no higher than six stories
- Buildings oriented towards the street
- Active street life created by mixed uses
- Small signs without internal illumination
- Public amenities such as drinking fountains & benches
- Nearby, attractive parks

Near the Torre dell'Orologio, Venice, 1997
This street in Venice is built at human scale. By the standards given here, it is nearly perfect. It lacks a bench, for which there is clearly no room. Public drinking water and toilets are available in Venice.

TRANSPORT MEASURES

A transport system is an integral part of a city and affects many spheres of life. Four points of comparison are especially important: travel time, area of land consumed, direct costs, and externalized costs; we will consider each of these in turn.

Travel Time

The total time each person spends on travel is affected by both the distances to be traveled and the average speed of the trips. The following characteristics reduce the total distance that must be covered:

- Compact development, so no part of the city is far away
- Basic shopping within walking distance
- Work, school, and health care close to home

The following attributes of any transport system, whether public or private, reduce the door-to-door travel time for a given trip:

Strip mall, Los Angeles, 1999
This public area was scaled for cars, not people. The paved area is at least ten times larger than what would be required for foot traffic alone. Nobody cares what this place looks like, so it looks awful.

- Short walking distance to transport
- No wait for service
- No need to transfer from one vehicle to another
- Direct routing without intermediate stops
- High acceleration
- High speed

Car drivers usually escape walking, waiting, and transferring, but in many urban areas these savings are overbalanced by the effects of suburban sprawl, which forces people to:

- Drive to all shopping
- Drive an hour or more to routine destinations
- Search for parking
- Wait in traffic

Suburban sprawl is typified by the US pattern of postwar development. Single-family houses are built on large lots. Nonresidential functions are located in specialized districts, far from home.

Land Consumed by Transport

Transport systems must be measured against the area of land they occupy. A road lane and a railroad track are each roughly 4 meters wide. About 2000 cars/hr can pass over one traffic lane. At typical occupancy rates, this is just 2500 people/hr. Trains, on the other hand, can carry 50,000 passengers/hr over a single track. Cars are therefore up to 20 times more land intensive than trains for the same capacity, before any allowance is made for car parking. While railroads can be built underground, roads are too wide for routine tunneling.

The Central Artery project in Boston will bury 257 lane-kilometers of highway costing $14.2 billion and will provide capacity for 190,000 cars each day, so the capital cost per daily car is $75,000.
http://www.bigdig.com

The American Automobile Association estimates the direct costs of a mid-sized car at $4504/year.
from "Transportation Cost Analysis"
Victoria Transport Policy Institute
http://www.vtpi.org/tcasum.htm

Direct Costs

The direct costs of passenger transport are easily measured. Transport is a large item in most family budgets, and this is especially true of families in sprawling suburbs, many of whom must own and operate several cars in order to meet their transport needs. Travel costs include mileage-based costs, per-trip costs, and periodic costs. The following table gives examples of costs paid by car and urban rail travelers:

	Car	Urban rail
Cost per unit distance	Gasoline	Nil
Cost per trip	Parking	Flat-rate
Cost per year	Insurance	Nil

Most urban rail systems charge a flat rate per trip, but some systems charge fares based on distance. Of course, if a passenger buys a season ticket, his entire cost is periodic and unaffected by usage.

Passengers usually pay at least some of the direct costs, but governments often subsidize much of the remainder. (In the USA, virtually every passenger transport mode is subsidized, directly or indirectly.) Most car drivers underestimate the out-of-pocket cost of driving and are unaware of the large subsidy they receive. Drivers tend to equate their costs of driving to the cost of gasoline consumed plus parking and tolls, but the driver actually pays much more than this: depreciation and maintenance are large costs that are not paid at the time of travel, so drivers are not particularly aware of them. The system is arranged in such a way that, once you have a car, the cost of driving additional distance seems fairly low, which tends to encourage more driving.

Proposals have been made to charge for insurance on a per-mile rather than a per-year basis, in order to discourage driving and charge drivers for their actual risk exposure.

Externalized Costs

While many externalized costs are difficult to measure, they are at least as important as direct costs. Every transport system externalizes costs to its neighbors and to the global ecosystem. For example, car drivers externalize the following costs:

Externalized costs are the monetary and nonmaterial costs imposed on society at large by the consumer of a product or service.

- Death & injury to bystanders
- Intimidation of pedestrians & bicyclists
- Diminished freedom for children
- Road maintenance costs in excess of road taxes
- Reduced availability of public transport
- Noise & vibration
- Air pollution & climate change
- Loss of beauty to visual clutter
- Deterioration of human-scale public spaces

THE YARDSTICKS APPLIED

Richard Risemberg was kind enough to share his local knowledge of Los Angeles. He and his son Jack took the photographs of Los Angeles, which are far from the worst examples that might be chosen: this is simply what Los Angeles looks like.

The next ten pages contrast various facets of life in auto-centric Los Angeles and carfree Venice, using our yardsticks. First a few words by way of introduction.

Each page contrasts one aspect of life in both cities, taking first Los Angeles and then Venice. For each city, the influence of transport on that aspect of life is taken up first, followed by the consequences for quality of life in that city.

Some reviewers held such a comparison to be unfair, and while this criticism may be accurate, it misses the point. The comparison merely highlights the extreme deterioration of public spaces characteristic of auto-centric cities and shows that repulsive public areas are not intrinsic to modern life.

The ugliness of Los Angeles stems quite directly from its auto-centric patterns. Other factors less germane to the subject of this book, such as the globalization of the world economy and the rise of multinational corporations, surely also affect Los Angeles. It is worth noting, however, that both McDonalds and international package express companies found ways to adapt their normal methods of operation to the unique requirements of Venice.

The miniaturized arches can be seen on page 157

Even though Venice is centuries old, nothing in Venice could not be replicated today: there are no technical barriers to the construction of new cities just like Venice. Doubtless, some aspects of Venetian construction would be seen as prohibitively expensive today, but the large majority of buildings in Venice are actually quite ordinary and require nothing more difficult or expensive than a modest amount of stone-cutting of a type still commonly seen in new and reconstructed buildings throughout southern Europe.

Indeed, the Fenice opera house, one of the jewels of Venice, was devastated by fire a few years ago, but the building will be completely restored. All of the necessary skills and materials are still available.

This chapter concludes with a tabular comparison of Los Angeles, Venice, and the carfree city as proposed in Part II.

Where Do the Children Play?

In Los Angeles, speeding cars make the streets too dangerous for young children, so they must play in fenced-in back yards and depend entirely on adults for all transport. Two small children who do not live next door can only play together if a parent drives one child to the other's home. Older children may be allowed to bicycle, but the constant danger from cars and trucks makes this a nail-biting event for parents. Few children get themselves to school because traffic makes it too dangerous to walk or bike, so children are driven instead.

The constant travel within the confines of a car delays the exposure of children to the adult world and retards their social development. Only later do they discover the larger world and its expectations regarding public behavior. Children don't get as much exercise as they need, one cause of obesity among American children.

Strip mall, Los Angeles, 1999
No place to play

Venice has relatively few gardens and parks, but the complete absence of cars makes it safe for children to play anywhere, even in the middle of the street. The entire city serves as their playground, and, as children grow, they can explore steadily more of it. Two children who want to play together can safely walk to each other's homes, even from a very young age. Younger children walk to school, and older children sometimes take the ferry.

Because all but the very youngest children can go to school on their own, without adult help, children begin very early to learn how to get along in the real world. If children on the street become obnoxious, a passing adult may correct their behavior, so children begin to absorb social norms from a young age. By the time they reach their teens, children have learned how to behave in public.

Campo Santa Maria Formosa, Venice
Carnival, 1997

STREET LIFE

In Los Angeles, almost anybody with enough money to own and operate a car drives nearly everywhere, and since parking garages are often integrated into the buildings they serve, drivers headed for many destinations never even set foot on the street. In most places and at most times there are relatively few people on the streets except for drivers sealed up in air-conditioned cars. Most of the people who spend much time on the streets are poor and even homeless.

The constant heavy traffic makes the streets noisy, smelly, and abidingly ugly. It is unpleasant and even difficult to socialize on the street, and few people do. What passes for street life takes place inside large, privately-owned shopping centers that have little incentive to permit or encourage activities that are not directly profit-making. Unlike city streets, malls close at night.

The Beverly Center, Los Angeles, 1999
The first five stories are mostly parking garage

In Venice, cars never intrude upon the streets except for a small area near the parking garage at the entrance to the city. Rich and poor alike use the streets at every hour of the day and night. Long trips begin and end with a walk between the door and the nearest ferry landing. Water taxis are for hire at stiff rates, but even their passengers usually begin their trips with a walk down the street.

The streets echo to human sounds: footsteps, voices, whistling porters, singing gondoliers. The stink, roar, and danger of car and truck traffic never inhibit street life. People dawdle without worrying about onrushing traffic. All day long, people are present on the street, which serves as a stage for an endless stream of interesting and sometimes amusing episodes. Restaurants put tables outdoors, from which their patrons watch and participate in the play of life.

Street musician, Venice, 1997
Better acoustics than some concert halls

Public Spaces

Los Angeles has as many public spaces as any other city, but few of them are arranged for anything but the convenience of cars and the imperatives they impose on commerce. The stores are set back from the street in order to provide parking in front, and huge signs pass terse messages to fleeting drivers. Traffic signs and signals further erode the quality of the area, and drooping overhead communication and power cables complete the picture. The organizational principles are fast automobile movement and convenient parking.

Another strip mall, Los Angeles, 1999

Beauty and the needs of pedestrians are given little thought, and the long strips of low buildings bordering wide streets fail to create a sense of enclosure. Comfortable places where people gather to enjoy city life scarcely exist. Attractive public squares can hardly be found. Graffiti and litter abound in an environment about which no one cares.

In Venice, public squares large and small are scattered throughout the city. These squares were arranged for the sole convenience of pedestrians, many of whom are intimately familiar with the area, so few signs are required. In Venice, the church acted as a major organizational force, and each parish has its own church, usually fronting on a square that once served as a water catchment and storage area, furnished with a well from which people drew their water.

Campo Santa Maria Formosa, Venice, 1997

While drawing water is no longer an activity that regulates daily life, the wellheads remain gathering places, and people cluster around them to enjoy the vibrant street life. Building facades almost entirely delineate these squares, giving them an interesting and comfortable sense of enclosure. A few squares, including the great Piazza San Marco, border on the lagoon, with its arresting water views.

MAJOR STREETS

Yet another strip mall, Los Angeles, 1999

In the photograph of Los Angeles, every person in the scene sits isolated in a car: of the 10 or 12 people present, not one is actually visible. These few people almost fully occupy the large amount of space and make the street look congested. In order to offer their customers "free" parking, the stores have dedicated large areas of land to parking. The resultant low-density land usage gives rise to the power poles; underground service would have cost too much. The overriding concern is to minimize capital and operating costs.

The street is no place to stop to look around or to chat with neighbors. Should a motorist stop for any reason, drivers would begin honking their horns almost immediately. Giant signs and power lines blot the scene. No thought has been given to the provision of any amenity except parking. The street fails to serve as a social space.

The steps of Rialto Bridge, Venice, 1997

In Venice, people sometimes nearly fill a street, but real congestion is rare. In this photograph of one of the busiest spots in Venice, many more people are present than in the photograph of Los Angeles. There is room enough for everyone, even though the way is partially blocked by a few people sitting on the steps. The businesses face directly onto the sidewalk and have no need to shout in order to advertise their wares. As in most of Europe, the high density made it practical to put power lines underground.

None of the people are isolated in steel cages, so everyone is actively present on the street. Many stores have no signs at all. Restaurants put their menu cards out on small stands, and the tables in the street are sufficient to announce the nature of the business to passersby. The street is attractive and serves as an active social area.

PASSENGER TRANSPORT

In Los Angeles, driving is the nearly universal way to get anywhere. This has led to terrible congestion on the streets and highways. The once-famous Red Cars (trams) operated over a vast network, but most public transport is now provided by bus. Faced with intractable air pollution, the city has resurrected some rail service and is building a metro of modest extent. Handicapped access is provided mainly by buses equipped with cumbersome wheelchair lifts, although the new metro system provides elevator access.

Traffic jam, Los Angeles, 1999

Air pollution remains a serious issue as traffic continues to worsen. People waste large amounts of time stuck in traffic. Those without a car must endure dreadful bus service in order to get anywhere. Those who drive spend a large proportion of their disposable income for relatively low-speed transport, which is, of course, faster than the bus.

In Venice, walking is the most common way to get around, and congestion is rarely an issue. At a reasonably brisk pace, one can cross the city in an hour. Pleasant, if slow, public transport is provided by ferryboats, but evening service is infrequent, and it is often faster to walk. (The gondola is little used as a serious means of transport today.) Those arriving by car must park in a large garage at the end of the causeway. A small area near the garage is the only part of the city in which cars, trucks, buses, or trains can be found.

Ferryboats, Venice, 1997

The atmosphere aboard the ferries is pleasant, and passengers enjoy excellent views of the city. Arched bridges, necessary to allow boats to pass beneath, abound in Venice. These bridges all have steps, making this one of the world's least accessible cities for those confined to wheelchairs. Lifts are now being added to the most heavily traversed bridges.

FREIGHT DELIVERY

Trucks, Los Angeles, 1999

In Los Angeles, freight is usually delivered by truck. Almost all merchandise arriving from overseas is containerized and delivered by ship, with final local delivery of the container by truck. Some bulk cargoes, such as crude oil, are also delivered by ship. There are no inland waterways, so delivery by water is only possible along the harborfront. Rail is seldom used for local freight delivery, although some larger shippers do have rail access. However, many of the containers arriving by ship are transshipped to trains for through delivery to the hinterlands.

The use of trucks to deliver so much freight aggravates the already-severe road congestion. Most big trucks are diesel-powered and emit clouds of stinking exhaust, and all trucks exacerbate global warming because they burn fossil fuels and waste energy.

Freight handling, Rialto bridge, Venice, 1997

In Venice, virtually all freight is transported by boat, except for a small area near the train station that has direct rail and road service. The narrow waterways and low bridges restrict the size of freight scows, so their capacity is quite limited. Freight must be transshipped between rail or road and the delivery boats, a time-consuming and expensive task. Final deliveries, except to destinations along a canal, must be made by hand cart. The steps on the bridges make this a chore for the very fit, and it is doubtless a bit dangerous as well.

Despite these problems, freight gets delivered in Venice, and even the overnight express companies have managed to cope. Street and water traffic never interfere with one another, and congestion on the water rarely becomes an issue. While the diesel-powered boats do emit some pollutants, they are reasonably quiet and rarely intrusive.

CIVIC BUILDINGS

The photograph shows one of the most important civic buildings in the Los Angeles region: the Los Angeles City Hall. This facility was clearly designed with the needs of cars and their drivers foremost in mind. The obvious expectation is that most visitors and employees will arrive by private car. This necessitates the huge parking facilities that swallow up the entire foreground. In the background, the city hall itself can just be seen.

City Hall, Los Angeles, 1999

The problem of car parking is insoluble. While multistory parking garages do reduce the amount of land required, they are never attractive structures. As long as the car remains the primary means of access, the design of beautiful public buildings in attractive surroundings will remain an impossible task. Despite its importance, this building could quite easily be mistaken for an ordinary office building.

In Venice, the Doge's Palace is clearly the most important civic building. No one arrives by car, so there is, of course, no car parking at all. One facade faces the Riva degli Schiavone, a busy waterfront where a variety of boats moor. This is as close to a parking lot as exists anywhere in the vicinity.

Doge's Palace, Venice, 1997

The moored and moving boats, rather than detracting from the appearance and habitability of the area, actually make it more interesting. While the monumental architecture of the Doge's Palace is best appreciated from other vantage points, even here on the back side, one sees the attention paid to making the building beautiful. The principal facade of the Doge's Palace faces the Piazza San Marco where it and the adjoining cathedral form the grandest architectural feature of the piazza, and thus of all Venice. The importance of this building is unmistakable from any prospect.

CHURCHES

In Los Angeles, churchgoers pile into the car and drive to church. There is no procession of people in their Sunday best through the streets. As with all public buildings in auto-centric cities, a vast parking lot must be provided, and, as usual, the most convenient and space-saving location is between the buildings and the street.

Oriental Mission Church, Los Angeles, 1999

Most of what is visible from the street is parking lot. In this instance, a few token trees were added to shield the expanse of sizzling asphalt and the mass of parked cars, but the entire arrangement inspires awe only by the breadth and depth of its ugliness. Only the cross marks this site as different from any other. The building itself is in no way remarkable (this one was probably converted from a failed store). The fence and the gate imply that only some people are welcome, and this church provides no amenities whatever to passersby.

In Venice, those going to church begin to meet each other in the streets during their walk to church. The social function thus begins well before their arrival at the church itself. Since everyone walks to church, there is no need to make any provision for parking. The street is narrow enough that the cost of stone paving was reasonable.

Church on the Záttere, Venice, 1997

This church faces directly onto the street. The rich architectural details are seen from close up and intended to be appreciated by passersby as a sign that this building is important enough to be worthy of decoration. (By Venetian standards, this church is only barely worthy of note.) Great care was lavished on the design and execution of the lovely stone paving. This particular church is generous enough to provide a pleasant amenity to the general public: a sunny place to sit and watch the world go past.

HOUSING

In Los Angeles, housing is designed with the assumption that all transport outside of the immediate neighborhood is by car. The extreme reliance on automobile transport means that most adults need a car, which explains why there is never enough parking, despite the city's requirement that developers provide parking spaces for all apartments.

A large percentage of almost every building site must be devoted to parking and access roads, leaving little room for public spaces. The ground floor may be dedicated entirely to garages, as here, so there is often no human presence at ground level, which makes the area hostile, forbidding, and even frightening. Few architectural elements can be more difficult to make beautiful than garage doors, and most housing is overwhelmed by these faceless artifacts of automobility, which foil every effort to design attractive buildings.

Nine cars and nine garages, Los Angeles, 1999

All residential buildings in Venice were designed with the assumption that everyone would arrive either on foot or by boat. No provision need be made for parking lots or garages. Most buildings that front on a canal are provided with landing stages for boats, although almost everybody makes all local trips on foot.

Absent the need for car parking, open space is invariably devoted to human uses. It is true that open space is scarce in the older parts of Venice, and much of this takes the form of private gardens. Parks are few and small, but the high quality of public spaces and the omnipresent water views offer a delightful alternative. The surroundings are never threatening. In the absence of the need for garages, the design of attractive buildings is a relatively straightforward matter, even here, where the style here has been kept rather simple.

Housing, Venice, 1997

SHOPPING

Bulk food store, Los Angeles, 1999

In Los Angeles, most retail sales are made by large enterprises housed in huge, featureless buildings from which a large staff serves a vast geographic area. Only inexpensive automobile transport made these enterprises economically feasible, and the traffic they generate exacerbates highway congestion. These businesses generally construct a new building to their own specification, complete with huge parking lot.

Because customers and store employees come from a wide geographic area, they seldom know or even recognize each other and rarely have any social contact outside the store. Should a customer burst into tears, no one would know why. The store is owned by a distant corporation and managed from afar. The business knows its customers only by their demographic profiles but does its best to accommodate them, for its livelihood depends upon it.

Green grocer and news agent, Venice, 1997

In Venice, small buildings house small enterprises from which a few people, or a family, serve a small geographic area. Transport is by foot, and the surroundings are always agreeable. These businesses may have located at their current address generations ago.

The people who work and shop in these stores know each other, sometimes quite well. Both customers and staff usually live within the same neighborhood, so sometimes they meet on the street. They know the local gossip and the recent misfortunes. A customer who is recently bereaved can expect to be greeted with compassion when entering the store for the first time since the death. The proprietor is present during opening hours. He has learned the special needs and desires of all his customers and does his best to accommodate them, for his livelihood depends upon it.

The Alpha & Omega

This table compares Los Angeles, Venice, and the carfree city as proposed in Part II. More stars indicate better conditions. Judgements are, of course, subjective.

Yardstick	Los Angeles	Venice	Carfree City
Priority for pedestrians	★	★★★★★	★★★★★
Human-scale development in downtown	★	★★★★★	★★★★★
Human-scale development elsewhere	★★★	★★★★★	★★★★★
Active street life in downtown	★★★	★★★★★	★★★★★
Active street life in residential quarters	★	★★★★	★★★★
Mixed uses	★	★★★★★	★★★★★
Attractive signage	★	★★★★★	★★★★★
Public amenities	★★	★★★★	★★★★★
Basic shopping in every neighborhood	★★	★★★★★	★★★★★
Short distances to routine destinations	★	★★★★	★★★★
Nearby transport	★★★★★	★★	★★★
Total daily time spent traveling	★★	★★★	★★★★★
Land occupied by transport systems	★	★★★★★	★★★★★
Availability of public transport	★	★★★	★★★★★
Quality of public transport	★	★★★	★★★★★
Direct cost of transport	★	★★★	★★★★
Externalized cost of transport	★	★★★★	★★★★★
Death & injury to bystanders	★	★★★★★	★★★★★
Intimidation of pedestrians	★	★★★★★	★★★★
Safety of very small children on the street	★	★★★★	★★★★
Mobility of older children	★★	★★★★★	★★★★★
Attractive, nearby parks	★★	★★	★★★★★
Street maintenance costs	★	★★★★	★★★★
Noise & vibration (plus wake damage)	★★	★★★	★★★★★
Air pollution & climate change	★	★★★	★★★★★
Exhaustion of nonrenewable energy	★	★★★★	★★★★★

Los Angeles is the archetype of the auto-centric city and so was chosen as the first element in this comparison. Venice, the only large existing carfree city, was chosen as the second element. The final element is a hypothetical carfree city based on the reference design presented in Part II of this work.

On statistical quality-of-life measures, Venice ought to fare as well as any city in the developed nations.

For administrative purposes, the mainland near Venice is part of Venice, but I have omitted the mainland (with its auto-centric patterns) from this comparison.

I have assumed that the car is used for all travel in Los Angeles; this reasonably approximates the current reality.

Venice scores poorly on transport because the ferries provide relatively slow and infrequent service and because the use of motorboats to provide private transport and freight service results in some noise, pollution, and wake damage to buildings.

New carfree cities will enjoy better passenger and freight transport than either Los Angeles or Venice.

"City car," Amsterdam, 1999
The Smart is the smallest of a new breed of city cars designed for urban drivers: these short-wheelbase vehicles can be parked almost anywhere. They impose about the same burden on other street users as full-size cars because they are driven at least as fast and make nearly as much stink and noise. They are more often parked on the sidewalk than larger cars, where they form yet another obstacle for hapless pedestrians.

CITIES & TRANSPORT

The form of the contemporary auto-centric city arises not from historical imperatives, nor directly from human needs. Rather, the auto-centric city takes its form almost entirely from the requirements imposed by the movement and parking of cars: all other needs are subjugated to this end. The medieval city, on the other hand, was shaped directly by human needs and aspirations. The most pressing need was to bring many people within walking distance of one another. Medium-rise buildings packed tightly along narrow streets allowed high human density and assured an active street life.

If we are to improve the form of our cities, we must first remove cars from urban areas, so that other needs can regain the primacy they once had. Only in this way can we build cities that meet human needs while minimizing the impact of human activities on Earth's ecosystem. This chapter considers how cities have been shaped by changes in transport technology during the past two centuries.

Montmartre, Paris, c.1900
The City of Light before the advent of automobiles

TRANSPORT SHAPES CITIES

Transport technology has always affected both the growth and form of cities, and each new transport mode has left its stamp on urban form. When a new mode is adopted, existing urban areas are forced into new uses and even new forms, and new development is arranged in accordance with the demands and capabilities of the new mode. This influence of transport on city form has not always been a positive one. Because city form greatly influences the nature of social life in public spaces, the prevailing transport technology exerts a strong influence on the congeniality of every city.

The rapid growth of 19th-century London was enabled partly by barge canals that were dug across England in the 18th century, but it was the British invention of the railroad in 1825 that enabled London to become the first metropolis with a population of two million.

Just as rail transport was the primary engine of urban development in Europe and North America between 1850 and 1900, automobiles determined the evolution of most cities in the latter half of the 20th century. Rail and road are the two principal alternatives for urban transport (leaving aside special cases such as Venice, where waterborne transport rules). The requirements and capacities of rail and road systems differ greatly and lead to widely divergent urban forms. Rail systems demand relatively dense human settlements with their centers connected to one another by a high-capacity system that usurps relatively small amounts of land. Road transport allows human settlements to disperse over wide areas, because all destinations are in principle equally accessible. This comes at a large cost: an enormous amount of land must be given over to roads and parking, and this exerts a centrifugal force on city form. Large parts of the city

A walking city, Amsterdam, c.1900

See both Goddard and McShane for the history of transport in the USA.

San Francisco, c.1900

In 1906, San Francisco was struck by a devastating earthquake. No sooner had the city been rebuilt than cars staged an insidious assault. Which did more the harm to this beautiful city, the earthquake or the cars?

center are demolished and paved over. The displaced tenants are usually relocated in new buildings farther from the center of town. This change is sometimes accompanied by a decline in population even as the physical extent of the city increases. With the scattering of homes and workplaces, the average trip length increases, and more road capacity is required as drivers rack up ever-greater annual mileage. The dispersed auto-centric city is the antithesis of cities throughout history.

We turn now to a brief history of the evolution of urban form as driven by the development and application of new transport systems. Since the effects are clearest in the auto-centric USA, we begin there.

Shaping Cities in the USA

Between the establishment of the first colonial cities and the present day, urban development in the USA passed through a series of forms, as discussed in the following sections. Compact, walkable cities were universal until the mid-19th century, when slow horse-drawn public transport began to appear. During the following 150 years, new transport technologies radically altered the form of US cities.

Walking Cities

Boston and Philadelphia were the largest 17th-century North American cities, with populations rising to about 10,000. As was everywhere the case at that time, they were densely-populated, compact walking cities. Few could afford to own a horse, and most people walked everywhere they went, so streets were usually crowded with pedestrians. The only attractive building sites were those within reasonable walking distance of the center. In these compact cities, casual social encounters on the street were a normal part of

Cleveland, Ohio, lost population between 1970 and 1990, but the geographical extent of the city increased by one-third during the same period.
"Paved Paradise," *Newsweek,* 15 May 1995

■ Very Dense
■ Dense
■ Moderate
■ Sparse

Walking city
The same key applies to the drawings below.

everyday life. These cities were always built at a human scale: buildings taller than about six stories were impractical until the advent of elevators.

Traffic congestion became an issue relatively early in the history of these cities: New York City already suffered from serious traffic congestion long before the arrival of cars. Draft animals, besides being dangerous and expensive, consumed even more street space than cars and trucks, because backing or turning a wagon and a team of horses or mules requires far more time and space than needed by a truck.

16th-century Nancy, France, 1997

Railroad Cities & Suburbs

By 1860, the construction of railroads permitted the well-to-do to live outside the city and commute by train to jobs downtown. The first US railroad suburb was Llewellyn Park, built in 1858 near New York.

Railroad suburbs usually cluster around the train station, and open space separates one town from the next. Most of these towns developed as independent geographic and political entities. The first of them were sparsely settled, but later examples were often built at fairly high densities, although still lower than the central city. The train station was a natural commercial and civic focus, giving rise to a clearly defined downtown. The development of railroad suburbs continued until about 1930, and included such towns as Radburn, New Jersey.

Railroad suburbs were built near most larger US cities, particularly in the northeast, and many remain agreeable places to live. The streets are relatively narrow, and the houses were built before cars had affected domestic architecture. When garages were built, they were set in the back yard. Houses had front porches that served a social function in the evenings, as people sat out to chat with passing neighbors.

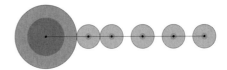

City with railroad suburbs

The San Francisco Bay area BART system uses metro technology but functions more nearly as a commuter railroad than as a metro: except in downtown Berkeley, Oakland, and San Francisco, the station spacing is closer to that of a commuter railroad than that of an urban metro. Another important difference is that many BART riders drive to the station. The competition of station parking facilities for land has impeded the development of commercial centers at these otherwise excellent locations.

City with linear streetcar suburb

Electric streetcars are variously known as trams, trolleys, and Light Rail Vehicles (LRV). Except in a specifically American context, I call these vehicles trams, their usual name outside the USA.

To get a feel for life in these towns, read "Knoxville: Summer of 1915," at the start of James Agee's *A Death in the Family*

Brill Bullets, 1977
This system was arguably the apex of the interurbans and still provides service today, although the Bullets are finally gone.

Streetcar Suburbs

Horsedrawn rail cars began to appear on US city streets shortly after 1850. The first electric streetcar line entered service in Richmond, Virginia, in the late 1880s. Streetcars encouraged suburban development almost from the beginning. The principal difference between streetcar and railroad suburbs was that streetcars were designed for relatively low speeds and stops at intervals of as little as 100 meters. This gave rise to a linear form of development, which led to the appearance of commercial strips along the streetcar lines, with residential districts constructed in continuous bands on both sides of the line. Streetcar lines were often the basis for real estate development projects, and some developers even built their own lines to channel development into areas where they owned land. Again, development took place only within reasonable walking distance of the streetcar stop: lots too far from a stop were hard to sell.

Notice that the definition of a clear community center already begins to fade in streetcar suburbs: the concentration of activities necessary for an active street life begins to diffuse. Each of the many tram stops is a minor center, but no center reaches the intensity of use necessary to support an active street life. Still, life in many of these suburbs was quite agreeable: they were free of noxious uses, the architecture was often quite good, and all buildings were still oriented towards the street and helped to build a sense of place. However, these relatively homogeneous communities were already somewhat closed in their outlook compared to the city center.

The interurban street railway is a US phenomenon. Starting around 1900, enterprises were established across the nation to build interurban lines based on tram technology. These lines operated relatively small, electrified vehicles on lightly-built track linking cities and suburbs. The nub of the matter is summed up by Stephen B. Goddard: "While inter-urbans traveled at two-thirds the speed of the hated railroads, they ran four to six times more frequently at half to two-thirds the fare." Some interurbans, however, operated at quite high speeds: the streamlined, lightweight Brill Bullets on Philadelphia's Norristown High-Speed Line operated from 1931 until almost 1990 at speeds over 140 km/hr.

Goddard, 76

Elevators: Vertical Transport

The widespread availability of electrical power in US cities at the end of the 19th century allowed the installation of elevators, and the height of buildings was no longer limited by the number of steps ordinary people could climb. The first tall buildings, such as the Flatiron Building in Manhattan, were richly detailed and of moderate height, but the rise of Modernism in the 1920s led eventually to faceless, towering glass-and-steel skyscrapers. People who live and work in tall buildings spend a lot of time in elevators, which to this day remain socially uncomfortable spaces. Notwithstanding the close proximity of passengers, conversation in elevators is the exception rather than the rule. Elevators actually damage the social fabric because they tend to make people awkward with one another.

Elevator buildings in Manhattan, 1999

The Metro

The first electrified metro was the London underground, which entered service in 1890, replacing steam-powered trains that had operated since 1863. Boston got the first US subway, which entered service in 1897. In large cities, horse-drawn trams were sometimes replaced by underground metro lines. This change permitted a large increase in personal mobility while actually reducing the surface area occupied by transport systems; New York's subway was

A metro is also variously known as an underground or tube (England) or a subway (USA). When speaking of specific places, I have used the local term.

essential to the city's rapid growth. Between 1904, when the first subway entered service, and 1940, when the subway system had assumed substantially its current form, the population of New York doubled, from 3.5 to 7 million. In most cases, the metro was a tool of city building: the construction costs were prohibitive for privately-financed suburban development. The boroughs of Brooklyn, Queens, and the Bronx were well served by the New York system and could perhaps be regarded as suburbs of much denser Manhattan. Without the easy connection to Manhattan, they could hardly have grown as they did. Nonetheless, construction density in the outer boroughs greatly exceeds what is commonly regarded as "suburban."

Cars Invade Cities

When primitive steam-powered automobiles were first introduced, their use in cities was strenuously and successfully resisted on the grounds that they were too dangerous, noisy, and dirty. The invention of a practical internal combustion engine a few decades later was a sufficient improvement to overcome these early objections, and cars began to show up in cities around 1895, first in Europe and soon afterwards in the USA. They arrived at the height of the bicycle craze, just as the first electrified subways and streetcars were appearing. However, with the exception of trains and steamships, draft animals still pulled most conveyances, including canal barges, trams, heavy wagons, and carriages. One reason cars found such ready acceptance was the painful familiarity with the manifold problems of animal traction, including danger, expense, congestion, slow speeds, noise from steel shoes, stench, filth, and equine epidemics. The end of widespread use of draft animals in cities eased the lives of city dwellers while helping to reduce traffic congestion, at least for a time.

McShane, 93-97

The great Boston fire of 1872 burned out of control for some 35 hours as the result of a raging equine epidemic, the Great Epizootic. The horses were sick or dead, and the fire engines could not be drawn to the blazes. 776 buildings were destroyed.

McShane, 41

Auto-Centric Suburbs

The first auto-centric suburbs appeared in the late 1930s. With this form, for the first time, the rail route network no longer dictated the pattern of development, which could and did occur anywhere. Explosive suburbanization began immediately after World War II and continues even today. Wider and faster roads linked the cities with the countryside, and suburbs sprang up wherever developers could find cheap land. This was not an event that was fated to happen: wild suburban growth was ignited by a variety of government policies that favored suburbs and spurned cities:

- Federal funds paid for infrastructure that was essential to suburban development, including Interstate highways.
- National and state governments maintained gasoline prices at subsidized levels.
- Income tax laws granted special treatment for mortgage interest payments and capital gains from the sale of a home.
- Banking regulators forbade lending in deteriorating downtown areas.
- Cheap, government-insured mortgages were made available only for new construction.
- Adherence to the 1938 US planning guidelines was a prerequisite for federal mortgage insurance; these guidelines expressly forbade traditional mixed-use development.

This last point is especially important, because it ended classic mixed-use development, in which all uses are assembled side by side. Uses were first separated in the late 19th century: nobody wanted stinking, smoky factories as neighbors, a circumstance that had become common by that time. Planners made the right decision in keeping heavy industry away from inhabited areas, but there was no need to separate all other uses from one another. Throughout history, residences have mixed successfully with businesses in cities.

City with auto-centric suburb

For more background, see Jackson, chapter 11

Moonrise, Phoenix, Arizona, 1983
The city lies decked in a thick mantle of smoggy air

"Snout" house, Los Angeles, 1999
This house typifies the kind of housing built in cul-de-sac development. The garage door gets pride of place.

The following table compares infrastructure and resource costs per dwelling unit for suburban single-family houses and medium-density condominiums.

	Single-family	Condominium
Roads, $	3,000	800
Utilities, $	5,000	950
Water, liters/day	1,514	757
Gas, therms/mo.	150	60
Power, kwh/year	10,000	6,000
	Zuckermann, 231	

The favored form of suburban development has been the cul-de-sac, because it is free from through traffic. When buying a house, families search for dead-end streets because they don't want to expose their children to traffic hazards, and low-density, cul-de-sac housing has become the hallmark of US suburbs. However, these low-density areas are far from school, shopping, and some place to hang out. When I speak of "suburban sprawl," I refer to these postwar auto-centric suburbs.

Devastated Inner Cities

Millions of families scraped together a 10% down payment and bought new single-family houses in the suburbs. These families took with them their culture and their money, leaving little behind except their jobs, to which they commuted by car. The millions who migrated to the suburbs had previously paid taxes to the city, helping to maintain its institutions and to provide services to fellow citizens in times of hardship. Most suburban towns had been chartered as separate political entities, and the taxes they collected were for their own use; this money did not find its way into the coffers of the central city. Instead, these taxes were used to pay for building and maintaining suburban infrastructure, and since infrastructure costs in sparsely-settled suburbs exceed infrastructure costs in densely-populated cities, suburban taxes tend to exceed city taxes. The high taxes to support local infrastructure, combined with the costs of operating two or more automobiles, are a crushing burden even for double-income suburban families, who reject any proposal to raise taxes to help the inner cities.

Large areas of most American inner cities turned into ghettos characterized by burned-out buildings, filth, crime, and grinding poverty. Without the stabilizing influence of the middle-class, social conditions deteriorated rapidly, initiating a self-perpetuating cycle of poverty and misery. But, as it turned out, it was not just the cities that turned into slums. As James Howard Kunstler puts it, the USA turned into a national automobile slum, in which grotesque buildings, elephantine signs, and endless parking lagoons replaced real buildings designed for people, not cars.

Suburban Shopping Malls

Another great change occurred in the USA around 1960: suburban shopping malls began to replace downtown commercial centers. Car use did not reach its current extreme levels for several decades after WW II, and throughout the 1950s, many people continued to use public transit to reach downtown shopping. Downtown commercial centers therefore survived the first wave of suburbanization. The appearance of suburban shopping malls was to change all that.

Road interests had begun to dismantle streetcar lines around 1935, and within 20 years, buses had replaced streetcars in almost all US cities. In big cities that once had both subway and streetcar systems, the downtown cores usually survived the replacement of streetcars by buses, albeit with some decline, because the subway still brought many people downtown for work, shopping, and recreation.

In smaller cities that had no subway, when the streetcars stopped running, the only remaining public transport was infrequent, slow, uncomfortable bus service. In these cities, shoppers abandoned the downtown centers to flock to new suburban shopping malls, initiating a cycle of urban decay that was reinforced by the rapid flight of middle-class families to the new auto-centric suburbs. Savannah, Georgia, typifies these cities: it was left with a beautiful but deserted downtown, which gradually fell into decay. Often, only those with

Victor Gruen is usually credited with the design of the first enclosed shopping mall (Southdale Center, Minneapolis, 1956). Gruen is a complex figure. In 1964 he published *The Heart of Our Cities* (Simon and Schuster). His book begins with a paean to cities not unlike the Introduction of this book. He was clearly aware of the vital function of pedestrian areas in cities and the damage done by cars to this function. However, he did as much as anyone to forward auto-centric urban development. His book includes plans for an idealized city in which public transport plays an important role and in which cars are mostly relegated to underground locations. In practice, it would probably have worked in a similar fashion to the auto-centric carfree city shown on page 294, even though the form is rather different.

The activities of the "Road Gang" are discussed starting on page 87.

no other choice remained in inner-city neighborhoods. Social conditions in these areas deteriorated rapidly.

What a Beautiful Strip Mall!

Worse yet was still to come. In the 1970s, entrepreneurs discovered that easy money was to be made by building "strip malls" along busy streets. Developers bought up land that was cheap enough to devote most of it to gigantic asphalt parking lots, invariably located between the street and the store, for the convenience of drivers. Tasteless one-story buildings were quickly thrown up on the site and "decorated" with huge, brightly-colored signs to lure in speeding motorists. The entire effect is even worse than suburban shopping malls, which are at least self-contained, huddled as they are amid vast fields of asphalt.

Strip mall, Los Angeles, 1999

Gated Communities

The ultimate expression of US suburban development is the gated community. The first of these appeared in the mid-19th century, but they remained rare until around 1970, when some rich people withdrew behind guardhouses and high walls. This is the ultimate abandonment of common ground. In some of these communities, all the houses are identical, so family incomes fall within a narrow range. Residents of these communities have little contact with people who are not much like themselves and they lack any real understanding of what life is like for other people.

Jailhouse modern, Los Angeles, 1999
The design of this apartment building flows from parking and security requirements. It is a gated community at the smallest scale.

Contemporary US Cities

Decades after the advent of auto-centric suburbs, it became evident that, while suburbs increased the inhabited area of the city, the demand for road space in suburban and downtown areas, combined with the low FARs typical of suburban development, caused population density in the entire metropolitan region to fall. (The extent of the metropolitan region had, of course, increased considerably.) The construction of highways through the city forced the demolition of old inner-city neighborhoods, whose populations were dispersed into the suburbs (in the less usual case that their residents had been middle class) or relegated to new high-rise buildings that quickly deteriorated into ghettos (in the more usual case that they had been poor).

While urban rail systems remain essential to the functioning of cities like New York and Chicago, newer cities, such as Los Angeles and Phoenix, depend almost entirely on road-based transport systems. Their streets and highways are notoriously congested, and these cities routinely violate air pollution standards. In fact, all large cities without a metro now suffer from terrible traffic congestion and severe air pollution. Bangkok is probably the worst case, but many other cities are nearly as bad.

In auto-centric cities, buildings turn their backs to the street, ignoring the possibility of street life, and indeed very little of it can be observed. Social systems in both the suburbs and the center city deteriorate as people spend ever more time in their cars. All across the USA, people are wondering what happened to the sense of community they had once enjoyed.

Sprawling suburban development precludes efficient transport, because populations are too sparse and destinations are too diffuse to permit practical application of either bus or rail transport.

Los Angeles has finally embarked on a program of metro construction.

Blind-sided, Los Angeles, 1999
Customers enter from the parking lot, not the street.

SHAPING THE REST OF THE WORLD

Most cities outside the USA have embraced the car with less enthusiasm and have altered their urban environments in a less extreme manner than the USA. We turn now to a brief consideration of the effects of cars on cities in nations other than the USA.

Australia & Canada

Australia and Canada most closely approach the US pattern, but public transport was not generally allowed to deteriorate to the extent that it did in the USA. Sydney has a vast rail system that provides reasonably effective public transport. Toronto planned most of its expansion around its metro system and retained its extensive streetcar network.

Western Europe

Western Europe showed a decided ambivalence about the car and the accommodations that it demands, but its cities still suffered considerable damage. New development was usually close to existing cities and considerably denser than in the USA. While tram tracks were ripped up to pave the way for buses and cars in many western European cities, the damage to public transport networks never reached the extremes seen in the USA. All European cities of any size still have reasonably good public transport systems that are widely used and essential to the smooth functioning of the cities they serve. As these cities come to grips with the reality of trying to accommodate cars in crowded downtown cores, tram systems are being restored and people are being asked to leave their cars at home when traveling into the city center.

Urban highway construction never reached the same fever pitch in Europe as in the USA. Instead, highway construction usually took the form of ring roads, because few cities were willing to consider destroying their ancient downtown cores in order to build roads. The new ring roads gradually siphoned development away from the center and out to the edge, where land is cheaper and access for cars is easier. This change somewhat diminished the vitality of the center cities, but most European cities remain reasonably healthy, if less pleasant as a result of the car and truck traffic that bathes these

Downtown Bologna, Italy, 1998
Once one of the world's most beautiful cities, it's now overrun by cars. And Bologna is often upheld as an example of good traffic management!

In just 25 years, the number of 7- and 8-year-old British school children going to school on their own fell from 80% to 9%; in the Netherlands, 83% of children still bike to school.

Two-thirds of all journeys within London are by car, and vehicular traffic is projected to increase by 142% over the next 25 years. Ironically, all this driving has reduced the number of rush hour highway users from 404,000 in 1956 to 251,000 in 1996. The reduction results from a shift from buses to private cars, which reduces road capacity.

Rogers, 120-122

cities in noise and air pollution. European city centers did not see the wholesale destruction so common in US inner cities.

European suburbs are smaller, denser, and house a smaller proportion of the population than those in the USA. The most desirable real estate in European cities is found right at the heart of the city, in the oldest districts.

Elements of the American pattern have been adopted in parts of Europe, however. France has seen the rise of "big-box" stores at the fringes of its cities, and Paris is now ringed by suburbs, the newest of which are of low density. Italian cities (with the sole exception of Venice) have been abandoned to the stink and roar of cars and mopeds. Northern Europe resisted these trends somewhat, but even cities like Amsterdam, which was relatively free of cars as late as 1960, have lost much ground to the automobile since then.

For years I have made a habit of checking real estate prices when visiting European cities. My impression has been that, per unit floor area, the most expensive districts are always in or near downtown.

Fouchier, 78-81

Eastern Europe

Throughout the former Soviet Bloc, trams were adopted as an important urban transport mode that remains in use today. Moscow is a huge city and boasts what is arguably the world's best metro, the crown jewel of the Communist era. No expense was spared in the construction of this system, replete with art and chandeliers. Even though powerful forces are now at work in Moscow to improve the road system, the city is completely dependent on its metro and almost certainly will remain so.

The Developing Nations

In the developing nations, the middle classes emulate the American model they see on television. Suburbs are springing up around Asian capitals, each house complete with parking spaces for two cars, and China has recently

Shanghai planned to put 7 million bicyclists into cars by the year 2000.   Rogers, 68

announced its adoption of the private automobile as the preferred means of passenger transport. (Fortunately, there has been some rethinking of the wisdom of this approach.) Asian cities were always crowded by Western standards, but now they overflow with cars, trucks, and motorcycles. The noise and air pollution have devastated tranquility and health.

Having considered the effects of transport systems on the patterns of urban development, we turn now to a more detailed examination of automobiles and their effects on life in the city.

Distant thunder, cold as stone,
a V8 screams down from its throne.
One by one, each car succumbs.
Something wicked
this way comes.

Naught-to-sixty in 5.7 seconds: Once a figment of the
imagination, now a fixture of intimidation. All courtesy of
the 300-horsepower, 32-valve V8 which seethes within
this, the fiercest automatic sedan in the world.

The new GS
Faster. Sleeker. Meaner.

Full text of a Lexus advertisement. The car is shown
hurtling through a burned-out forest. What an odd
way to sell a car.

The New Yorker Magazine
2 February 1998, inside cover

Mating season, Amstelveld, Amsterdam, 1998
While a car, as a sculptural object, may even be beautiful, cars bring only ugliness to city streets, as here at the Amstelveld. These two shapely automobiles blot this tree-lined square in the heart of Amsterdam's canal district. This is but a mild example of the harm cars do to urban environments.

By "urban automobile" I mean any mechanically-propelled private passenger car that is routinely driven at speeds above 30 km/hr.

See the bibliography for sources. The most up-to-date information is often to be found on the Internet, where most environmental organizations maintain useful sites.

WICKED CARS

There is a multitude of reasons to remove cars and trucks from our cities. While technology may eventually solve or at least ameliorate many of the problems with cars, some of the worst problems are inherent, and urban automobiles will always remain a serious nuisance at best. I believe that the real solution to these problems is to remove cars and trucks from our cities. This chapter has as its goal to persuade the reader that this is the most reasonable course of action.

The past few years have seen the beginnings of a serious dialog about the effects of cars and trucks on urban life. This reflects a dawning awareness following a century in which we blindly accepted the harm caused by motorized vehicles riding on rubber tires. While air pollution gained attention in the 1960s, many other problems related to automobility were not widely recognized until quite recently, and some are still not generally understood. We begin by reflecting on the war between cars and other street users.

CARS VS. PEOPLE

Cars are merely tools, and in rural areas they certainly have appropriate uses. In cities, however, life becomes a contest between cars (and their drivers) and everyone else. In most cities, of course, many people are also drivers, so many of us share in both the blame and the harm. Some of the problems discussed in this section apply primarily within cities, but the slaughter wrought by cars is a problem everywhere.

Slaughter

Practically everyone in the industrialized world knows someone who was killed or maimed in a road collision, and it seems that we have resigned ourselves to this carnage. Road traffic accidents are the leading cause of death worldwide among males aged 15-44. Traffic claims appalling numbers of children: some 300,000 die every year in road crashes around the world.

The USA is one of the safest countries in the world in terms of deaths per distance driven, but in 1998, despite safer cars and highways, US motor vehicle crashes caused almost precisely one death per 100 million vehicle-kilometers traveled, for a total of 41,471 lives lost. In 1994, car crashes were the ninth most common cause of death among all Americans.

By comparison, railroads, with their dedicated rights-of-way, passive guidance, trained operators, and automated safety enforcement, are perhaps the safest form of transport ever devised (airlines may be safer on a passenger-mile basis). Between 1894 and 1994, a total of 9678 people died in railway disasters worldwide, including 543 soldiers killed in the crash of a jam-packed World War I troop train (a wreck that peacetime operational procedures would have prevented).

Central Amsterdam, 1999
Amsterdam is known as the "Venice of the North" because of its canals, but unlike Venice, cars hurt the city's quality of life and besmirch its beauty.

"Global Burden of Disease," 1999, page 19

Archives of Diseases in Childhood, September 1999; 81:200-201

Pucher & Lefèvre, 26

"Traffic Safety Facts 1998," National Highway and Traffic Safety Administration (NHTSA), page ii

NHTSA, National Center for Statistics and Analysis, March 1998

Railroads operate on exclusive rights of way; conflicts with other traffic only arise at grade crossings.

The World Almanac and Book of Facts, 1995. While this is not a comparison of deaths per passenger-kilometer, it does give an indication of the relative safety of trains and cars.

This 100-year global toll is about equal to the number of Americans killed by car crashes in a three-month period.

Danger to Pedestrians and Bicyclists

While car drivers may be said to enter into an implicit agreement to risk life and limb in order to get somewhere in a hurry, many victims of hasty drivers are defenseless bicyclists and pedestrians who have no choice but to use the streets. Some of them never drive and so gain no benefit from the risks they must accept. Many victims are children and elderly people. In Britain, pedestrians represent a shocking one-third of all road deaths. London is notoriously dangerous for children and the elderly.

Out of My Way... Or Else

An enormous power imbalance exists between a pedestrian and a car driver. If anything goes wrong, the pedestrian is likely to be seriously injured or killed. The car driver is unlikely to suffer anything worse than a dent in his car. Nothing can rectify this fundamental injustice, and many drivers still act like schoolyard bullies when they encounter a pedestrian.

Dr. Jekyll and Mr. Hyde

When I used to drive, I noticed that I became a different person behind the wheel of a car, a person I didn't much like. Driving seems to have that effect on many people. It is otherwise hard to explain how so many people, who are polite and considerate in their usual dealings, become highly aggressive once behind the wheel of a car. Multiply this by millions, release the result onto the highways twice a day, and watch as shattered parents return home after a hard day's work and grueling commute. This does not help parents to be nice to their kids or to spend very much time with them.

"Federal data shows that 5,157 pedestrians were killed on the nation's streets in 1996. 69% of those fatalities occurred on neighborhood streets. 837 children died on the street in 1996, 16% of the total pedestrian deaths. This is a significant public health and safety problem that is killing more Americans than headline-grabbing causes of death such as accidental shootings, airbags, or the e-coli bacteria."
Mean Streets '98: http://www.transact.org/mean98/p2.htm

Freund & Martin, 36

The extreme cases of this are known as "road rage"

WRECKING COMMUNITIES

Apart from the danger that cars impose on city streets, traffic also damages the social systems of almost every city. Traffic is a direct contributor to the breakdown of social systems in the USA, both in the inner cities and in the suburbs. In rural areas, cars do actually improve social systems, by making it easier for friends and neighbors to associate, but in cities with decent public transport, cars contribute little to the health of social systems while doing great damage. We consider in this section some of the ways in which cars harm society.

Destruction of Social Systems

The work of Donald Appleyard has established that as automobile traffic on a street increases, social life on that street dies. The noise, danger, and pollution slowly drive people off the street.

People will tolerate quite a lot before they finally abandon the street. In Madrid, for example, people still patronize sidewalk cafés despite the stink and roar of passing diesel trucks. That people will tolerate such conditions shows how highly they value the social functions of common public areas. When conditions finally become so bad that people are driven from the street, chance meetings between neighbors rarely occur, and they are more likely to remain strangers. This lack of contact does grave damage to the social fabric of the neighborhood.

On streets with really heavy traffic, people do not even inhabit the rooms that front on the street, and they make every effort to shut the street out of their lives. Traffic noise makes conversation difficult, even indoors. On streets with such heavy traffic, many people do not even know who their neighbors are.

Carfree street, Bologna, Italy, 1998
This street looks bald, for the simple reason that it isn't carfree at all: I waited for a break in traffic to take the picture. If it were carfree, the street would draw in people and activities.

Sidewalk café, Siena, Italy, 1998
Guests gaze out over the grand Campo, the Gaia fountain, and the campanile. Occasionally a car passes through the square along the far side, but usually all you hear is people talking.

By contrast, in Venice, people don't look over their shoulders, because they know nothing is bearing down on them. The streets are quiet, so there is no need to shout just to be heard. People relax and are more willing to talk to strangers, which leads to a comfortable feeling in the streets.

Isolation of Drivers

If you regard car drivers as gladiators wearing two tons of self-propelled armor, you gain a better understanding of the social dynamics of automobility. Drivers are not part of the landscape through which they pass. They gaze serenely upon the scene while being insulated and protected from it. Drivers thus have no investment in what happens outside their cars and little sense of responsibility. This insulation has permitted the American middle-class to tolerate appalling conditions in the inner cities. People on foot or bicycle or public transport are more aware of conditions around them, more likely to be affected by a bad environment, and hence more likely to take responsibility for maintaining and improving the areas in which they find themselves. This tends to make deteriorating social conditions self-correcting. Among the rich nations, only the USA has accepted the destruction of its inner cities, probably because no other nation depends on cars to quite the same degree.

I lived for several years adjacent to a devastated neighborhood in Oakland, California, riddled with derelict buildings and plagued by crime. Public transport service was marginal despite the large number of people too poor to own a car. Many people with jobs in downtown Oakland had to drive through this neighborhood every day on their way to work, but little action was taken, and conditions in this area never seemed to improve.

Isolation of Non-Drivers

The automobile has isolated the young, the elderly, and anyone who does not drive, particularly in suburban areas lacking any other form of transport. Most suburban children grow up with a very narrow experience of the world and remain dependent on their parents for mobility until they reach driving age. This delays the development of their independence and self-reliance. It also delays their entrance into their community:

> A healthy community is one where children can play outdoors on their own, and where they have the freedom to move around their neighbourhoods without fear. Children learn right from wrong by interacting

with others: friends and neighbours as well as family and teachers. Keeping children off the streets can only hinder their moral and social development. It stops them mixing socially with their neighbours and learning the importance of respect for others, and leads to them having less sense of responsibility for their actions. As for abductions by strangers, while they are tragic events, it is important to remember that they are very rare (which is why they get so much media attention). Home zones will reduce the risk of abduction, because there will be more people out and about in the street and more contact between residents. Family, friends and neighbours will all be keeping a watchful eye out.

Because the car often provides the only means of mobility, older people tend to keep driving long after their vision and reflexes are really up to the task. In most of the USA, giving up one's driver's license amounts to a de facto resignation from the community's social life. Those who can no longer drive are sometimes imprisoned by traffic, as in the case of the Tamiami Trail, which debouches into Port Charlotte, Florida, as a street 14 lanes wide at some intersections. Many old people live nearby, and, despite the traffic islands in the middle of the crosswalks, those who are frail cannot cross from the curb to the island during the interval that the light is with them: they can no longer cross this street *at all*.

Nancy, France, 1997
This street is dangerous for kids to play on, and, with all those cars blocking the view, neighbors can't keep an eye out.
Quote courtesy the Children's Play Council
"Home Zones: Reclaiming Residential Streets,"
National Children's Bureau, London, 1997.

Disturbing the Peace

In most cities, traffic is the worst source of noise, but in the pedestrian precincts of Amsterdam and Copenhagen, the loudest sounds are often people's footsteps. Venice is entirely free of automotive noise, and quiet usually reigns in carfree downtown areas in other cities. Once cars vanish, people

I once attended a meeting in a new office building located near a busy California highway. The building was sound insulated and had triple glazing. Throughout the meeting I was distracted by the peculiar whine of the attenuated traffic noise. Outdoors it was difficult to hold a conversation.

tend to speak more softly and life becomes more peaceful. Even worse than cars are motor scooters and motorcycles, many of which make simply shocking amounts of noise. No attempt at regulation has had any lasting success at quieting these miserable things.

Not in My Back Yard

In the developed nations, public opposition now makes it nearly impossible to build new urban highways. Societies that have lived with cars for a generation or more have a clear understanding of just how much damage a highway does to the quality of life. Nobody wants a highway running through the back yard: the noise alone is reason enough. Local opposition to the intrusion of a highway, and to the demolition of entire neighborhoods to make room for it, has become so vociferous that few cities even dare to propose such schemes. To skirt the conflict, governments instead build new ring roads, ever farther from downtown. This leads to still more sprawl, even worse highway congestion, and yet more damage to the economic vitality of the inner city, as jobs and housing are lured away by the ring road.

AUTOMOBILITY DOES NOT WORK

When the first cars were sold little more than a century ago, it was not foreseen that this curiosity would become the dominant transport mode in richer nations. Cars initially provided only entertainment and recreation; they had yet to become a serious means of getting about. Top speeds were low and breakdowns routine. As auto manufacturers solved these problems, people began to expect that cars would improve mobility, but better mobility is not provided by higher speed alone. Cars improve mobility in rural areas and

Highway interchange, Los Angeles, 1999
Nobody wants one of these in the backyard, or even anywhere near by.

Mobility can be defined simply as getting people where they need to be.

small towns, but in metropolitan areas, cars actually *reduce* mobility. It is crucial to understand why this occurs. It has to do with the astonishingly large amount of space consumed by roads and parking lots in auto-centric cities.

Cars Demand Too Much Space

A single traffic lane can carry only 2000 cars an hour under ideal circumstances. (A rail line can move up to 20 times as many people over the same amount of land, before any allowance is made for parking.) As more roads are built to carry increased traffic, less land is available for other uses, forcing development into rural areas far from downtown. The resulting sprawl increases the length of many trips, causing yet more demand for highway capacity. The results of this vicious circle can be seen in any large auto-centric city.

Cars can only provide fast transport if an extensive system of highways is constructed. This, however, requires the construction of interchanges where two major highways intersect. These interchanges sometimes have six levels of traffic crossing one another, and the space required for elevation and direction changes becomes enormous. These interchanges can take a decade to construct and cost hundreds of millions of dollars.

In addition to road space, each car also needs several parking spaces. (It seems that nobody really knows just how much parking is needed. The figure of eight spaces per car is often quoted, but the source of this number remains elusive.) Under ideal circumstances, just 400 cars can be parked at ground-level on one hectare. Multilevel parking garages can increase this value considerably, but garages are expensive to construct (and must be the ugliest structures ever made by man). Even multistory garages occupy large amounts of land.

Parking garage, Los Angeles, 1999
For a given amount of land, many more cars can be parked in a multilevel garage than on a simple, at-grade parking lot. The difference is not as great as it might seem, because the dual access ramps (one up, one down) consume much space.

Finally, there is the space required by the automobile infrastructure itself: car washes, service stations, tank farms, body shops, junk yards, and dealerships. To this we could add the space required by hospitals to treat those injured in wrecks.

Perpetual Traffic Congestion

Contemporary wisdom on roads and traffic holds: "build a road and they will come." New roads in urban areas are almost instantly filled to capacity and beyond. It seems that no matter how many roads we build, they will always be congested at rush hour. Since the demand for transport is finite (presumably, people want to spend some time at their destinations), there must exist some capacity at which demand is fully supplied, but building this much capacity is almost beyond contemplation. In fact, roads would expand to occupy most land in the city center.

Traffic engineers have recently concluded that the best way to relieve congestion is to *reduce* road capacity. This runs contrary to common sense, but it works, after a fashion. At first it was assumed that the traffic was merely being displaced to other routes, but it now appears that about 20% of the traffic simply disappears. What is happening, of course, is that some people are either not making the trip at all or going by another means. The difference between the number of trips people would like to make and the number of trips they actually do make is the "mobility gap." Clearly, traffic congestion now imposes mobility limitations on Americans, especially in the suburbs. Some activists want to limit mobility in order to reduce environmental damage. However, I see no reason to deny people the access to the social, cultural, educational, and employment opportunities that quick, convenient, sustainable transport can provide.

"Relationships Between Highway Capacity and Induced Vehicle Travel," Robert B. Noland, U.S. Environmental Protection Agency, 16 November 1998, paper no. 991069.

On any road, as traffic begins to thicken, speed diminishes, vehicle spacing shrinks, and more capacity becomes available at the slower speed. This appears to be a stable feedback condition. However, once speeds have fallen to the optimum level, any further increase in traffic results in snowballing delays, and traffic grinds to a halt. This condition now regularly occurs on streets and highways around the world.

Building new roads is no longer an option in many cities. The Century Freeway, the last major new superhighway built through central Los Angeles, cost a staggering $200 million/kilometer.

Newman & Kenworthy, 60

The Limits of the Auto-Centric City

As more and more people move into an auto-centric city, the area covered by the road system increases without limit once the population reaches around five million. In order to keep all areas of the city within a 90-minute rush-hour drive, roads, parking, and other auto-related services must expand to cover all available ground. Some auto-centric cities in the American West and South are actually approaching this absurd condition: up to 70% of downtown land in Houston and Los Angeles is devoted to the automobile.

Beyond a certain point, however, the demand for more road capacity becomes practically impossible to meet, for the following reasons:

- The land area required by roads becomes enormous and exerts a further centrifugal effect.
- Air pollution caused by the large number of cars traveling long distances becomes an intractable problem.
- The cost of new highways becomes so high that their construction is not even considered.
- The energy costs of transport become insupportable.

Without rail transport, a growing metropolitan region will eventually occupy so much land that it becomes a constellation of contiguous cities. Los Angeles and Atlanta are vast agglomerations, more than 100 kilometers across. It is impractical to live at one extremity of Atlanta and work at the other extremity: these agglomerations no longer function as single, unified cities.

FOULING THE NEST

We are making a mess of the Earth. While cars are not the only culprits, they account for a large share of the damage we are doing. Aside from the problems of their direct emissions,

In Lancaster and Palmdale (on the fringes of Los Angeles), one-third of commuters drive more than 80 km to work.

"Shaping Cities: The Environmental and Human Dimensions," Marcia D. Lowe, Worldwatch Paper 105, page 19

Atlanta recently reached a crisis. Air pollution had become so bad that the US government threatened to withhold vital highway funds. In the 1998 elections, a new governor was elected on the promise of tackling the problem. His proposal for a regional body with broad powers over transport and development won wide support and was easily adopted in the state legislature.

Pollution emitted from typical USA work commutes, in grams per 100 passenger-km.

Mode	Organics (VOC)	NO$_x$
Metro	0.2	30
Bus	12	95
Single-occupancy car	130	128

"Alternatives to the Automobile: Transport for Livable Cities," Marcia D. Lowe Worldwatch Paper 98, page 14

While it is true that newer cars are cleaner per vehicle-mile traveled, total US highway emissions during the period 1960-1995 have increased 73% for NO$_x$ and 1% for CO. Volatile organic compounds (VOC) did actually fall, by 41%. The increase in vehicle miles traveled is negating improvements in emissions control.

From a posting by John Holtzclaw of the Sierra Club to the cons-spst-sprawl-trans list

The combustion of hydrocarbons under pressure, as in an internal combustion engine, also generates a potent family of greenhouse gases, NO$_x$.

Solar sources include wind energy, hydropower, and biomass, as well as direct solar conversion devices such as solar cells and sun-fired steam generators.

cars also consume huge amounts of raw materials in their construction. The extraction and smelting of metal ores causes a great deal of pollution and consumes large amounts of energy, as does the production of plastic and glass. The disposal of junked cars and worn out parts (batteries in particular) also contributes to the burden. The transport and refining of petroleum further taxes the global ecosystem. When all these burdens are taken into account, the problem becomes large indeed.

Poisoning the Air

Air pollution problems are exacerbated in cities because of the extreme concentration of cars and trucks. Every large auto-centric city has been faced with horrific air pollution problems, and while vast resources have been committed to cleaning up automobile emissions, little progress has been made in improving air quality.

Global Warming

Cars are fueled, directly or indirectly, by fossil fuels, and therefore aggravate the global warming problem by their CO_2 emissions. Only electric cars recharged from nuclear or solar energy sources and vehicles burning renewable fuels do not contribute to global warming. Most energy today comes from carbon-based fuels (mainly coal, oil, and natural gas), and all of these emit CO_2 when burned. Energy derived from non-fossil sources is currently expensive and of limited supply, but both the cost and supply picture are improving.

Poisoning the Land & Water

Cars are not usually mentioned in connection with water pollution, but they are a source of two serious pollutants: oil and salt. Cars release more oil than tanker spills, and winter road salt finds its way into drinking water. Cars also cause heavy-metal pollution. Lead is released in huge quantities because it is added to gasoline as an octane booster; leaded fuels are still used in many areas of the world. Even tiny amounts of lead inhibit the mental development of children.

Car exhausts and motor oil changes dumped down drains account for more oil entering the oceans than any other source.   Greenpeace

Resource Consumption

The global automobile fleet now numbers about 500 million vehicles. In rich nations, every second person owns a car. If this rate of car ownership were extended to a global population of 6 billion then we would have 3 billion automobiles, or six times as many as now. Even if vehicle weights decline dramatically, our planet may not harbor enough natural resources to build and fuel this enormous fleet of automobiles.

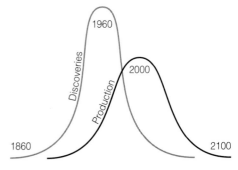

The March 1998 issue of *Scientific American* carried an excellent series of articles entitled, "The End of Cheap Oil." Hubbert's work figures prominently in the discussion.

The End of Cheap Oil

American oil geologist M. King Hubbert spent a lifetime considering the relationship between petroleum supplies and industrial economies. He paid particular attention to the question of the extent of supplies and was the first to warn that the oil age would be a short one. In 1956, Hubbert accurately predicted that oil production in the 48 lower US states would peak around 1970. His method is deceptively simple: when half of the total supply has been extracted, the peak of production has been reached. In 1974 he predicted that global production would peak around 1995. Using his very simple methodology, others have applied contemporary data and predicted a global peak soon after 2000. Other experts give dates as late as 2020. One thing is certain: oil reserves are finite. We have already burned at least a third of all the recoverable oil that ever existed, and consumption is doubling every 35 years.

Oil production from all non-OPEC nations has already peaked, as has production from all of the world's 37 largest fields.
Walker & Kanaki, *Chemical Engineering in Australia* 14(4): pp6-9, 1988 (from Newman & Kenworthy, 50)

Even some big oil companies now admit that the peak will come between 2010 and 2020.
                    Newman & Kenworthy, 50

Almost the entire world has now been intensively explored for oil using technologies that didn't exist a few decades ago. During the period 1982-1992, the 30 largest oil companies invested US$417 billion in oil and gas exploration and development, but only found oil and gas worth US$170 billion.

Some 75% of all oil has been found in giant fields, ones larger than 500 million barrels, and we have found very few giants since the 1980s. Oil consumption is about 23 billion barrels per year and rising, while discoveries are running about 7 billion barrels per year and falling.

From a posting to the SusTrans list
by Charlie Richardson

For those who say that new discoveries will save the day, the news is bad: oil discoveries peaked in 1962 and now run at only a third the rate of consumption. It is true that Saudi Arabia sits atop a vast pool of oil, and Saudi production may peak as late as 2020. By then, however, oil production from all other nations will be in fairly rapid decline.

It is therefore only a question of time before the rate of oil production begins to fall. Petroleum prices will probably rise inexorably after 2010, perhaps much sooner.

CARS ARE DRIVING US POOR

The monetary costs of transport have a large effect on standards of living. The prosperity of the industrialized nations has made it possible to provide most adults with their own cars, fuel to run them, and roads enough to drive on, but the direct economic costs are high. The cost of private automobile transport is a substantial fraction of most family budgets in the USA. While the capital costs of rail systems are high (although not particularly so in comparison to the costs of roads), their operating and energy costs are relatively modest in comparison to private cars. The difference will become steadily more important in the years ahead, as energy becomes scarcer and therefore more expensive.

The Myth: Drivers Pay Their Way

Who pays for automobility? Many people think that drivers pay the full cost of their driving. Researchers agree that this is far from being the case. John Holtzclaw of the Sierra Club summarized various research studies of what the pump price of a gallon of gasoline would have to be to cover the costs of driving. When the externalities are considered, the true cost of a gallon of gasoline rises to over $10.00.

$4.00/gallon is equivalent to $1.06/liter, which is roughly the price of gasoline in western Europe.

Researcher	Real cost of fuel, $/gal
Ketcham & Komanoff	5.53
Litman	7.08
MacKenzie, Dower & Chen	3.03
Moffet & Miller	2.86 - 5.00
Vorhees	4.78
Delucchi	3.13 - 7.55
US Office of Technology Assessment (OTA)	3.39 - 6.81
OTA, including non-monetary personal costs	11.17 - 16.11

http://www.sierraclub.org/sprawl/transportation/subsidies.asp

The Reality: The Public Subsidizes Drivers

The following costs are often omitted in calculations of the costs of automobility:

- Damage to the social fabric
- Subsidies to public transit due to reduced ridership
- Capital & maintenance costs of parking lots
- Injuries to other street users
- Petroleum production subsidies
- Military actions to protect petroleum supplies
- Reduction in real estate values caused by nearby roads
- Lost property taxes on land occupied by streets
- Vibration damage to structures
- Noise-related stress
- Additional police, fire & ambulance services
- Global warming & coastal flooding
- Air, water & land pollution

Capital and operating costs for parking are much higher than one might expect. Capital costs for simple surface parking lots are $7967 per space, with an annual operating cost of $995. Multilevel parking structures can cost as much as $60,857 per space to build, with annual costs of $4504. Drivers often do not pay these costs themselves: the costs are absorbed by employers and merchants. This means, of course, that non-drivers also pay part of the cost of parking, since these costs are reflected in higher prices.

Warren, 15, quoting
Shelley L. Smith, "The Stuff of Parking,"
Urban Land, Feb. 1990, page 38

TRAFFIC CALMING

Much work has been done to tame the car in the city. These projects, generally known as "traffic calming," attempt to curb the worst excesses of drivers, but many of these measures bring unexpected side effects. For instance, while speed bumps do slow passing cars, most drivers will brake hard just before the bump and stomp on the accelerator as soon as they are clear of it. This results in more noise, more energy consumption, and more air pollution than is the case with a steady high speed. Pedestrians may be a little safer, but the overall result is not much of an improvement.

TECHNOLOGY TO THE RESCUE?

Technical fixes for the automobile are held out as the solution to the problems cars cause, and the coming decades will probably see several advances that would reduce the burden of automobility. Keep in mind, however, that even if cars become quicker, safer, cheaper, quieter, more efficient, and less polluting, they still impose enormous burdens on the city, its inhabitants, and the global ecosystem.

Computerized Guidance

Computer-guided automobiles are likely to see large-scale trials. These systems would pilot cars without human attention on superhighways. In larger cities, computer-controlled cars might double their current rush-hour speeds, and the capacity of highways would increase. Safety would improve and pollution would decline if the number of vehicle-miles remained constant. Experience shows that the increased capacity will be rapidly absorbed, leading to still more vehicles traveling ever farther, with congestion delays soon returning.

Safety Enforcement

Computerized cars offer many possibilities for regulation and taxation of use. While local streets will probably never see full automation, onboard computers can restrict speed and stop the car if the driver's behavior is dangerous.

For a thorough review of traffic calming measures, and particularly their many unintended consequences, see Zuckermann's *End of the Road.*

A test of computer-guided cars was recently conducted on an unopened stretch of highway in the Netherlands. A string of Buicks blazed past at 100 km/hr, with just 6 meters separating the cars.
"Handen van het stuur; blik niet op de weg"
NRC Handelsblad, 16 June 1998

Stationary Power Generation

Power for battery-powered cars could be supplied from static sources, thereby relocating pollution away from the automobile itself. Conventional lead-acid cells are adequate for slow speeds and short distances. Major breakthroughs in battery technology may make long-range electric cars practical.

See the *Scientific American* special issue, "The Future of Transportation," October 1997, for an interesting look at transportation technology and the future of automobiles.

Advanced Motive Power

Many auto manufacturers have embarked on programs to develop advanced hybrid and fuel-cell cars that are expected to achieve far higher fuel efficiencies than conventional cars. When hydrogen-fueled, the tailpipe emission of a fuel cell is pure water. Given the certain need for continued car use in rural areas, and given that hydrogen is likely to be the fuel of choice in a sustainable energy infrastructure, the development of practical fuel-cell cars is in any case nearly essential.

Victor Wouk, "Hybrid Electric Vehicles," in *Scientific American*, October 1997

Underground Roads

The entire automobile network of a city could be buried at huge expense. Major improvements in tunneling technology are ongoing, and the cost of such an enormous project might someday fall just within our means.

Hollywood Freeway, Los Angeles, 1999
This segment of highway is already close to being underground. If it were decked over, the space above could be reclaimed and the noise nearly eliminated, but the cost would be very high.

And Suppose It Works?

Technology might solve the congestion, safety, pollution, and energy issues related to automobile use in cities. Underground roads might even solve the social and aesthetic issues. This still does not mean that the car is the best solution: it will remain the most expensive, most resource intensive, and least sustainable method of urban transport.

We consider next a better means of moving ourselves and our goods within cities.

Lisbon metro station, 1999
What isn't polished marble is decorated tile.

BETTER PUBLIC TRANSPORT

An externalized cost is a monetary or non-material cost that is borne neither by the producer nor by the consumer of a product or service.

By removing cars from cities, we can improve urban mobility while also reducing its direct and externalized costs. Better public transport is essential to this task, and people will need assurance that all of their transport needs can be met by the proposed system. The technical difficulties are fairly easy to overcome, but convincing people that it would work is more difficult. Most Americans and many Europeans regard public transport as a third-rate way of getting around, suitable only for those who can't afford a car. It wasn't always like this.

A SHORT HISTORY OF URBAN TRANSPORT

Most rail systems were profit-making until the rise of the car, but today it is doubtful if any passenger rail system in the USA operates at a profit. It was the widespread adoption of cars that made it essentially impossible for US rail systems to pay their direct operating costs from farebox revenues alone:

- Subsidies for cars were so large that rail systems could not compete with them while maintaining fares at a level high enough to turn a profit.
- Cars siphoned off traffic from rail systems, reducing their economic base.
- Heavy car use caused traffic congestion, which delayed trams, raised operating costs, and made public transport service even less attractive to riders.

If drivers had never received the enormous subsidies they do, cars would never have displaced rail systems for urban transport: we would today have extensive tram networks in most cities, and large cities would have built metro lines instead of urban highways. Suburban development would have occurred on a much smaller and denser scale, in the form of railroad and streetcar suburbs. How, then, did it come to pass that cars replaced trains?

The Evil Empire: US Railroad Monopolies

Had railroads not become the villain of the age, road transport might never have supplanted rail transport in the USA. The railroads had been a great boon to US westward expansion, and the government offered huge incentives to those daring enough to build railroads into areas that lacked sufficient economic activity to support profitable service at the time of construction. Once built, the railroad offered both reason and means to occupy the lands near it. As the young nation grew, the railroads profited handsomely.

Railroading is by nature a monopoly business, and it was the first monopoly of national importance. Most rural areas were served by a single railroad, and the railroads so abused their monopoly positions that, by 1900, they were widely despised. It was decades before the USA decided to regulate

See Goddard and McShane for a detailed history of the downfall of railroads and the rise of cars and trucks in the USA.

monopolies and instituted the necessary reforms. Ironically, road transport began to offer serious competition to railroads around 1930, just as government regulation was finally hitting its stride. The Great Depression struck simultaneously, and the railroads never recovered. But the decline of railroads was driven by more than the hatred they had engendered:

- The usefulness of cars in rural areas
- Complacent management
- Greedy unions
- Excessive debt
- Price wars resulting from overbuilding
- Competition from interurban street railways

At one time, the Pennsylvania, the New York Central, the Erie, the Nickel Plate Road, and the B&O all provided service between New York and Chicago.

The Road Gang Takes the Wheel

Starting around 1920 in the USA, trucks, buses, and cars began to displace rail-based systems, which ceased to be the linchpin of transport. Henry Ford succeeded in making a practical automobile at a price that eventually fell within the reach of most Americans. There was one problem, however: the deplorable state of US roads. Road networks in Europe and North America actually deteriorated during the 19th century because railroads offered such good transport. When cars first appeared, rural roads were in a dismal state. The hatred of the railroads, combined with mass-produced cars, free roads, and cheap gasoline, set the stage for a consortium of highway interests (the Road Gang) to dominate US transport politics right up to the present.

McShane, 86

Cars were first adopted in cities, where streets had already been paved to facilitate cleaning them. Ironically, the city was the one place cars weren't really needed: US urban public transport in the early 20th century was relatively good.

Under pressure from the Road Gang, highway building became a favored Depression-era public works project that

"To counter the perceived drift toward White House control, the highway coalition went underground in 1942 to seek common ground. Meeting for lunch each Thursday behind closed doors in Washington, 240 oil, rubber, and auto bigwigs, top highway bureaucrats, trade association executives, and public relations specialists debated how to maintain hegemony in the highway field. No press releases issued from this secret society, referred to by Washington insiders as simply the 'Road Gang.'"

Goddard, 171

finally made intercity travel by road a practical proposition. But it was the 1956 launch of the Eisenhower System of Interstate and Defense Highways that really set the stage for unbridled road transport. The Interstates gave truckers a subsidized route network that allowed them to compete successfully with railroads despite the labor and energy inefficiency of trucking. It also gave real estate developers the high-speed arteries leading to downtown that made large-scale suburban sprawl possible.

But not even the widespread public support for better roads was sufficient to further the interests of the highwaymen. Treachery was also necessary.

Road Interests Kill US Public Transport

Beginning in the 1930s, a grim story played itself out on the streets of almost every US city: members of the Road Gang conspired to destroy public transport. These criminals bankrolled the systematic destruction of streetcar lines throughout the nation, and by the 1950s, buses had replaced streetcars in almost every US city. Public transport ridership plummeted: people chose to drive rather than take the slow, uncomfortable buses that replaced the trams. As ridership fell, levels of service declined and fares increased. Bus systems became unprofitable and eventually insolvent. Cities ultimately found it necessary to buy up and operate urban bus lines, and large subsidies became universal in an environment where high-quality, profit-making public transport service had become impossible.

Elsewhere in the World

Outside the USA, similar problems have beset most cities. In Western Europe, tram lines were closed in many cities between 1945 and 1965. Massive road construction, along

In the USA, trucks pay only a small portion of the costs of repairing the damage they do to roads, whereas freight railroads are not subsidized. Heavy trucks are believed to do 95% of the damage to US highways. (Lowe [1994], 39)

Anti-railroad bias in the USA is so strong that even today few see the incongruity of deep subsidies to the trucking industry while railroads must pay taxes on their rights-of-way to every community through which they pass.

US prosecutors secured a conviction against several members of the Road Gang in 1949. "Yet for their roles in concocting and perpetrating a criminal conspiracy–which helped change the dominant urban energy from electricity to less-efficient petroleum and to alter American urban life forever–the Court fined the corporations five thousand dollars each and the individuals one dollar."

Goddard, 135

New York City once had the world's largest streetcar network. The Road Gang converted the entire system to buses in just 18 months.

Goddard, 127

the US model, began in the 1960s, and car usage in Europe has risen nearly to US levels. There are a few bright spots in this picture, however. As mentioned earlier, trams are enjoying a major revival. Metro lines are being constructed and extended. France pioneered high-speed rail service in Europe, and travel time on some routes was slashed so much that both highways and airlines lost passengers to the train.

Eastern Europe used trams as an important urban transport mode, but after the collapse of the Soviet Union, cities in the region started to copy the "success" of their Western cousins. Cars now terrorize pedestrians from Estonia to Bulgaria. A massive program of highway construction is under way, and intercity rail lines are being abandoned as cars take over.

Japan's rail system was rebuilt after wartime devastation, and it is today arguably the most advanced and heavily used system in the world. Development in Tokyo has remained centered on rail systems. In Sydney, an extensive suburban rail network continues to provide decent service, although cars have become the dominant mode of transport.

Developing nations seek to adopt Western patterns of car use (with help from international development agencies, which still see cars as the centerpiece of economic development). Cities like Bangkok have bus systems that cover the whole city and once offered reasonable service. Widespread car usage in Bangkok and many other Asian cities has now brought rush-hour traffic to a standstill, so neither drivers nor bus passengers can get anywhere.

A peculiar situation affects nations that were formerly colonies of European powers, which often built rail systems in their dependencies during the late 19th and early 20th centuries. These systems are still in place, but many have seen little improvement since the colonial powers withdrew. The newly-independent nations have often invested their scarce

In 1971, the sparkling new Mexico City metro broke with this trend by providing efficient, attractive, and cheap metro service. By contrast, technical problems plagued the new BART system in the San Francisco Bay Area, although these problems were eventually resolved, and BART now provides reliable service to many people.

Rail infrastructure is often incredibly durable. When I was traveling in Thailand in 1989, most of the signaling and control equipment was nearly 100 years old and still seemed to be functioning reliably.

capital in improving road networks and airports while neglecting railroads.

Rail has come to be seen by many as a costly anachronism. This is unfortunate, because, for a given investment, rail systems provide greater capacity than road systems.

Except in a few large cities such as Paris and Tokyo, public transport typically does not function very well. We must improve our public transport systems, using trains, not buses, in order to provide service that competes with cars on every point of comparison, with an eye to gradually moving cars out of cities.

Do Rail Systems Measure Up?

Rail-based transport systems do not always measure up as well as they might by some of our yardsticks. We need to understand why this is so and what might be done about it.

Advantages & Limitations of Rail Systems

Rail systems enjoy a number of intrinsic advantages over road-based transport but are also affected by several significant limitations. The advantages have favorable effects on urban form, and it is possible to design around the limitations without adversely affecting the resulting city. The following considerations affect the planning of a city and the design of its rail system:

- Trains occupy far less land than cars and trucks, and much of their infrastructure can be placed underground or removed to unpopulated areas.
- Rail systems only work when origins and destinations are densely-populated areas that can generate enough ridership to justify the capital investment and operating costs.
- Rail passengers must walk between the doorstep and the

station, which must therefore be located within reasonable walking distance.

- Trains achieve excellent point-to-point speeds, quite often higher than cars, but the route network is inflexible, and transfers from one line to another are often required to reach a particular destination, whereas a car driver can select any destination and route he may wish.
- When trains run on grade-separated rights of way, they are never affected by road congestion. Trams operating on surface streets can offer good service in smaller cities, but road traffic must not be permitted to cause delays.
- Trains use comparatively little energy per passenger-mile, permitting longer distances between stations, thereby allowing the establishment of natural areas near downtown.

Working Around Rail's Limitations

The limitations can be mitigated by adopting a city plan that locates all destinations near a station and that limits the number of transfers to one at the most. The reference design for carfree cities is predicated on a densely-populated city with a route network that never requires more than one transfer. Such a design employs the powerful advantages of rail systems while circumventing their inherent limitations.

FASTER PUBLIC TRANSPORT

The most common and most serious complaint about using public transport is that it is slow in comparison to driving. In some large cities with good rail systems, the reverse is true: it is faster to take the metro than to slog through heavy traffic. But in the main, the charge of slow door-to-door service is justified, especially where service is provided by bus. A crosstown bus in Manhattan can often be overtaken by a fit pedestrian. Public transport must achieve at least the average speed of a bicyclist and preferably better. This is, in fact, a difficult design goal: in many urban areas, bicycling is actually the fastest door-to-door transport mode. Several strategies to improve door-to-door transit times are discussed in the following sections.

New Attitudes

Transit managers need to think in terms of shaving *seconds* off journey times. The prevailing attitude is that minor delays and slow service are not problems worth worrying about, and that no solutions exist, anyway. Without a fundamental change in this attitude, real improvements are impossible.

I once phoned the management of the Boston MBTA to inquire why trains on the new Quincy line never exceeded 80 km/hr even though the line was built for 110 km/hr service. The answer was shocking: "That would only save a couple of minutes." Two minutes a passenger, twice a day, for 50,000 passengers is a *lot* of man-hours.

Short Waits

Waiting for the vehicle to arrive is often the largest single component of a public transport journey, and one that does not arise when driving. There's nothing to do, and transport stops are rarely pleasant places to hang around. Having endured the wait for the bus, passengers are then subjected to the indignity of watching cars stream past, first as the bus lumbers along and then while it sits, sometimes for minutes at a time, as people board. Average bus speeds are dismal, and the numerous transfers involve long waits.

Tram service in Amsterdam operates only four times an hour in the evenings, at which time it may be faster to walk several kilometers rather than wait for the tram to come, especially when you know that they occasionally just skip a scheduled trip.

In an ideal world, a bus or tram would come along every few seconds to whisk you directly to your destination. In reality, public transport is generally scheduled to run no more frequently than is necessary to provide service with full vehicles (usually with some passengers standing). From the viewpoint of maximizing revenue and minimizing direct costs, this is a sensible strategy, but it is unlikely to attract customers who have any other choice. If the goal is to entice

The interval between one trip and the next is known as "headway."

people out of their cars, then the system must move people quickly to their destinations at all times of day, not just rush hour. On heavily-used routes, it is economically feasible to provide frequent service at most times of the day. Automated metro systems can reduce the costs of frequent service.

The newest metro line in Lyon is fully automated, allowing more frequent evening service than is provided on the other lines, which require drivers.

Grade separation, Venice, 1997
Passenger and freight transport is waterborne, and the pedestrian network crosses above the canals. This unusual example of grade separation demonstrates the principle: different kinds of traffic never interfere with each other.

Elevated metro, New York, 1999
How *not* to do grade-separation

Higher Speed

Obviously, the higher the maximum speed a vehicle attains, the shorter the trip. What is less obvious is that the maximum speed is usually limited by acceleration: the short distance between stops caps the maximum speed that can be attained. Speed is, however, often limited by other factors.

In many cities, public transport is provided by buses and trams that must compete with cars for right-of-way. Since transit vehicles must stop to load and unload, their average speed is much lower than that of cars. Only when high priority is given to transit service can it achieve better speed than cars. Cities should decide to make transit faster than driving by allocating street space first to transit, then to bicycles, and next to trucks. Cars could use any space that remains, as long as they did not interfere with public transport. This is a much more efficient use of resources: buses and trams carrying many people will move at good speeds, free from competing traffic. The real solution is the provision of a grade-separated right-of-way, as for a metro: surface traffic congestion never delays the trains.

Cities with population below 500,000 do not absolutely require grade-separated systems: ordinary streets can provide reasonable passenger and freight service provided those streets are free of cars. In the absence of competing car traffic, trams (buses, if you must) will make good time, and freight can be trucked over streets of normal width. In larger cities, the need for grade separation becomes nearly inescapable.

For safety reasons, the speed of vehicles running on city streets should be limited, and I have assumed a maximum of 50 km/hr for buses and trams running on the street. In practice, higher speeds are often accepted. The speed of metro trains, running as they do on grade-separated rights-of-way, need not be limited for safety reasons, and BART trains reach speeds as high as 130 km/hr.

High Acceleration

Vehicle acceleration should be as high as possible within the limit of what is safe and comfortable for riders. That limit is well below the traction limit of steel wheels on dry steel rails. It is actually jerk, not acceleration itself, that is the principal limiting factor for passenger comfort and safety. With precise computer control of motors it is possible to achieve quick, smooth starts and stops. If jerk is kept low, then relatively high acceleration is quite acceptable, leading to a large improvement in average speed. When accelerating from a stop, PCC streetcars take about 0.75 seconds to reach a peak acceleration of 0.22 G. They maintain this acceleration for only a few seconds, because at higher speeds the motors cannot produce enough torque to sustain such a high rate. After extensive testing, the designers of the PCC streetcar specified 0.22 G as the maximum acceleration, and this value can be taken as the upper limit for any vehicle with standing passengers. This relatively high figure is contingent on very low jerk, which can now be provided simply by installing computerized motor controllers.

There is one loophole in the acceleration limitation: acceleration due to gravity imposes little strain on passengers. If metro stations are located just below the street, tracks can be arranged to slope down on either side of the station. This gives an acceleration boost, helps braking, and saves energy. For a variety of reasons, this arrangement is not always feasible, but it should be applied when possible. A drop of just 5 meters gives a speed of 35 km/hr; this is about the largest drop that can readily be arranged with short station-to-station distances.

PCC cars weighed about 16,000 kg and were powered by four 55 HP motors. By contrast, NJ Transit's heavy-rail Arrow I cars had four 225 HP motors.
PCC figures from Kashin & Demoro

Short Dwell

Dwell time must be kept short. Long articulated buses with single-door boarding and onboard fare payment sometimes experience dwell times of several *minutes* when dozens of

Dwell time is the duration of a station stop

EuroTram, Strasbourg, 1997
Huge doors and level-loading platforms keep dwell times short.

It is common practice in Europe that door opening is *enabled* by the driver or door tender, but the door does not actually open until a passenger presses a button on the door.

passengers board at once. The steep steps are an obstacle, but new low-floor vehicles are making life easier for everyone. With metro trains, dwell times are short because plenty of doors and level-loading platforms are universal and make for speedy boarding. Fares are collected before entering the platform, so fare collection never delays the vehicle.

The speed with which doors open and close also affects dwell times. With intelligent sensors, doors could close more quickly than they now do, but without endangering passengers. Doors should in any case open very quickly. A further reduction is possible by applying a technique still sometimes seen in older equipment, which permits the motorman to enable door opening at a slow speed, once the train is committed to a stop. The doors are fully open just as the train stops. Correctly applied, this is an entirely safe technique and saves about two seconds per stop.

Nearby Service

Long walking distances to the nearest stop make transit less convenient to use and increase door-to-door travel times. I regard ten minutes as the outer limit of an easy walk. A five-minute walk, a distance of 380 meters, is much better.

Few Stops

Stops bring the average speed down quickly. The route should have the minimum possible number of stops consistent with keeping all destinations within easy walking distance of stations.

Compact Network

The shorter the distance, the faster the journey. In compact, dense cities all destinations are relatively close, so journey times are held to a minimum.

Better Reliability

Paradoxically, reliability has declined in the last 30 years. One might think that a door that failed to close properly once in a million operations would be sufficiently reliable, but this failure rate leads to system delays about once a week. Better design and maintenance should make a 10-fold improvement an easy goal to attain.

I'm especially aware of this because Amsterdam took delivery of a new fleet of trams that suffered from frequent door failures. Large parts of the system would shut down while the offending vehicle was taken out of service.

Redundancy

Delays cannot be entirely avoided, if only because medical emergencies are inevitable. If a train must wait while a passenger is evacuated, service is going to stop. With the topology proposed in the reference design for carfree cities, riders can take a train in the other direction and arrive about ten minutes late. (The closed-loop design provides an alternate route.) Should both tracks be blocked, the system can enter a shuttle mode, running in both directions on both tracks. Capacity remains nearly the same, but the numerous transfers increase travel time. Such outages should be rare.

See the drawing on page 130

SAFE & CONVENIENT PUBLIC TRANSPORT

Many transit managers and politicians who set the policies that govern public transport seem content to offer service that is not only slow but also inconvenient and even dangerous. If we expect the public actually to use public transport, these shortcomings must be eliminated to the greatest possible extent. We consider in this section methods of making public transport use as attractive as possible.

We must never underestimate the importance of the simple fact that most of the decisions about transport are made by people who drive to work. When I worked as a public transit manager, I drove to work because the bus service was so bad. So did most of my colleagues.

Of Ferryboats, Cable Cars & Buses

The ferryboats plying the waterways of Venice are a pleasant, if slow, means of public transport. People are cheerful and the

Inland steamer, Stockholm, 1985

The lovely British word "posh" is actually an early acronym that means "port out, starboard home." These were the cooler sides of the ship on voyages between England and India.

EuroTram, Strasbourg, 1997
First-class public transport

scenery is excellent. San Francisco's cable cars also provide slow service that is popular with tourists, who enjoy the panoramic views from the hills and the good-humored banter of the gripmen and conductors who operate this anachronistic system. If all public transport were this agreeable, I'm sure buses and trains would be filled with happy passengers. As it stands, most public transport is a much grimmer reality, particularly in the USA.

Traveling Posh

People want to travel posh. Planes, trains, and ships offer luxury accommodations for the rich. So, too, can urban rail systems: the Paris metro has first class cars. Private compartments and even private trains are possible. But no public transport should be "hard class." Everybody deserves a comfortable seat, reasonable quiet, and a clean window.

Some public transport operators are thinking creatively in an effort to meet the public's needs and desires. For example, Danish intercity trains are segmented by use: a family area with playpen, a place to chat, somewhere to work quietly, a corner to have a smoke. If the passenger chooses the right area, the environment is likely to suit him. In Strasbourg, the sleek new EuroTrams show how pleasant trams can be. These new, easy-to-board trams offer a smooth, quiet ride. We need more of the creative, customer-oriented thinking that makes these systems so nice to use.

Have a Pleasant Trip

Taking the bus or metro is not usually a pleasant experience. It needs to become more like our Venetian ferryboat trip or San Francisco cable car ride. A change in attitude on the part of transit managers will be required before public transport systems provide comfort levels equivalent to private cars.

None of the necessary measures is difficult to achieve. Hard seats, lurching vehicles, and excessive noise can all be overcome with existing technology. Clean, well-lit stations free of graffiti and advertising should be within the grasp of any city. Artists can help make stations attractive and interesting, as was done in the Moscow metro. Well-trained personnel can offer courteous service. The required attitude is that public transport is a first-class service.

Metro station, Lisbon, 1999
Portugal has a long tradition of decorated glazed tiling. The newest metro line was graced with this art form, using a contemporary idiom. You could eat off the polished marble floors, so clean are they kept.

The recent rash of carjackings and road rage attacks means that motorists have also become vulnerable to violence by strangers.

Personal Safety in Public Spaces

People no longer expect a clean, safe, cordial environment when using public transport. They fear many of the people who would be their fellow passengers and think that horrible deeds occur routinely in the metro. In fact, however, even during the worst of the high-crime era in New York City, you were statistically safer in the subway than you were on the street. Many people feel safer driving than aboard public transport, although statistics do not support their beliefs, and perhaps the time has come to publicize the facts.

It is true that people are occasionally murdered while using public transport. On the other hand, more than 100 people die in traffic accidents in the USA every day, and thousands more are injured. People tend to underestimate the risks of driving and overestimate the danger of being in public places. There is also the matter that drivers are the masters of their own fates. Public transport passengers don't enjoy this false sense of control, but, in reality, unpleasant external events sometimes overtake car drivers.

In the days when everybody rode public transport, the atmosphere aboard was not threatening and often congenial. Even today, systems like the PATH in New York and BART in San Francisco are high-quality systems with a civil clientele. These systems are used by thousands of professional people during rush hour, when unpleasant incidents are nearly unknown.

We must restore personal safety in public places, a circumstance that prevailed in most of Europe and the USA as recently as a few decades ago. During the 1980s, many US cities saw increases in street crime, and with the accompanying media bombast, many people assumed that most cities had undergone dramatic increases in street crime. While the actual increase was usually not extreme, people began to fear the street and other public spaces. In the USA, this trend has now been reversed in many cities. New York City, for instance, had serious public safety problems in the 1980s, but street and subway crime have recently declined considerably.

Eliminate Fares

Paying the fare is a huge inconvenience for the passenger. Most systems require exact change, and if you arrive without it, you can figure on missing at least one bus while you try to find somebody willing to make change. Buying, stamping, and retaining a ticket is a further annoyance, and on systems using the so-called "honor system," your trip may be interrupted by controllers wanting to see your ticket. When a passenger refuses to pay his fine, the tram is delayed until the police can remove him.

The irritation of fare collection for passengers can be seen in an experiment in Hasselt, Belgium, where a free-fare system was implemented. Use of public transport increased 800% in a year.

"Hasselt rijdt gratis met de bus, uit geldgebrek" *NRC Handelsblad,* 16 September 1998

While some systems operate with farebox revenues that pay only 20% of operating costs, virtually all systems charge a fare. I think most urban public transport systems should abandon fares entirely. Fare collection is expensive because it causes loading delays, thereby increasing the number of operating personnel and vehicles required. (Metro systems, however, almost invariably collect fares before passengers reach the boarding platform; fare collection delays passengers but does not slow vehicle boarding.) Fare-based systems

The range of "fare recovery ratios" for 37 large cities is 19% (Denver) to 136% (Hong Kong). The fare recovery ratio is simply the farebox revenues expressed as a percentage of operating expenses.

Newman & Kenworthy, 346-347

also require additional staff to sell and check tickets. More convenient, no-fare service attracts more users, reducing the per-rider subsidy. The cost of the no-fare approach is thus lower than it first seems.

Seats for Everyone

Car drivers are sure of one thing: there will always be a seat. Public transport riders often stand under jerky and crowded conditions during rush hour and sometimes at other times as well. Public transport systems should provide a seat at all times, and the use of higher-capacity vehicles makes this possible without raising labor costs. Bus routes with enough traffic to require the use of high-capacity articulated buses are ripe for tram or metro construction. A metro system almost always has sufficient capacity to run enough trains that everyone can have a seat. If the passenger is seated and the ride is smooth, useful activity is possible aboard a train. In the car, however, the driver can't (or at least shouldn't) do anything except drive.

You *Can* Take It with You

You can take almost anything with you in the car, including the kitchen sink if you must. That's difficult by bus. We must arrange public transport so that a parent with small children in tow can still move fairly heavy objects around. The new low-floor trams are the beginnings of a solution: just put that kitchen sink on a pushcart and roll it aboard.

BUSES AND THE COMMON MAN: NO THANKS!

Everybody hates buses. They're slow, they stink, they're noisy, they take forever to board, they lurch, and the small, hard seats pinch your butt. When the Road Gang set out to

These double-deckers of the Dutch Railways can seat many passengers but are used only for shorter routes because they are somewhat cramped for long trips.

In Lisbon, rush-hour metro service is very frequent, but the trains are still crowded. Only an increase in train length above the current four-car limitation can relieve the problem.

kill public transport, their weapon was the bus. Trains, on the other hand, once were glamorous. The food was delicious, the service elegant, the ride comfortable, and the view excellent. For a century, trains were the fleetest, finest transport. No bus ever offered such amenities. No bus was ever glamorous. Nobody with a choice ever took a bus anywhere.

Mayor Jaime Lerner Fixes Buses

That having been said, it must be admitted that Jaime Lerner fixed his local bus system. A long-time mayor of Curitiba, Brazil, Lerner is an architect and planner with vision. Working with meager resources, he and his staff set out to make city buses work, and they succeeded beyond any reasonable expectation. Lerner and his team:

"Urban Planning in Curitiba," *Scientific American,* March 1996. Bogotá, Columbia, developed its TransMilenio system along the lines of the Curitiba system, and also saw a rapid improvement the quality of life for residents, at fairly modest costs.

- Laid out a sensible route network
- Gave buses priority over cars
- Built level-loading platforms with fare prepayment
- Achieved excellent speeds and high capacities
- Lured 30% of automobile commuters onto buses
- Spent a tiny fraction of the cost of a new metro

Notwithstanding Lerner's successes, the system is still not as good as a metro. It occupies considerable amounts of land, the buses are noisy and smelly, and performance is not quite up to metro standards. It is, however, an excellent interim step. A later upgrade to a rail system becomes feasible once the traffic and routes have been developed by the bus system. Indeed, Curitiba is now considering the replacement of some bus routes with tram lines.

Newman & Kenworthy, 200

THE PEOPLE MOVER OPTION

Roxanne Warren's *The Urban Oasis: Guideways and Greenways in the Human Environment* is an excellent source of information on people movers.

A plethora of transport modes falls under the general rubric "people mover." These disparate systems have a wide variety of attributes. Some systems are akin to automobiles (on-demand service, flexible direct routing, private vehicles) while others resemble an ordinary tram or metro system (scheduled service, fixed routes, intermediate stops, shared vehicles). Many of these systems exist at least as pilot projects but others remain just concepts. Although some systems have been operational for about 30 years, this is still a young technology, and standards have yet to emerge.

The most common application so far for people movers has been local transport within large airports, and many such systems now operate successfully. Most of them operate over fixed routes and many have only two stops on each line. They are highly suitable for moving large numbers of people between outlying satellite gates and the central terminal.

Many vehicles use conventional steel-wheel-on-steel-rail technology with onboard electrical propulsion, but other systems use cable drives or pneumatic propulsion. The vehicles are typically fairly small, ranging in capacity from just a single rider to 30 or more passengers, but some vehicles used at airports have capacities equal to that of a tram.

Guideways are typically elevated above ground level in order to provide the grade separation required for safe automated operation. Experience with elevated urban transport systems has been poor because they are noisy, intrusive, and create dark, inhospitable areas beneath. Developers of people movers have proposed designs that are quiet and cast narrow shadows. The loss of privacy is a problem without a solution.

People movers might become a useful supplemental means of transport in carfree cities, especially in later phases when further growth beyond the original design is required. Given that the technology is not yet mature, I have not relied upon it in the development of the reference design. If and when people movers become inexpensive, energy-efficient, and

Automated people mover, Newark Airport, 1999

The wide diversity of approaches is reflected in the variety of names:

Personal Rapid Transit
Automated Guideway Transit
Shuttle/Loop Transit
Group Rapid Transit
Automated Guideway System
Light Guideway Transit
Automated People Mover
Automated Light Metro
Horizontal Elevator

However, the people mover in Morgantown, West Virginia has provided good service to the university population it has served for decades.

reliable, they could help in reaching the goal of carfree cities, especially in existing urban areas.

Warren's Oasis

Roxanne Warren's *The Urban Oasis* proposes the application of people movers in urban development. She has reached some conclusions similar to my own regarding human-centered development and effective urban transport systems. Warren does not propose to remove cars from urban areas, but she does believe car use can be reduced by connecting new, small urban centers to the existing matrix of public transport, using people movers. In her vision, medium-sized buildings would be sited in a garden environment, with car parking facilities located away from inhabited areas and accessed by the people mover. Three problems affect the Urban Oasis proposal:

- The freestanding buildings and their small garden do not create the enclosure that forms "outdoor urban rooms."
- Cars still enter the area, with all the problems that brings.
- Trucks are used to provide freight transport.

Warren's approach clearly improves on conventional urban planning in the USA, but does not offer all the advantages provided by a completely carfree design.

Personal Rapid Transit

People movers based on small, personal vehicles are known as Personal Rapid Transit (PRT), which is the rail transport system that most resembles the private automobile or taxi. As such, it has many of the same advantages and disadvantages, and it is not yet clear whether PRT will ever develop into a mature transport system. These systems still exist only as concepts and prototypes. Some serious problems remain to be overcome:

Outdoor urban room, Strasbourg, 1997
A lovely spot that would be further improved by a sidewalk café. The chain indicates that cars sometimes use this street, probably the reason for the absence of tables.

One daring initiative is the "SkyTran" system, which its promoter terms "Personal/Mass Transportation." The design is based on two-passenger vehicles traveling at 160 km/hr along a very lightweight magnetic levitation (maglev) guideway suspended from ordinary lighting poles. Acceleration would be at 0.5 G, requiring passengers to strap in prior to departure. Exceedingly low costs and energy consumption are claimed. Stations would be "880 steps" away from all urban destinations. This probably translates to about 650 meters, which is rather far but not unreasonable. To my knowledge, the technical feasibility of the system and the soundness of the cost estimates have yet to be verified by a third party.

http://www.skytran.net/old/04Technical/pod01.htm

- Capacity limitations compared to a metro
- Expensive guidance and control systems
- Reserve vehicles requiring parking facilities
- Vehicles returning empty during peak hours
- High energy consumption, nearly comparable to cars

THE COSTS OF URBAN RAIL SYSTEMS

The cost of operating public transport has become a major burden for most cities in the industrialized nations, although in the USA, the cost of maintaining highways dwarfs the subsidies granted to public transport systems. As we have seen, subsidies are essential because of the huge subsidies given to car drivers. There are, however, some other causes.

Holding Cities for Ransom

Transit workers' unions gained a stranglehold on the public. Unions have secured, through what amounts to coercion, labor contracts that do not permit operators to run efficient organizations. We need a solution to this problem that respects the rights of workers while removing their ability to blackmail an entire city: transit systems upon which an entire economy depends can never be allowed to go on strike. This was formerly the case in many cities, but no-strike laws and contract clauses no longer seem to prevent strikes.

Direct Costs

Most public transport systems in the industrialized nations were profit-making just 50 years ago, but today fares would typically have to double to recover costs. Public systems have generally done poorly at managing costs. Municipal civil servants, not a group widely known for innovation, run most systems, and have been slow to adopt measures to contain

In the past few years, it has become apparent that some of the many difficulties that beset the Amsterdam system stem from corruption.

http://www.carfree.com/metro.html

The following table gives energy consumed per passenger-kilometer by various transport modes.

Mode	BTU/passenger-km
Intercity rail	442
Light rail	639
Single-occupancy car	4576

"Alternatives to the Automobile: Transport for Livable Cities," Marcia D. Lowe Worldwatch Paper 98, page 13

Only waterborne bulk transport uses less energy per tonne-kilometer than rail freight. In the USA, a three-man train crew can move 10,000 tons of freight. It would take more than 250 trucks, each with its own driver, to move this much freight, and freight trains now often travel faster than trucks.

costs. In some jurisdictions, corruption bleeds off money.

Metro systems have earned a reputation for being expensive to build and operate. To a certain degree, this reputation is justified, although the per-rider costs are generally not so terribly high. Measures that can reduce the operating costs of rail systems are summarized at Carfree.com.

All the problems notwithstanding, public transport in general remains a fundamentally sound undertaking, and especially metro systems, where one driver can operate a train carrying many hundreds of passengers. It is, however, difficult to put more than about 70 seats on a bus, so bus operations are intrinsically labor-intensive and relatively expensive. The low average speed of buses further increases labor costs.

Externalized Costs

All transport modes externalize significant costs. All modes except maritime transport are noisy, and all systems except sailing ships and electric trains powered from renewable energy sources (such as hydropower) contribute to air pollution and global warming in some degree. The external costs vary greatly by mode, however, and reductions are easier to achieve with some modes than with others. Rail systems enjoy two fundamental energy efficiencies:

• The low rolling resistance of steel wheels on steel rails
• The intrinsically low wind resistance of long, thin shapes
Road-based transit systems will probably never offer either of these advantages. Since global warming is directly related to the amount of energy consumed, the fundamental energy efficiency of a transport mode has a large effect on the size of this external cost. It must be said that the efficiency of trains (and all other public modes) depends on high load factors: there shouldn't be too many empty seats. Fluctuations in

demand can be handled by running trains of a length that comfortably meets the demand.

Air pollution is largely, but not entirely, related to energy consumption. In the USA, most trains are diesel powered, and emit plenty of pollutants, as do all vehicles powered by internal combustion engines. In Europe, most busy rail lines are electrified, and a stationary power plant is the easiest energy source to clean up because heavy, bulky equipment is not in itself a burden that must be transported with the vehicle.

Noise is a large external cost. Sound barriers are routinely erected along urban highways and help reduce the noise burden somewhat. Rail lines, being narrower, gain more benefit from this treatment. Rail systems can be put underground if necessary, and recent research suggests that the application of a thin layer of cobalt to train wheels may greatly reduce wheel noise, a large component of total noise.

FURTHER ADVANCES IN RAIL SYSTEMS

The Presidents' Conference Commission (PCC) streetcar of the 1930s was a brilliant design. These cars are comfortable, quiet, energy efficient, and fast; designers also paid careful attention to human factors, to ease the driver's workload and ensure a comfortable ride for everyone. The service life of these trams sometimes exceeded 50 years, and San Francisco has a lovingly-restored stable of PCC cars operating a popular service along Market Street. Replacements, such as the 1970s-era Boeing-Vertol cars used by San Francisco and Boston, were less satisfactory and required replacement within 20 years.

The best of the new tram designs meet every requirement that could reasonably be imposed. These trams are fast, com-

Freight scows, Venice, 1997
These boats also impose external costs, including wake damage to buildings, noise, and exhaust emissions from their diesel engines.

"Zachtjes sporen," *NRC Handelsbald,* 20 December 1997

PCC streetcars, Newark City Subway, 1999
Fifty years on, these PCC cars were still providing reliable daily service, although they have finally been replaced.

fortable, quiet, easy to board, attractive, and energy efficient. That having been said, many cities are even now taking delivery of new trams that in no way meet this standard. Amsterdam recently bought a fleet of trams and metro cars of poor quality. The doors fail to close properly, the cars are unacceptably noisy, the ride is harsh, and some of the metro cars have an unpleasant rolling lurch when they stop. There is no excuse for these faults: the engineering problems were solved decades ago.

Whereas improvements in trams are ongoing, subway vehicle design matured in the early 1950s, and only minor improvements are still needed. Metro speeds are now largely limited by human factors: tolerance for acceleration and speed of boarding and disembarking. Metro vehicles should, however, be equipped with regenerative braking to reduce energy consumption.

We move now to a consideration of why carfree cities must necessarily become a cornerstone in the development of cities that can be sustained indefinitely into the future.

Regenerative braking slows trains while recovering the energy used to accelerate them. The motors are used as generators and the electricity is fed back into the overhead or third rail. Energy savings are appreciable and the technology is simple.

Manarola, Italy, 1998
For generations, this town
took its living from the sea.

Leiden, the Netherlands, 1998
Bicycling is far more sustainable than driving, but I regard it as only a partial solution. Not everyone can ride a bike, and it really isn't very pleasant when the weather is sweltering, frigid, or wet. We need other means of sustainable transport besides bicycles.

SUSTAINABLE CITIES

Contemporary cities consume energy and resources at a rate that cannot long be sustained. Supplies of fossil fuels and minerals are finite, and we will eventually have to live within this constraint. Modern auto-centric cities are the least sustainable urban form ever devised because of the exorbitant amounts of energy consumed by transport.

By the end of the 21st century, most energy will have to come from renewable sources (or nuclear fusion, still a tantalizing dream after 50 years of intense research). Eventually, we will have to recycle 100% of all but the most ubiquitous minerals. The prudent course is to begin to build a nearly steady-state society based on sustainable energy sources and recycled minerals. In such a society, energy production must be based primarily on solar sources such as wind and solar cells. Raw materials must be either recycled or derived from renewable sources such as wood. It is now time to begin designing and building cities with this in mind.

Planning Sustainable Societies

We have recently learned that we must limit our emissions into the atmosphere or play Russian roulette with global climate change. While the 1997 Kyoto Accords amount to a de facto acknowledgment that anthropogenic climatic change has already begun, sustainable management of the atmosphere lies far in the future. To achieve it, we must make deep cuts in our greenhouse gas emissions. This signals not only the end of fossil fuels as our primary energy source but also the limitation of many industrial and transportation practices that release CO_2 and other greenhouse gases. Initial reductions will come from a shift away from coal and petroleum to natural gas (methane). But natural gas is also of limited supply, and even it emits significant amounts of CO_2 when burned, so a methane-based economy is only an interim step on the way to a truly sustainable energy system. Current thinking holds that hydrogen will become the fuel of choice; fortunately, it can use substantially the same infrastructure as gas.

Some fairly detailed blueprints exist for sustainable societies. Some plans are based on small towns surrounded by sufficient farmland to grow all necessary food and fiber. The reference design for carfree cities, presented in the next part of the book, presumes a much larger population. It, too, includes expansive green areas near the city, but these areas are not devoted exclusively to agriculture; nature reserves, parks, and forests would also find places near the city. The reference design does not provide enough land to grow all of the city's food within the range of human-powered transport, although a large portion of perishable foods could be grown nearby. Perishable food is usually transported by truck, sometimes even by air, so producing it locally yields an

Anthropogenic means "caused by human activity"

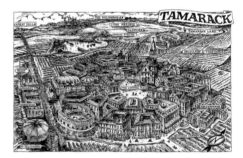

Ken and Roberta Avidor have developed a quite detailed plan for a sustainable community called Tamarack in the US Midwest. The population of the town would be limited to about 30,000, with access only by rail or bike.

It is worth remembering that, well into the 20th century, grain was transported from Australia to Europe in square-rigged sailing ships not equipped with any form of mechanical propulsion.

John Whitelegg believes that a good environment, and not good road access, is what attracts new businesses to a city; Covent Garden in London and Manhattan have poor highway access but thriving economies.

Personal communication

"My advice to local authorities is to go for clean air, protected countryside and quiet residential areas. These are the assets that stimulate economic development. Unfortunately, too many authorities are providing the opposite: an area with terrific accessibility, but which is noisy, polluted and crisscrossed with motorways."

Whitelegg, quoted in Newman & Kenworthy, 53

important improvement in energy efficiency. Grains and fibers can just as well be transported by ship or rail, at low energy costs. I expect that we will develop enough sustainable energy sources to move bulk agricultural products over long distances using efficient transport modes, and that it will not become necessary to grow all food within a few kilometers of where it is consumed.

The Not-So-Dismal Science

Economics became a less dismal and more useful science after John Maynard Keynes developed the theories that are now used to manage the economies of industrial democracies. Economists understand how money works and can adjust monetary and fiscal policy to guide an economy. The wild economic swings characteristic of capitalist economies prior to 1950 have been dampened. We have enjoyed 50 years of relative economic stability; those who lived through the Great Depression recognize this for the blessing it is.

Unfortunately, money is the only thing Keynesian economics understands, for money is the only yardstick it recognizes: no value is ascribed to things that are not worth money. However useful Keynesian economics may be, it is of little help in attaining a sustainable society. We must now develop economic theories to support the transition to a sustainable economy. We need techniques that measure the non-monetary costs of every activity and account for these costs in ways that help preserve the planetary ecosystem and improve the quality of life. Consumers must be charged for the external costs of products and services in ways that tend to improve the total efficiency of the economy while protecting ecosystems. Of necessity, this requires disincentives for the consumption of resources and the emission of pollutants, in order to encourage more sustainable alternatives.

Resource-Added Taxes

Europeans have long been familiar with Value-Added Taxes (VAT). Every organization adding value to a product or service collects a tax from the next buyer on the total accrued value. Intermediaries pay to the government all the taxes they collect and receive a full refund of the taxes they pay to suppliers. At each step in the process, the VAT on a product increases. The final consumer ultimately pays the total tax.

Resource-added taxes might work better. Taxes on raw materials would replace taxes on income, on the basis of:

- Scarcity
- Adverse effects of extraction, transport & refining
- Difficulty of waste disposal
- Recyclability

Such a system would result in products that are stingy in their use of nonrenewable and toxic resources but relatively generous in their use of labor. This would reduce environmental damage and improve the employment picture in the unskilled labor force. A resource-added tax, however, applies no pressure to companies and individuals to reduce such external costs as noise. Some other means of accounting for these costs will be needed.

Resource and Pollution Rationing

If we must limit both resource consumption and pollution, we will soon confront the question of how to allocate the rights to consume and pollute. It is difficult to imagine any fair way of distributing these rights except simply to give every human being equal rights. A system for trading these rights could be established, so rich nations could buy extra rights from poor nations. If the total supply of these rights were adjusted to what the planet can bear, then such a system could safeguard ecosystems while bringing some measure of

On 1 October 1999, Germany raised fuel taxes and reduced social security taxes in a move that is consistent with resource-added taxes.

If it ever becomes practical to mine the asteroid belt at a reasonable cost, we will have an inexhaustible supply of some very useful metals. Of course, intensive space exploration will require vast amounts of energy, perhaps from nuclear fusion. Whether this will ever happen at all is debatable, but it seems most unlikely to happen soon enough to prevent resource shortages by the end of the 21st century.

economic equity to the international realm. Such an arrangement would clearly force large and painful reductions in consumption in the rich nations, especially in the USA, which consumes and pollutes more per capita than any other nation. The auto-centric development of the USA will place it in an unfavorable economic position when resource consumption and pollution become subject to limitation.

Sustainable Energy

We must eventually develop an energy infrastructure that is indefinitely sustainable. With careful use, coal, oil, and gas will get us through the 21st century, but beyond that we must either turn to sustainable sources or resort to nuclear fission (itself a finite resource because the supply of fissile elements is quite limited). A number of sustainable systems already provide energy, and some installations now operate at commercial scale. The most important approaches are discussed below, but others, such as wave power, also exist.

Hydropower
Most hydropower resources have already been developed, and there is even pressure to blow up some dams for environmental reasons, so it seems unlikely that we will see great increases in hydropower.

Photovoltaic Cells
Power from photovoltaic (solar) cells has become steadily cheaper and may soon compete head-to-head with fossil-fueled power plants. (Pumped storage facilities can provide reserves for nights and cloudy days.) The manufacture of photovoltaic panels still consumes considerable amounts of energy, but improvements in technology have lowered both

Deuterium, the fuel for fusion reactions, exists in enormous quantities in the oceans and will be an infinite resource if fusion ever becomes practical.

The Dutch Energieonderzoek Centrum Nederland recently made an interesting proposal for handling nuclear waste. Actinides (which have long half lives) would be chemically separated from other fission products. The actinides are fissile and would be consumed in special reactors (the only safe way to dispose of the plutonium in nuclear warheads). The other fission products have fairly short half lives and would decay to safe levels within a few thousand years, instead of the million years now regarded as the period for keeping these materials out of the biosphere. However, the wisdom of building more nuclear power plants has become highly questionable in the wake of the terrorist attacks of 11 September 2001.
"Actiniden aangepakt," *NRC Handelsblad*
14 November 1998

A pumped storage facility uses two reservoirs, one substantially higher than the other. When surplus electricity is available, water is pumped into the upper reservoir. When demand exceeds supply, water flows backwards through the pumps, generating electricity. Losses are fairly high but tolerable.

the energy and economic costs of manufacture, a trend that continues. Flexible panels may someday be used for roofing.

Wind Turbines

In windy areas such as the Netherlands and California's Altamont Pass, large wind turbines already supply substantial amounts of energy at prices only slightly above that of electricity from fossil-fueled power plants. Given that wind turbines do not externalize the cost of greenhouse gas emissions, the real cost to society may already be lower from wind energy than from conventional sources, although there is as yet no useful way to conduct this accounting. Early installations were unreliable and many designs have had to be scrapped. Much has been learned, and newer models are both larger and more reliable. A serious proposal has been made by Greenpeace to supply one-third of the electricity consumed in the Netherlands from a wind farm in the North Sea. The offshore location avoids problems with neighbors and enjoys higher average wind speeds.

Old & new windmills near Groningen, the Netherlands, 1997
The new mills are generating significant amounts of power. Except for an interlude in the 20th century, wind power was always important here.

"Greenpeace: windparken op zee moeten door-braak forceren," in *Duurzaam Energie,* (Dutch) August 1997

Biomass Conversion

There are many ways to convert plant matter into energy. Rapeseed can be processed into clean-burning diesel fuel; wood can be burned directly or converted into methanol; grain can be fermented into ethanol. Some of these conversions are fairly efficient, but others consume nearly as much energy as they release. There is another serious problem with biomass conversion: we are soon going to need all the food and fiber we can grow. Arable land will be in very short supply in the coming century as the world population continues to increase. However, agricultural waste products can be burned without serious difficulty, and this may supply modest amounts of energy. Managed forests planted on terrain too steep to farm can supply wood for space heating and cooking in rural areas. The biggest advantage of biomass conversion is that it is neutral as far as the CO_2 budget is concerned: the plants take as much CO_2 out of the atmosphere as is released when the fuel is burned.

Waste Decomposition

Sewage and some other waste products can be anaerobically decomposed to methane. Early digesters were unreliable and required constant attention, but more recent efforts have produced useful amounts of methane without undue difficulty. Farmers can use this technology to digest manure, with the added benefit that neighbors no longer need endure the stink and adverse health affects of rotting manure.

Geothermal Energy

Heat from the earth's crust can be used to generate steam. Iceland, a highly volcanic island, gets large amounts of its energy from geothermal sources. This source of energy is only available in limited areas and can also release SO_2 (the principal constituent of acid rain) into the atmosphere.

Active & Passive Solar Heating

Active and passive solar design can provide a significant fraction of the energy needed to heat and cool buildings and provide domestic hot water. In Southeast Asia, hot water from rooftop collectors is already cheaper than from gas-fired boilers. As external costs such as global warming are added to the equation, the balance will increasingly favor such installations. Much has also been learned about design and construction techniques for houses employing passive solar heating. These buildings shed excess heat in the summer and absorb solar energy during winter months. Construction costs are higher than for conventional buildings but the extra expense seems to be justified, even at current energy prices.

Cogeneration

While not actually a sustainable resource in itself, cogeneration has been used for decades to improve the overall thermodynamic efficiency of energy installations. Waste heat from a turbogenerator is used to provide process heat, air conditioning, and space heating. The net efficiency of cogeneration systems is much higher than that of stand-alone generating plants, which discharge more than half the total energy consumed directly into the environment in the form of low-grade thermal energy. Small cogeneration plants are a proven technology, providing a city district or even an individual housing project with both electricity and space heating. Cogeneration offers the further benefit of greatly reduced electrical transmission losses because the power is consumed near where it is generated. These plants can be fueled by practically anything that burns, including trash and biomass.

Cogeneration efficiencies as high as 90% have been attained. It is important to remember that transmission losses from large power plants to the point of usage are quite large, and that these losses essentially do not occur with cogeneration.

The Hydrogen Economy

The hydrogen-powered sustainable economy has become a topic of discussion. Hydrogen is the cleanest fuel of all and emits no CO_2 when burned. Unfortunately, hydrogen does not exist as a free element on Earth. All of it must be manufactured, which always consumes more energy than is released by burning the hydrogen. If renewable energy is used to manufacture the hydrogen, there is in principle no net global warming effect. (However, when hydrogen is burned by aircraft, the resultant contrails may somewhat affect the Earth's heat balance.) Natural gas can be used as a feedstock for the production of either hydrogen or liquid fuels. The

The cheapest method of making hydrogen is to inject steam into incandescent coke (refined coal). The products of this reaction are hydrogen and carbon monoxide plus impurities. The carbon monoxide can be burned (in a power plant, for instance), but this process releases huge amounts of CO_2 and a whole medley of pollutants into the atmosphere.

Safaa A. Fouda, "Liquid Fuels from Natural Gas," in *Scientific American,* March 1998

processes currently in use are relatively expensive and wasteful of energy, but near-term improvements are likely.

If hydrogen is going to provide clean, sustainable energy, it must be produced from sources other than fossil fuels. We may be able to build an energy infrastructure based on wind turbines and solar cells, but the ultimate production capacity may not be sufficient to maintain current levels of consumption in industrialized nations, let alone to meet rising demand in developing nations.

Energy Allocation

The only energy available for automobility will be that which remains after essential uses have been supplied:

- Food production & transport
- Electrical power generation
- Industrial process energy
- Space & water heating

Modern agriculture, which has managed to feed mankind despite enormous increases in numbers, depends on petroleum to fuel tractors and irrigation pumps. Petroleum is also a principal feedstock in the production of fertilizers and pesticides. Genetic engineering may make farming considerably more efficient but it will probably remain a large consumer of both energy and raw materials. We can expect continuing improvements in the energy efficiency of non-farm activities, but we will face an enormous demand for energy as the world population grows and standards of living rise. Cars will have to come last in line for energy supplies.

CITIES AND ENERGY CONSUMPTION

Human density and energy consumption are inversely correlated: the higher the density of an area, the lower its per-capita energy consumption. There are several reasons for this, as discussed below.

Compact Cities

Dense cities cover a small area, so transport lines are few and short. If density and population are high, rail systems can be used to transport both passengers and freight within the city. The inherent efficiency of rail transport, combined with short travel distances, yields dramatically reduced transport energy consumption.

Larger, more complex cities are more diverse and more efficient (ecologically and economically) than smaller ones.

Newman & Kenworthy, 14-15

Sustainable Transport

We must make a commitment to developing sustainable urban transport systems characterized by:

- Rapid transport of both passengers and freight
- Efficient use of land
- Efficient use of renewable energy sources
- Inexpensive service

Existing rail technology meets these requirements admirably, but most existing urban areas in North America lack the necessary density to support efficient use of rail systems.

Because cars and trucks require so much space, their removal from the city is essential to the change to rail-based transport systems. Only when cars and trucks are removed does enough land become available to permit high-density living while still maintaining an excellent quality of life.

Common Walls & Multiple Stories

Most Europeans would not regard an area without multiple stories and common walls as a city at all: low density cities like Phoenix and Los Angeles are essentially a North American phenomenon. When buildings touch other buildings on two sides, they use far less energy for heating and cooling.

For example, consider a 144 square meter single-story detached house with a flat roof. The house is 18 meters wide and 8 meters deep (typical values for smaller North American suburban houses). Assuming the walls are 3 meters high, the building has 156 square meters of exterior wall and 144 square meters of roof, for a total exposed area of 300 square meters. If the same floor area is provided in a building 4 meters wide and 4 stories high, then the building is 9 meters deep. If this building adjoins its neighbors on the two long sides, then it has only 44% of the exposed surface area of its single-family detached cousin. Small four-story buildings of this type can be highly desirable: in central Amsterdam, they fetch more than $500,000.

Sunset, Siena, Italy, 1998
Siena is old and nearly carfree. It is surrounded by rural areas beginning at the foot of the city walls.

The common walls are at roughly the same temperature as the building interiors and so impose little heating or cooling load. Similarly, multistory buildings use less energy than single-story buildings because of the reduction in roof area per unit floor area. The combined savings can exceed 50%.

Getting Away from It All

I live in the heart of Amsterdam, a major European capital. I enjoy life in the city and often go for months at a time without leaving town. I do get worn down by the heavy traffic: the noise, the dust, the stench, and the need for constant vigilance. If these stresses were removed, I would travel even less often. Absent the menace of cars, I would bike a great deal more than I do, getting into the countryside and exercising at the same time, all at essentially zero energy cost.

When people go on vacation they usually want some respite from heavy traffic. If we lived in more hospitable surroundings, we might enjoy more vacations at home, which in itself represents a considerable energy saving. People also go on vacation to get back in touch with nature. Neither cities nor suburbs offer real contact with nature. The carfree city can and should be arranged so that wide-open natural areas, even wilderness, lie just a few minutes away by bike.

SUSTAINABLE CARFREE CITIES

The reference design for carfree cities offers a large contribution to sustainable development because it:
- Uses less construction material than suburban sprawl
- Uses less energy for space heating and transportation
- Generates reduced atmospheric emissions
- Supplies perishable food at low transport energy cost
  Some thinkers on sustainability see civilization dispersing

into millions of small communities, each numbering a few thousand people. These communities would be largely self-sufficient, and international trade would decline to a tiny fraction of its current levels. I do not believe this to be a viable route to sustainability. Many of the tools we need to achieve sustainable societies are precisely those high-tech products that cannot be manufactured by cottage industries. A substantial global trade in these goods is probably essential to a sustainable global society.

I also do not believe that humanity would benefit from an urban diaspora. Many valuable human activities require large groups of people for their support. If we abandoned our cities, we would also be abandoning many important cultural institutions. Furthermore, cities also offer a depth of social resources that rural areas can never match.

We must reduce the required energy and raw-material inputs for all human activities. If we start soon and achieve substantial reductions within a few decades, we will have gained a breathing spell to plan the next phase of the transition to a sustainable society. The single greatest contribution to achieving large reductions would be the elimination of urban automobile usage. For this reason, I view the carfree city as a cornerstone in sustainable development.

This brings us to the end of our consideration of cities in general. The next part of the book presents a reference design for carfree cities that is based on the principles established in this part.

If everyone used as much energy and as many resources as the average North American, we would need a planet three times as big as the Earth to supply food, energy, and raw materials.

Newman & Kenworthy, 20

Lago di Como-Bellagio, Italy, c.1900

Campo San Bartolomeo
Venice, 1997

PART II

CARFREE CITIES

A reference design is a benchmark, used as a measure and a point of departure. Normally, reference designs are not actually built, although they should in principle be employable in some real situation. The reference design for carfree cities could be built without appreciable modification in several Dutch polders (large, featureless tracts created when land is reclaimed from the sea) and other flat, sparsely-settled tracts. Usually, however, local conditions will dictate substantial deviations from the reference design.

DESIGN PARAMETERS
Establishes design goals and standards for the "reference design" for carfree cities as presented in this Part.

CITY TOPOLOGY
Describes and explains the reference topology for carfree cities; proposes alternate topologies for larger and smaller cities.

CITY DISTRICTS
Presents the reference district for carfree cities along with a number of variations on the reference district.

CITY BLOCKS
Examines the requirements for blocks in carfree cities and presents a reference block design.

PASSENGER TRANSPORT
Proposes a variety of passenger transport systems that meet the requirements of the reference design.

FREIGHT DELIVERY
Explains the design and operation of a dedicated freight system suitable to the needs of the reference design.

Zeitglockenthurm
Bern, c.1900

A small business with its own wharf
Venice, 1997

DESIGN PARAMETERS

A serious exploration of the feasibility of carfree cities requires the declaration of design goals for cities in general and specific design standards for the project at hand. That is the purpose of this chapter. You may, of course, disagree with either the goals or the standards I propose. In that event, please consider how your own preferences would affect the reference design and whether the design could be modified to accommodate your own vision of an ideal city. In many cases, other goals and standards can be accommodated in the carfree design. Some changes would, of course, require major alterations to the reference design.

When evaluating both the standards and the reference design, please consider whether it is worth sacrificing an important element of the reference design in order to accomplish some other end. While it is true that carfree cities will require some compromises with the convenience of the auto-centric city, these compromises should not be large.

DESIGN GOALS

In my view, urban planners must fulfill the following design goals to the greatest possible extent:
- Support vigorous, diverse, sustainable economies
- Reduce consumption of energy & resources
- Minimize construction & operating costs
- Create a high quality of life
- Build beautiful urban areas
- Generate pedestrian traffic to assure safe, lively streets
- Establish natural areas near the city
- Provide quick, inexpensive passenger transport
- Deliver freight promptly & cheaply

DESIGN STANDARDS

The following design standards derive from the design goals and are used in developing the reference design for carfree cities.

Diverse Economy
- Ample space for small businesses
- Workable sites for heavy industry
- Broad range of infrastructure to support innovation
- Practical delivery of standard shipping containers

Energy & Resource Efficiency
- Basic services located in every district
- Short runs for utilities
- District heating
- Shared walls
- Multiple stories
- Efficient transport of people & goods

Gondolas for tourists, Venice, 1997
Venice no longer has a diverse economy. The enormous volume of tourism drives up the value of land, forcing industry to leave the city. The high cost of freight delivery compounds the problem.

Family bakery, Greenwich Village, 1999
Mom & pop shops serve important social functions

Low Construction Costs

- Low per-capita paved surface area
- Short runs for pipes & cables
- Short transport lines

High Quality of Life

- Regular opportunities for informal social contact
- Safe, early independence for children
- Continued self-reliance of the elderly
- Ease in meeting life's daily needs
- Routine destinations located within the district
- Minimal externalized transport costs
- Mixed uses in every neighborhood
- Low noise levels
- Active street life

Rapid Access to Nature

- Small gardens behind most buildings
- Open natural areas adjacent to every district

Beauty

- Human scale
- Carfree streets
- Richly-textured buildings
- Well-proportioned streets & squares

Good Passenger Transport

- Maximum 5-minute walk to transport
- Frequent service
- Single-transfer journeys
- Minimal land occupation by transport
- Dense utilization of public transport
- Low capital & operating costs

Urban park, Nancy, France, 1997
Parks are terribly important to city-dwellers, who need attractive green areas within easy reach.

- Energy-efficient transport
- Minimal externalized costs
- Car parking at the periphery

Efficient Freight Transport

- Truck-free city streets
- Fast & economical freight delivery
- Minimal land occupation
- Minimal externalized costs
- Efficient energy use
- Intermodal exchange with the global freight network

Freight handling, Rialto, Venice, 1997
This kind of labor-intensive sorting and routing must drive up the cost of freight delivery in Venice. Carfree cities need better arrangements than this.

Note that many of the design standards enumerated above are easier to achieve in a compact city. Notice also that the transport system affects the attainment of a great many of these standards.

In the next chapter we consider the topology of the reference design for carfree cities. Keep these design standards in mind when evaluating the reference design.

Frankfurt am Main, Germany. The stamp
on the postcard was cancelled in 1903.

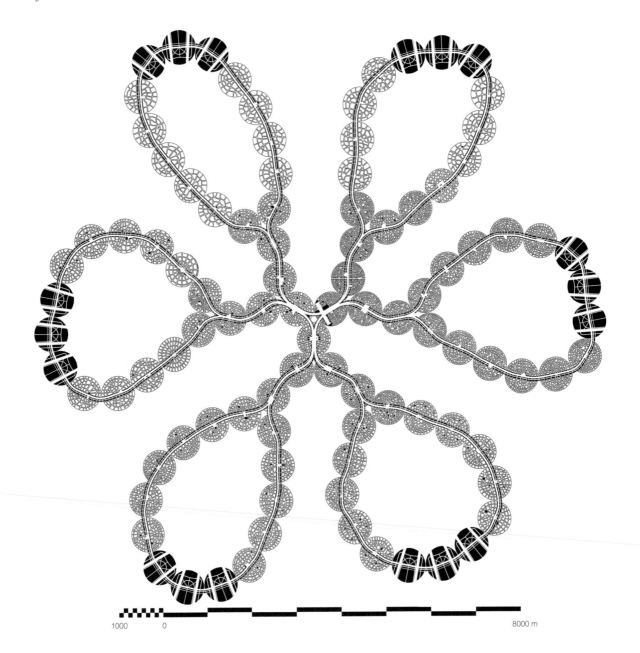

Detail of the downtown area. The intercity train station and tracks cut diagonally through the drawing.

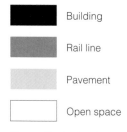

⬛	Building
▨	Rail line
▨	Pavement
☐	Open space

Above: Key to drawing on this page

Opposite: The reference topology for a carfree city includes 81 inhabited districts and 18 utility areas. Buildings are shown in black; for clarity, all other uses are shown in white. Only about 16% of the site is urban; nearly all of the remainder is devoted to a variety of open-space uses.

CITY TOPOLOGY

Topology is the branch of mathematics that deals with spatial relationships. City topology is thus the study of the spatial arrangement of various urban elements and the relationships of these elements to one another. Virtually every aspect of city life is affected by the topology selected, in particular the transport arrangements: changing a topology alters the route structure of the transport system, usually with large effects on its effectiveness and efficiency. This chapter considers the topology of carfree cities as a whole; later chapters consider successively smaller-scale elements of the city, from entire districts down to blocks and individual buildings.

The topology of the reference design was selected for a variety of reasons, including the creation of a clearly-defined downtown area and the availability of green areas close to each district. The most important single concern, however, was the optimum arrangement of the transport system. The reference topology permits the use of a modified hub-and-spoke route system, which provides the fastest service for most trips. No trip requires more than one transfer (even though there are three transfer stations in the downtown area). The dense utilization of the few transit lines permits frequent service while keeping operating costs under control. A few trips would be better served by a system with tangential routes in addition to the routes radiating from downtown, but this would greatly increase the length of the transit system that must be constructed, maintained, and operated. The tangential routes only slightly increase the number of passengers who enjoy direct service. Even with tangential routes, most trips are actually faster through the hub, and the concentration of ridership on the radial lines results in higher utilization, better efficiency, and more frequent service, with its attendant shorter waiting times.

Reference Topology

While any set of parameters might have been selected for the reference design, I thought it most useful to choose attributes for a medium-sized city, as explicated in the sections that follow.

1,000,000 Residents

A million residents is a reasonable balance between small and large cities. A city of a million is big enough to require the solution of difficult transport issues. A city of this size can support major cultural institutions such as orchestras, museums, and sports teams. It is not so big that it creates extreme concentrations of pollution, nor does the supply of water and other necessities become a terribly difficult issue. The reference topology is useful for cities ranging in population between about 300,000 and 3,000,000. While the size and

Tangential routes would cut across the radial routes and would not pass through the downtown area.

The reference topology superimposed on the city of Amsterdam (population 700,000).

Increasing maximum walking time from 5 to 10 minutes quadruples the area of a district. This allows 4,000,000 people to live in 81 districts, and the maximum travel time increases to 50 minutes, but the long walks to transit and green space are less than ideal. Increasing the number of districts to 260 gives room for 3,000,000 people, with a maximum travel time of 58 minutes, while the longest walk stays at 5 minutes. In cities larger than 2 or 3 million people, a more complex topology will work better.

number of districts will change, the basic 6-lobe topology can be adapted to cities within this range. Carfree cities with much smaller or larger populations are also possible but require different topologies, as shown later in this chapter.

256 Square-Kilometer Land Area

The reference design occupies a roughly square parcel of land about 16 kilometers on a side. A parcel of this size allows the city to be separated from adjoining uses by a greenbelt at least two kilometers wide.

In order to provide ample green space, only 16% of the parcel is developed. Broad expanses of green space comprise the remaining 84% of the site, excepting only a small amount of land occupied by the connections to the external rail and road systems. Green space can and should be used for a wide variety of purposes, including parks, garden allotments, lakes and streams, playing fields, golf courses, farms, forests, nature reserves, and wilderness.

The green space nearest the city center is best reserved for parks and garden allotments; more distant areas are suitable for uses that draw a smaller public, thereby minimizing the aggregate time spent in transit.

6 City Lobes

The city is divided into districts, which are in turn arranged into "lobes," each of which is similar in form and function. Six lobes form the complete city. This arrangement conveys several advantages:

- All areas of the city are within quick reach of the center.
- Each district is almost entirely encircled by open space.
- There are only three metro routes, each beginning in one lobe, running into downtown, and back out to an adjacent lobe.

Park in Siena, Italy, 1998

- The closed-loop metro arrangements provide redundant service in the event of an outage; some journeys can only be made by way of a longer route, but all destinations remain accessible.
- The metro routes never cross one another, but each can be brought adjacent to the others for transfers. The walk at the transfer points is short, there are three transfer points instead of one crowded central location, and only one transfer is ever required.
- The transport system is efficient, densely utilized, economical to construct, and holds travel time to an almost irreducible minimum.

The importance of getting the topology right was brought home to me when I lived in Quincy and commuted to East Boston (Massachusetts). I had to take an intermediate metro because the line from Quincy did not connect directly with the line to East Boston, even though they came within a few hundred meters of each other. This fault cost me 15 minutes a day.

81 Districts

The city comprises 81 districts. Faster public transport could be provided with fewer, larger districts (requiring fewer intermediate stops and permitting higher top speeds), but walking distances become excessive and door-to-door times for the longest journeys actually increase. The optimum number of districts for a city of 1,000,000 is about 80.

The three most central districts are "downtown districts." The "inner districts" are those that lie between downtown and the point where the lobe splits. The remaining districts are "outer districts."

18 Utility Areas

Nonresidential utility areas are reserved for various infrastructure requirements, heavy industry, and parking for residents and visitors alike. Utility areas are located at the extremities of the city because they require direct access to the external rail and road networks. Siting the utility areas at the periphery keeps the heavy transport infrastructure away from inhabited areas and mitigates noise problems. It also helps conserve valuable land near the city center. The actual number of utility areas constructed will depend on the needs of a particular city and might be considerably more or less than 18.

The range is 31 to 39 minutes depending on the time spent waiting.

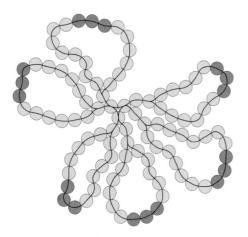

A topology is not affected by deformation. This city has the same topology as the reference design, even though it differs in shape. Geographic features will often force such changes.

35 Minutes to Any Doorstep

Assuming that an underground metro is selected to provide passenger transport, the longest transit time between any two points in the reference design averages only 35 minutes. This occurs when the origin of the trip is at the outside edge of the outermost utility area of one lobe and the destination is at the edge of the outermost utility area located on a different metro line. Many trips are within the district (since basic shopping is located at the center of every district), and the walking time to the district center does not exceed 5 minutes from any doorstep.

The typical trip outside the district is shorter than 15 minutes door-to-door. Popular destinations are located near metro stops to reduce the aggregated time spent walking. Many trips outside the district are to destinations in the three downtown districts, and in two out of three cases this trip does not involve a transfer, in which case the average travel time does not exceed 22 minutes; a transfer to reach the other downtown district adds no more than 5 minutes to the trip. These times are predicated on walking to the transport halt and riding public transport. In many cases, bicycling will be faster still, especially if the origin or destination is near the edge of the district or if the journey is to an adjacent lobe. It would be possible to bicycle anywhere in the city in under an hour. Bicycling will be especially attractive for trips between adjacent lobes; often these trips will be considerably faster by bike than by public transport.

VARIATIONS ON THE REFERENCE TOPOLOGY

An infinite number of variations can be made on the reference design, some more useful than others. Some alternative topologies are shown and discussed in this section.

Alternative Lobe Design

One obvious variation on the reference topology is to graduate the size and density of the districts, with those districts farthest from the city center being the largest and least densely populated, as shown in the marginal illustration. In this design, the downtown districts and inner districts are all the standard 760 meter diameter, and this part of the drawing was simply copied from the reference design. These districts would be built at the standard density. The districts in the left-hand branch increase in diameter to a maximum of 1500 meters. These districts would have the lowest building densities, possibly even as low as single-family, two-story houses on small lots. This arrangement somewhat lengthens the maximum travel time, but the increase is moderate: about 12 minutes. The density remains considerably above that for contemporary US suburban development, because the building lots are fairly small and relatively little land is devoted to streets.

Geography

With few exceptions, cities are greatly affected by the nature of the site upon which they are built: rivers and hills have shaped almost every city. A few cities in the Netherlands developed almost entirely free from topographic constraints, but in these cases, soil conditions have exercised a considerable influence. The reference design will almost certainly have to be adjusted to local geography, and in many cases substantial changes will be necessary. In particular, the closed-loop topology may have to be abandoned if a particular site does not lend itself to this arrangement. The lobes would then be open at the ends, which only slightly degrades the design and somewhat complicates the operation of the transport system.

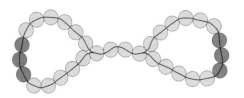

Topology for a city of 400,000

Topology for a city of 4,000,000

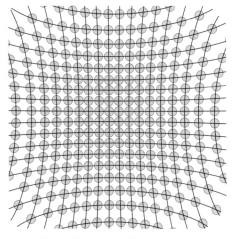

Extensible topology for a mega-city

Small Cities

Cities with a population of less than about 400,000 can employ a very simple topology, with just a single transport line arranged as shown. Such a city can also grow by the addition of more lobes, eventually assuming the reference topology.

Larger Cities

Cities with a population between 3,000,000 and 5,000,000 can be arranged as shown, using a second, outer lobe around the usual inner lobe. Maximum transit times for this topology rise to about 52 minutes. While the capacity of a four-track metro is very high, it is not infinite for the purposes of very large cities, and metro capacity problems may begin to arise at this size. This limitation is probably the governing condition for the maximum population that can be supported by the 6-lobe topology. Above this size, a more complex topology will be required.

Mega-Cities

Cities with populations over 5,000,000 present a special case. A completely different topology becomes necessary to support the enormous transport requirements of such a large city. The simple, extensible topology shown here supports very large cities. Such cities must be polycentric: a single center cannot possibly be large enough to support all the demands placed on it. This can be seen in other megacities, such as Tokyo. Instead, some districts near the center will have to assume specialized functions, as is the case in New York, where downtown Manhattan is the financial center, midtown has its agglomerations of electronics stores, its diamond district, and so forth.

It is worth noting that this grid pattern still never requires more than a single transfer to reach any destination within the city. It does require the construction of twice as many kilometers of metro per district as the reference design, but this additional mileage will be necessary to provide sufficient capacity in a huge city, so it is not wasted. The distances between the districts can be adjusted from none to any amount for which there is room. A regular grid need not be maintained, which permits more open space to be located around districts located some distance from the city center.

Metropolitan Agglomerations

There is another approach to building very large carfree urban areas. Rather than building a single, integrated city, it would be possible to establish several smaller cities. The centers of these cities would be connected by high-speed rail. If six cities were established, each in accordance with the reference design, then the agglomeration has a population of 6 million. A circular rail line with a top speed of only 200 km/hr yields a maximum travel time between any two points in the agglomeration of about 50 minutes, assuming the interval between trains is only a few minutes. This allows the entire region to function as a single socioeconomic entity.

A metropolitan agglomeration of 6,000,000

Denser Cities

It is possible to increase the percentage of built-up area as much as necessary. When land is extremely valuable or scarce, the built-up area can approach 100%, although the absence of open space is not a desirable condition. The spiral topology shown here occupies most of the area of the site but still leaves room for parks of reasonable size in the interstitial areas. This topology does require a single-point transfer station at the center: three levels of metro must be built, and transfers are more difficult due to the need to change levels,

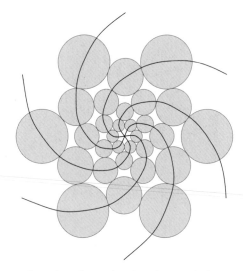

A topology denser than the reference design

but the arrangement can be made to work if necessary.

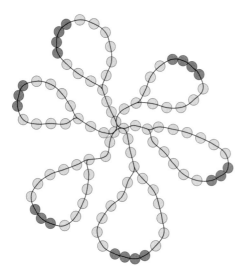

A topology with 300 meters between districts

Less Dense Cities

The addition of 300 meters of open space between each district adds only three minutes to the maximum travel time, because the extra distance is covered at top speed. Even with a full kilometer of open space between districts, travel time only increases by 10 minutes. If the maximum speed of the metro is increased to 120 km/hr (from the usual 100 km/hr), three kilometers of open space between each of the districts still permits maximum travel times below one hour; downtown remains less than half an hour away. This is about the practical limit. Another approach, of course, is to make the districts themselves less dense by increasing their diameter, up to a maximum of about 1500 meters.

Very Low Density Cities

If people will accept a 10-minute walk to the transit halt, then very low density carfree cities are possible. Because of the greater distance between district centers and the longer walks required, the maximum travel time increases to 50 minutes. This form is only 25% as dense as the reference design and permits the arrangement of two-story, single-family houses on very small lots.

I believe, however, that the duplex is a better solution at this level of density. In the Town of Mount Royal, a railroad suburb of Montréal, there was great demand for the duplex housing that had been built within about a 10 minute walk of the train station. These duplexes were built at roughly the same density as single-family houses on very small lots but resulted in what I find to be a more attractive and habitable form, with gardens large enough to be useful.

It would be sensible to build more densely near the center

Duplex, Town of Mount Royal, Quebec, 1999
As a child, I lived briefly in this railroad suburb of Montréal. I found it an agreeable place despite the bitter cold winters.

of the district, which allows a further reduction in the density of outlying areas.

When all is said and done, such low-density living is to my mind a less attractive arrangement than the considerably higher densities of the reference design. It involves much more walking (or perhaps biking—the streets would provide ample room for bicyclists) and requires four times as much land to house the same number of people. It is true that gardens of a decent size are possible at these lower densities, but it is worth remembering that the reference topology provides gardens 4 by 20 meters behind the townhouses (buildings near street corners do not have as large a garden as this). The walk to open green spaces outside the district is twice as long in the low-density pattern, and so these areas no longer easily serve the day-to-day needs of many district residents.

As a matter of intellectual honesty, I am compelled to present in an Appendix, The Auto-Centric Carfree City, a design for an auto-centric carfree city. I do not advocate this design, although it certainly improves on contemporary auto-centric cities. This design provides better automobility at lower construction costs than current practice and also provides sufficient rail capacity to fill the entire need for personal mobility. The road network could simply be abandoned at any time. This design reduces the cost of major freeway intersections by an order of magnitude.

It is with considerably more pleasure that I present in an Appendix, The Bicycle City, a design for a bicycle-centric carfree city.

We turn now to an examination of the districts that comprise a carfree city.

Grote Markt, Groningen, the Netherlands, c.1900.

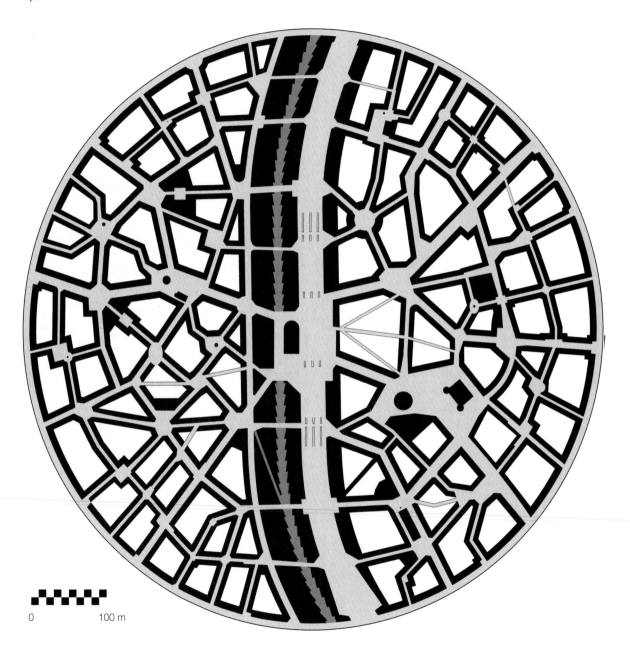

0   100 m

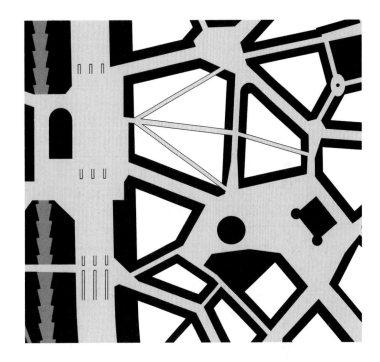

Detail of the reference district, showing the central square and part of the adjoining area. The metro exits can also be seen where they emerge onto the central boulevard.

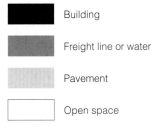

Building

Freight line or water

Pavement

Open space

Above: Key to all drawings in this chapter
Opposite: The reference district design. Buildings are shown in black (38.3%), streets in light gray (28.9%), and the metro-freight line in dark gray (1.8%). White areas are open space (31.0%). The percentages given relate only to the area inside the district boundary.

CITY DISTRICTS

As discussed in the previous chapter, the city is organized into districts, 81 general-use districts and 18 utility areas. This chapter begins with a description of the reference district design illustrated on the facing page; variations on the district design are taken up later. The reference district is a typical mixed-use district in a carfree city, located about midway between the city center and the utility areas. While the reference district cannot be directly applied when converting existing cities to the carfree model, a close approach should usually be feasible. The two critical points are:

• Transport stops within walking distance of every doorstep
• Density high enough to support good public transport

Please keep in mind that the reference district design is only a model: every district in a city should be unique. An infinite variety of district designs is possible, and each district can have its own character. In addition, each district has its own particular needs, and the design of a district must necessarily take these needs into account. The margins of this chapter carry drawings of several designs that are possible within the constraints of the reference design; also included are two districts of different sizes, one larger and one smaller than normal. These latter do not meet the requirements of the reference design but are suitable for use in cities whose design standards differ from those of the reference design.

The organization of the city into discrete districts, as opposed to continuous bands or a solid mass, conveys several important advantages:

- People prefer communities with clear boundaries, which the circular pattern naturally provides.
- Each district will tend to assume its own identity in the course of time.
- Each district is large enough to support basic services at the core and so within easy walking distance of every doorstep.
- Circular districts with a radial street pattern minimize walking distances to the central transport stop.
- Green space almost completely surrounds the district and lies within easy walking distance of every doorstep.

The reference topology shows a considerable variation in the density of the districts in the city: districts near the city center are denser than districts near the periphery. Some of the most dense districts have populations double the average, while other districts support populations about half the average. Much wider variations are possible. The reference district gives a FAR of 1.5 and a building footprint of 0.38, the average for the reference design as a whole.

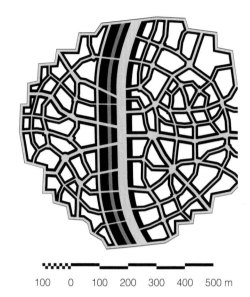

100   0   100   200   300   400   500 m

There is no intrinsic reason that districts must be perfectly circular.

The remainder of the drawings in the margins of this chapter are all drawn to the same scale as the drawing above.

The reference topology also shows a considerable variation in the average density of the lobes.

REFERENCE DISTRICT

The design standards for the reference district are given in the sections below.

12,000 Residents & 8000 Workplaces

The population of the district is 12,000 residents. Each circular district divides naturally along the central boulevard into two communities of roughly equal size. Each of these communities has a population of about 6000 residents, which is small enough that people feel they belong to a community in which their voices can be heard.

Community of 7000, Pattern 12

The reference district also provides workplaces for 8000 people, counting each school desk as a workplace. (School is where children work, and they need space for their work. While most schools probably allocate less space per student than most businesses, there will doubtless be businesses with higher-than-average space requirements. Also note that additional workplaces are provided in the utility areas.)

Radial Design

Streets radiate from the central transport stop in order to minimize walking times to the center of the district and the transport stop. A radial plan also provides quick access to the open space surrounding the district.

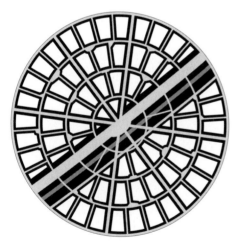

The radial design principle carried to its logical extreme. The regular pattern is easier for strangers to navigate but is rather boring.

5-Minute Walk to Transport & Green Space

The best practice is to keep every doorstep within a 5-minute walk of a transport stop; many people regard longer walks as excessive. Housing for the infirm should be sited very close to the center, allowing them to reach basic services and the transport stop with a minimum of walking. Expansive green space almost completely surrounds the district.

Many people are not happy without regular contact with the earth and living plants. The courtyards inside each block are large enough for lawns and gardens. Expansive green areas are never more than 5 minutes away; some of this land can be devoted to garden allotments.

760-Meter District Diameter

The 760 meter district diameter stems directly from the requirement that the central transport stop lie within a 5-minute walk. The area of a circle having a diameter of 760 meters is 45 hectares (112 acres). A population of 12,000 living on 45 hectares has a density of 264 residents/hectare, as compared to central Paris at 331 residents/hectare. In addition, the 8000 workplaces located in the district give a density of 176 workplaces/hectare, compared to 276 work-places/hectare in central Paris. The overall density is thus significantly below that of central Paris. Given that cars do not occupy any room in a carfree district, its perceived density is appreciably lower than that of central Paris. I make this comparison because many regard the older districts of Paris as a nearly ideal city form and also to show that high densities do not preclude the arrangement of highly agreeable urban spaces. The lower density of the carfree district permits the arrangement of somewhat more green space than is possible at Parisian densities, even though the streets are generally narrower than those in central Paris.

Wide Central Boulevard

The centers of the districts are connected by a boulevard about 33 meters wide. The metro (or tram) route follows this boulevard. (In the inner districts, the central boulevard is 40 meters wide in order to accommodate a 4-track metro beneath the boulevard.) The boulevard is also wide enough

Walking speed is 76 meters/minute, which gives a radius of 380 meters, or a diameter of 760 meters.

Vincent Fouchier (1997), 81

Opposite: The reference district compared, at the same scale, to three other well-known city forms.
• Top left: carfree reference district
• Top right: 17th-century canal district, Amsterdam
• Bottom left: San Marco district, Venice
• Bottom right: midtown Manhattan, New York
The variations in block size are large, and Manhattan is by no means the most extreme example. (Some blocks in Manhattan are built solid, as shown here, but others do have interior gardens.) Estimated Plot Ratios and FARs are given below:

	Plot Ratio	FAR
Carfree district	0.38	1.5
Amsterdam	0.43	1.7
San Marco	0.67	2.7
Manhattan	0.63	above 6.0

to serve as a bicycle expressway with lanes in both directions, and a median strip separating oncoming bicyclists makes it safe and easy for pedestrians to cross. A row of trees can be planted on each side of the 33-meter boulevard, but the 40-meter boulevard does not allow tree planting because the metro occupies the full width of the boulevard.

Central Square

Every district should have a focus. The metro stop is located at the center of the district and forms an obvious focal point, where a square is established in most districts. Basic services such as grocery stores and child care are sited here, along with important public buildings and other uses that draw a large public. Each of these squares should have its own shape and character.

I prefer organic designs like this one. They create suspense and mystery.

Freight Line Aside Central Boulevard

A freight delivery line is constructed parallel to the central boulevard and separated from it by a row of buildings (mainly stores) some 20 meters wide. The freight delivery line is constructed below grade level, and streets cross it at frequent intervals on short bridges. The question of freight delivery is discussed starting on page 195.

Mixed Uses

Jane Jacobs contends that the long-held urban planning doctrine mandating the separation of uses is not only unnecessary but actually antithetical to the creation of lively city districts. The move to separate industry from residential areas dates from a period around 1900 when smokestack industry caused great hardships for those forced to live nearby. The change was largely driven by the work of Ebenezer Howard, founder of the Garden Cities movement. It was Howard

Near San Marco, Venice, 1997
A mixed-use area with restaurants, shops, offices, and residences.

This district is smaller than normal

who maintained that each class of use should be grouped with its own kind: residences and commerce must be rigidly separated. The Garden City movement was the death knell for the traditional city, in which everything was arranged cheek-by-jowl and all manner of uses mixed in together.

Smokestack industry has in any case become much less important, and environmental controls now make factories considerably better neighbors. Nonetheless, it remains sensible to separate most heavy industry from residential and commercial areas. Space for this use is therefore allocated in the nonresidential utility areas. With judicious safeguards, commerce and light industry mix well with residences. Almost all areas of the city are occupied at all times of the day, which helps reduce both street crime and break-ins. Mixed uses also make for interesting, vibrant neighborhoods.

High-Density Occupation

The district occupies relatively little land in comparison to the amount of activity that it supports. This is assured by the high FAR of 1.5, which results in low land occupancy for a given amount of floor area.

VARIATIONS ON THE REFERENCE DISTRICT

An infinite variety of district designs is, of course, possible. All designs must meet the standards given at the beginning of this chapter if they are to satisfy the requirements of the reference topology, but within these limits there is great flexibility. The design standards and topology of a particular city are themselves subject to wide variation, depending upon the needs of that city, and alterations to a city's topology will usually also impose some changes on the design requirements for districts.

The district designs shown in the margins of this chapter are all drawn to the same scale. They give some idea of the range of designs that is possible within the constraints of the reference topology. Larger or smaller districts would also be useful in specific situations. Almost anything is possible within the limits of reasonable walking distance.

This district is considerably larger than the reference district. Walking times from the periphery to the center would be about 7 minutes. Such districts can provide lower density and more open space.

Granularity of the District

The scale of construction in a given district can be adjusted within a wide range. A coarse grain is created by large, deep buildings with wide interior courtyards and relatively broad streets. A finer grain arises from small, shallow buildings surrounding small interior courtyards and narrow streets. Either approach can meet the standards of the reference design but gives districts with quite different appearance and feeling. There is no reason why a mixture of styles cannot be applied to separate blocks in the same district. In general, larger buildings with public functions will tend to be located nearest the central square, so the granularity will tend to be coarsest in the center and finest at the edges. This tendency is partially reversed by the desirability of larger interior courtyards in the more residential parts of the district (located closer to the district edge), leading to larger blocks.

As the granularity gets finer, every element must also be scaled down in order to maintain the necessary balance among streets, buildings, and open spaces. In some cases, this will lead to very narrow streets, which in themselves pose no difficulties in a carfree city. Attention must be paid to the occasional need to bring large construction vehicles into the district. The requirement for emergency access also dictates that some streets be wide enough to accommodate emergency vehicles and that these streets are never more than about 75 meters away from any location. Within these limits,

A district denser than the reference district

almost anything is possible; see page 157 for a further consideration of these matters.

It is worth noting that streets in ancient cities were very narrow indeed, and this can still be seen in Venice today. In Pompeii, some streets were only 2.5 meters wide, and the broadest streets were less than 12 meters wide. In Venice, the Strada Nuova, the widest street that runs for more than a short distance, is only about 9 meters wide. The wonderfully comfortable feeling of Venetian streets results from their unusually narrow width, which give a sense of enclosure and turns the streets into spaces in their own right.

We turn next to an examination of the blocks that make up a carfree district.

Allan Jacobs, 136

Positive Outdoor Space, Pattern 106

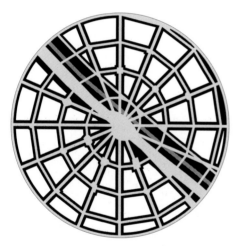

This design is derived from a plan by Francesco di Giorgio Martini, who pondered ideal city forms between 1451 and 1464.

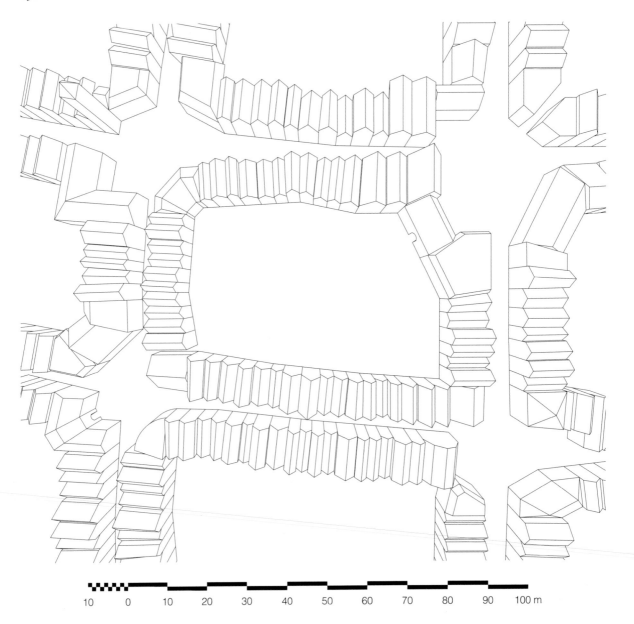

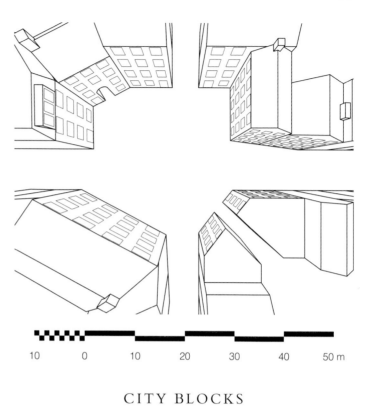

Detail of a small neighborhood square
(Scale at ground level)

10   0   10   20   30   40   50 m

Opposite: Bird's-eye view of the reference block, which is 85 meters long and 62 meters wide, measured to the centerlines of the bounding streets. The interior courtyard is about 61 by 39 meters, the buildings average 8.5 meters deep, and the streets are 5 meters wide, usually flaring near intersections. (Scale at ground level.) About 86 blocks of this size comprise one district.

CITY BLOCKS

City blocks are often perfectly uniform, as in large gridded areas of Manhattan and many other US cities. Blocks can also be highly irregular, as in most European city centers and the oldest parts of Boston. The grid form does simplify the task of finding your way around, and few urban areas are easier to navigate than Manhattan above 8th Street, with its nearly perfect grid of numbered streets and avenues. This is, however, a mechanistic form. I find the highly varied blocks typical of European cities endlessly interesting and usually attractive. There is, however, no reason why districts of both types should not be constructed in the same city.

Reference Block

In this chapter we consider the reference design for a block in a carfree city. Just as the districts should be unique, so too should each block within a district have its own character. This is possible even in cases where a rigid geometric street layout is adopted for a particular district: even though the shape and size of the blocks may be identical, the style of buildings can vary from block to block, as can their height. Clearly, there should be as much variety in the blocks of a carfree city as in its districts. What is presented here as the reference block design is simply a typical block, neither large nor small. The size and shape of other blocks will depart considerably from the reference design, as can be observed in the drawing of the reference topology and in the drawings of districts in the previous chapter.

Each district contains many blocks, ranging from as few as 30 to as many as 500. Because of the circular shape of the district, few blocks can be perfect rectangles or squares, as can be seen from the reference district design in the previous chapter. The reference block design is a roughly rectangular block 85 by 62 meters (measured to the centerlines of the encompassing streets, which are 5 meters wide). The interior courtyard is 61 by 39 meters. About 86 blocks of this area would fill one district (of course, only a few of these blocks could have the same shape as the reference block). The following table gives some statistical measures of the reference block:

	$meters^2$	$feet^2$
Surface area	5259	56,591
Footprint of buildings	1914	20,593
Gross floor area	7656	82,373

Gross floor area includes the space occupied by walls, stairs, utilities, etc. Net (usable) floor area runs about 25% less than gross floor area.

See page 36 for an explanation of FAR

The reference block is somewhat less dense than the district as a whole because of the especially high density of areas near the central boulevard.

FAR	1.456
Average number of floors	4
Building footprint ratio	.364
Open space ratio	.434
Paved area ratio	.202
Inhabitants	139
Workplaces	93

New carfree street, Amsterdam, 1999
This new construction in the heart of Amsterdam fills the bill for a carfree block. I don't much care for the architecture, but the block looks livable enough.

Historical Museum, Amsterdam, 1998
Very small blocks lead to very small interior courtyards; the reference block is considerably bigger.

The figure for paved area is based on the surface area of the streets only. When small squares are added at the intersections of streets, the buildings are pushed back into the interior courtyard to make room for the square. The green space is thus slightly reduced and the paved area correspondingly increased. The gross floor area remains unchanged. Squares, if carefully arranged, provide especially high quality space and thus improve the overall quality of the district, at a small cost in green space adjacent to buildings.

The following sections describe specific aspects of the reference block design.

Short Blocks

In *The Death and Life of Great American Cities,* Jane Jacobs devotes an entire chapter to the need for small blocks. She cites the example of Manhattan blocks, typically 240 meters long and 80 meters wide (measured from the centerlines of the streets). The avenues at the ends of the blocks are the major thoroughfares and prime commercial areas. The lack of intermediate, secondary streets running parallel to the avenues greatly reduces the number of routes that people follow to their destinations, with the result that people who live on one cross street rarely walk along cross streets parallel to their own. She advocates narrow connector streets, parallel to the avenues, to cut block lengths in half, to about 120 meters. This would provide redundant pathways, allowing a choice of routes to most destinations. People would become more familiar with the neighborhood in which they live, which helps to foster a sense of community.

The largest normal blocks proposed for the carfree city are about 80 by 120 meters. Most blocks are considerably smaller than this. Blocks as small as 24 meters square are entirely practical and can lead to a lovely, rich texture if laid out with some artistry. These small blocks house fewer than 25 people and are suitable for small cohousing developments. In hot, dry regions, another useful pattern has been found throughout history: individual family courtyard compounds. These can be as small as 14 meters square, with very narrow streets on two sides and a small interior courtyard. Each of these tiny compounds has enough floor area to house about 8 people in comfort.

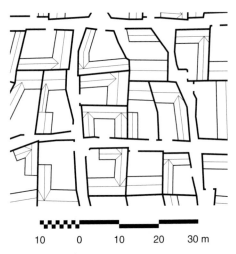

Traditional Arab family compounds, each with its own tiny courtyard.

1.5 Average FAR

Site Planning gives the following FARs as typical of various development types:

Housing Type	FAR
13-story elevator apartments	1.8
3-story walk-up apartments	1.0
Row houses	0.5
Two-family detached	0.3
Single-family	0.2 or less

Cohousing is a relatively new form of housing, a cross between private dwellings and communal living. Each family has its own quarters, but the community shares a large kitchen and dining area. Meals are taken communally several times a week. See McCamant & Durrett, *Cohousing: A contemporary Approach to Housing Ourselves* for a thorough treatment.

Lynch & Hack, 253

It will be seen that a FAR of 1.5 is quite high. However, the figures cited above are for developments in which large amounts of land are allocated to automobiles. A FAR of 1.5 can be realized by constructing 4-story buildings on 37.5% of the site area. If none of the remaining space is consumed

Narrow Street, Burano, 1997
There are many ways to achieve a FAR of 1.5. This area in Burano is only 2 to 3 stories high, but the plot ratio is high, and the FAR may even exceed 1.5.

Mixed uses in Venice, 1997
This is a main street just off the Piazza San Marco in Venice. It's about 6 meters wide and probably gets very crowded in the summer.

by automobiles, then there is adequate room for streets and yards. For the reference design, the FAR of the entire 256 sq-km site is only 0.24, or roughly the upper limit for detached single-family housing (the FAR for most US suburbs is considerably lower). The carfree city, however, leaves more than 80% of the site as expansive green space, contrasted to none for the suburban pattern (at the FAR given in the table; of course most suburbs include park land, which still further reduces the overall FAR). The relatively high FAR of 1.5 is selected because dense areas:

• Permit high-quality public transport
• Provide enough customers to support local services
• Can offer excellent quality of life
• Help conserve energy

A FAR of 1.5, combined with a district residential population of 12,000 and a workforce of 8000, gives the following average per-capita gross space allocations (usable space will be reduced by the area of walls, stairs, and mechanical spaces, typically about 25%):

Per-Capita Gross Area Allocation	meters^2	feet^2
Residence	36	387
Work	18	194
Shopping, health, recreation, etc.	9	97
Infrastructure (sited in utility areas)	20	215
Total	83	893

7-Meter Average Street Width

Most streets in a carfree district range between 4 and 8 meters wide. Streets as little as one meter wide are acceptable under some circumstances and are found in the oldest districts of Venice. Such narrow streets must be short and link directly to wider streets for emergency access. Streets wider than about

6 meters permit ready access by emergency vehicles and are in all other respects adequate for the expectable level of foot and wheeled traffic.

Except for the central boulevard, no street need be wider than 12 meters. The adequacy of this width is demonstrated throughout Europe by the continuing livability of medieval streets, many of which are just a few meters wide. These narrow streets are often the most inviting and comfortable parts of the city, provided that no motorized traffic intrudes.

A narrow residential street in Parma, Italy, 1998

A few straight radial streets of about 10 meters width permit views of the countryside from the heart of a district. Every district should have at least two streets of this width leading from the central square to the district edge, thereby providing a route to move mobile cranes and other specialized, large vehicles into the district on the rare occasions when this is necessary. These streets also provide fast access for emergency vehicles.

Many Small Squares

Where streets converge, it is natural to arrange small, comfortable squares that provide a gathering place for residents and visitors alike. These squares vary in size from about 8 meters square to 25 by 40 meters. The smallest squares are generally found near the edge of the district, reflecting the light foot traffic passing through them. Most districts have a fairly large square at the center.

Lively Ramo San Zulian, Venice, Italy, 1997

Interior Courtyards

Interior courtyards are found inside all but a few unusually dense blocks near the center of a district or where a large enclosed space is required (such as a theater). Courtyards admit daylight to building interiors and provide green space adjacent to most buildings.

Tiny courtyard, Bologna, Italy, 1998

A Pattern Language is introduced on page 19

A particularly nice sottoportego, Venice, 1997

A Pattern Language stresses the importance of *"Positive Outdoor Space"* (Pattern 106). This pattern calls for spaces largely enclosed by buildings, with narrow openings leading to the outer world. The interior courtyards proposed for the carfree district are of a comfortable size, consistent with the requirements of this pattern. While many residents will want to allocate this space to the occupants of the adjoining buildings, I think it would be desirable to arrange at least some of these courtyards as semiprivate areas, with pathways connecting them to the street network. The courtyard would belong to the block as a whole, which would be responsible for its maintenance. Such an arrangement permits the use of these courtyards as pedestrian shortcuts. The Venetian *sottoportego* (a narrow passageway underneath a building) provides the right combination of separation and linkage, making the interior courtyards clearly defined spaces that are still part of the web of the larger city. Both the private and semiprivate patterns can be accommodated, in different blocks.

Graduated Internal Density

Densities near the district center can be higher than the 1.5 FAR for the district as a whole; densities near the edges can be a little lower. The concentration of density at the center increases the number of people who have very short walks to the transport stop. In addition, public functions should logically be clustered around the transit stop, further reducing the amount of walking required.

The main street, Siena, Italy, 1998

Now we move on to the next level of detail in the reference design: individual buildings.

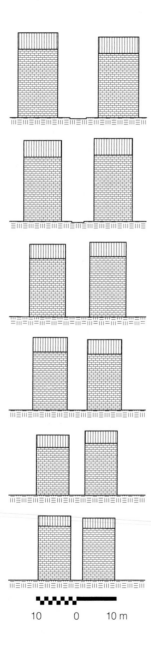

Freiburg, Germany, 1998
The buildings on this street are an ideal form for construction in a carfree city. Most of the buildings have an additional floor contained within the roof, bringing the average height to about four stories.

Opposite: Profiles of streets and buildings. The streets shown here range in width from 3 to 10 meters. Note that the heights of the houses vary but are similar on any given street. Lower buildings are desirable in the case of the narrowest streets, as this arrangement admits more daylight to the street. The reference design uses only a few streets of 3 meters width, and the inner districts each have several streets of 12 or 15 meter width. Everywhere, the boulevards are 33 or more meters wide, and the three downtown districts each have a 300-meter length of boulevard 100 meters wide.

BUILDINGS

Buildings in a carfree city can be designed in a limitless range of styles and types, although certain commonalities must be achieved in order to meet the requirements imposed by the reference design. In particular, a FAR of 1.5 must be reached, which requires dense construction and common walls. Within these limits, however, great freedom exists. I would prefer buildings that resemble those constructed for centuries in Europe and in most older US cities. These buildings are characterized by narrow frontages, moderate depths, and limited heights, usually no more than 5 or at most 6 stories. Customarily, each building differs from its neighbors, although most of the buildings on a block bear a family resemblance.

Small buildings offer several advantages. A single family can own an entire building, in some cases with a small income-producing rental apartment on an upper floor, perhaps with a store or small office on the ground floor. This arrangement prevents many conflicts among neighbors, because the resident family exercises considerable control over what happens in the building. Small buildings also support small enterprises by providing a large stock of relatively inexpensive street-level commercial space. Larger enterprises can occupy an entire building or even a string of buildings. The flexibility of small buildings has been demonstrated through the ages.

Clearly, however, the sorts of buildings constructed in North American strip malls have no place in the carfree city. These buildings are almost all one-story buildings (always surrounded by large amounts of parking) and often do not even touch adjacent buildings. Single-story buildings can never even reach a FAR of 1.0 (since in any case some amount of street area is always required), so they can never achieve the required density. Buildings of this sort only became common in the postwar era and stem directly from auto-centric urban planning.

Commerzbank, Amsterdam, 1999
Some large businesses occupy several adjacent buildings. The small buildings never lose their individual character even though they are occupied by a single tenant.

Mass-Produced Buildings

The world's population has exploded in the 20th century, and we have resorted to economical construction techniques in order to house our rapidly increasing numbers. At the same time, rising personal incomes have led to a demand for much larger living quarters in richer nations. These two phenomena have combined to create an enormous demand for new residential space. In the past, many buildings were designed, in the local vernacular style, by the same artisans who built the structures, often in direct consultation with the future occupants. These styles were developed over the course of centuries and were well adapted to local conditions and locally available materials.

Christopher Alexander argued convincingly in *The Production of Houses* that houses tailored to the needs of individual owners can actually be cheaper than mass-produced houses. He describes an entirely different approach to building houses.

In the postwar era, the USA built millions of inexpensive wood-frame single-family houses. However, wood is no longer inexpensive, and its combustibility precludes its use in dense urban areas, as shown by conflagrations throughout history. In the USA, carfree cities will have to adopt the European practice of building masonry houses, suitably reinforced in earthquake zones.

The end of the apprentice system and the gradual disappearance of artisans during the 20th century has brought us to the point where construction in vernacular styles without detailed plans has virtually disappeared in the industrialized lands. Authorities insist on the delivery of full construction drawings prior to the issuance of a building permit, and in most jurisdictions these plans must carry the stamp of a registered engineer or architect. This new expense has been minimized by developing a single design and using it repetitively, sometimes thousands of times in succession. The result has been the virtual disappearance of buildings designed *and* constructed by the same small team of artisans. Instead, we have rows, and even fields, of identical buildings (or huge structures with endlessly repeating elements). To the greatest extent possible, building construction has been turned into a mass production process.

Unique Buildings

Every building in a city should be unique. It is dehumanizing to force people to live in massive structures composed of hundreds of identical repeating elements. A friend of mine once lived in such a building. The only way to pick out his apartment from the ground was to count down 7 stories from the top and over 12 balconies from the left. This does nothing to enhance a person's self-esteem or to help him feel that he has a real home. The identical design of each apartment assumes that each family's needs are exactly the same, which is, of course, false. A wide-ranging variety in housing stock helps families to find housing that fits their needs.

The difference between these mass-produced neighborhoods and cities built piecemeal in vernacular styles is especially apparent in Europe. Districts built before about

Bijlmer district, Amsterdam, 1999
The explanation for the popularity of low-density suburbs: when auto-centric suburbs are built at high density, the streets become vast, ugly parking lots. High density living can only be pleasant in the absence of cars.

An exception to the rule is twin buildings, often seen in Europe. This pleasant variation should not be too frequently repeated.

The most extreme instance was Le Corbusier's Machine for Living. The thousands of identical units were to have been identically furnished in the manner prescribed by The Master.

Hall, 209

1880 are characterized by unique buildings in the prevailing style of the period. This led to districts with a feeling of integrity but without the deadly aura of mass production. Districts built since that time, and especially those built in the postwar era, are typified by numbing monotony. It is almost impossible to construct lively city districts in these circumstances. The vast fleet of cars that dominates the streetscape does nothing to help the situation.

The industrialized nations are rich enough to resume the practice of constructing unique buildings that give families a place they can really call home. Recent advances in computer-assisted design, engineering, and manufacturing should reduce the cost of making unique buildings. Whether the design of buildings will ever be permitted to revert to the former practice of close collaboration between owners and artisans remains to be seen. The results were usually highly satisfactory, but a long period of on-the-job training is essential, along with greater respect for highly skilled people who work with their hands.

Unique buildings are not essential to the carfree design, but I do believe that they improve it.

LIVING CLOSER TOGETHER

Noise is the most powerful argument against denser living arrangements. In much of the world, recent construction has taken the form of large apartment blocks. These buildings are relatively inexpensive to construct (although the need for elevators negates some of the savings). Each apartment may abut as many as eight other apartments. Concrete floors are used almost universally, and they transmit noise readily. The acoustic isolation of the demising walls between the apartments is usually poor, and noise often makes life in these large apartment blocks unbearable. Often, the people making the noise have never even met those suffering from it.

Denser living, Burano, Italy, 1997
People have always lived close to one another on this small, carfree island in the Venetian lagoon.

A demising wall separates one tenant's space from another's. In modern apartment buildings, loads are often carried by heavy columns; the demising walls are thin and have little strength in themselves.

If the crack between the buildings is sealed at the edge with an elastic compound, the energy saving advantages of common walls are preserved, but the acoustic isolation between the buildings is maintained.

Small buildings separated by a narrow air gap provide quite good acoustic isolation, and a single family can occupy an entire building and exert considerable influence over what goes on in the building. In the case of small families and those living alone, small buildings permit each household to occupy an entire floor. The residents of small buildings share a common stairway, so occasional meetings between residents are likely, and minor problems can be ironed out during these chance encounters, before matters get too far out of hand.

BUILDING DESIGN REQUIREMENTS

We turn now to a general discussion of building design issues. A handful of reference building designs could never meet the widely differing requirements of various uses, and I have not attempted to develop reference designs for buildings. Our architectural heritage is vast and can meet virtually every requirement for buildings of various types and sizes. Instead, we will consider general building design requirements imposed by the reference design for carfree cities.

Four-Story buildings, Amsterdam, 1999
All references in this section are to *Four-Story Limit* (Pattern 21). Remember that Alexander is counting the ground floor as the first floor. Most Europeans will need to think in terms of *three*-story buildings.

Alexander (1977), 115

Four-Story Buildings
This is one of the most controversial aspects of the proposal for carfree cities, so it is worth spending some time on this point. Christopher Alexander argues forcefully for buildings no higher than four stories:

There is abundant evidence to show that high buildings make people crazy.

He cites several research studies showing that people living on high floors display more symptoms of mental illness than people living closer to the ground. People living on high floors are, quite literally, beyond reach and out of touch. From the fourth floor, it is still possible to make out individual faces in the street below and even to hold a brief conversation. From higher floors this is difficult or impossible. Alexander concludes:

> In any urban area, no matter how dense, keep the majority of buildings four stories high or less. It is possible that certain buildings should exceed this limit, but they should never be buildings for human habitation.

There is another powerful argument that especially affects smaller buildings: up to about four stories, elevators are unnecessary, which saves both construction and operating costs. Buildings higher than five stories essentially require the installation of elevators, and so necessitate the construction of large buildings in order to spread the cost of elevators across many tenants. These larger buildings damage the texture of the neighborhood and force many families to live in the same building.

The reference design for carfree cities is therefore based on the assumption that virtually all buildings are between three and five stories high. In the heart of the downtown districts, some buildings may be a few stories higher than this. Every city, however, should have high places that provide views out over the city, but these structures should not be inhabited. The Campanile fulfills this function in Venice.

Connected Buildings

Unless buildings are very tall, a high FAR can be achieved only if most buildings abut other buildings on both sides. As previously noted, this arrangement also greatly reduces the

Children living on high floors begin to play outdoors by themselves at a much later age. One study cited by Alexander showed that, by age 5, all children living in low-rise buildings play outdoors by themselves, but 29% of those living in high-rise buildings still do not. In another study, 90% of the children from the lower 3 floors played outdoors alone, while only 59% of the children from the upper 3 floors did so. The reason is simple: parents can't keep an eye on a child playing outside (or reach him quickly in an emergency) if the building is too high.

Alexander (1977), 119

Consideration must be given to those with mobility limitations. It should be possible to house all those who cannot climb stairs at street level.

Connected buildings, Nancy, France, 1997

energy needed for heating and cooling. This connection of buildings with one another also supports another pattern, *Connected Buildings.* In support of this pattern, Alexander cites Camillo Sitte's study of 255 churches in Rome. Of these, all but 6 have at least one wall that abuts other buildings. In fact, 110 of these churches abut other buildings on three sides. Sitte continues:

> ... Regarding *Rome,* then, it can be taken as a rule that *churches* were *never* erected as *free-standing structures.* Almost the same is true, in fact, for the whole of Italy....
>
> As is becoming clear, our modern attitude runs precisely contrary to this well-integrated and obviously thought-out procedure. We do not seem to think it possible that a new church can be located anywhere except in the middle of its building lot, so that there is space all around it. But this placement offers only disadvantages and not a single advantage. It is the least favorable for building, since its effect is not concentrated anywhere but is scattered all about it. Such an exposed building will always appear like a cake on a serving-platter. To start with, any life-like organic integration with the site is ruled out....

Sitte, 27-28. Emphasis in the original.

Alexander concludes:

> Connect your building up, wherever possible, to the existing buildings round about. Do not keep set backs between buildings; instead, try to form new buildings as continuations of older buildings.

Alexander (1977), 534

9-Meter Maximum Building Depth

Wings of Light, Pattern 107

In order to provide natural light and ventilation, buildings should not be too deep. *A Pattern Language* calls for buildings

25 ft deep. Nine meters is just under 30 ft, which Alexander gives as the upper limit for good daylight within a room. In buildings of this depth, many floors can be open from front to back, providing light from two sides, and the use of bay windows further improves the quality of illumination. A further advantage of through-floors is the excellent cross-ventilation they provide.

I have not held rigorously to the 25-foot standard. Buildings along the broadest streets are deeper than 9 meters. The following standards have been used in developing the reference design:

Major street, Siena, 1998
This street is just 6 meters wide. The buildings along it have high ceilings and as many as 6 stories, which makes for rather high facades. Some may find this arrangement confining, but I think the proportions are very comfortable.

Street Width (meters)	Building Depth (meters)
3	7.5
4	8
5	8.5
6	9
8	9
10	10
12	12
15	15
Central boulevard	20
Factories along freight line	30

Particularly in the case of factories, I thought it necessary to allow for much deeper buildings. The buildings along the central boulevard serve important functions and also need more space than the shallower depth would allow. Generally, residences do not deviate far from the 9-meter standard.

Ground-Floor Commercial Space
Apartments located above ground-floor retail spaces are commonplace in Europe. While we do not need so many

Ground-floor commercial spaces, Venice, 1997

stores that every building would have one on the ground floor, we can also use this floor for small offices and any other kind of small business. This space is more valuable than the upper floors because it has direct access to the street, and it makes sense to use it for functions that require frequent access, especially by the general public. This pattern, once common in the USA, is now expressly forbidden by zoning ordinances in most American municipalities. The pattern also accords with the doctrine of mixed uses, which add life and interest to a street while improving security. Fortunately, the New Urbanism movement (NU) has made people aware of the desirability of this arrangement, and some municipalities have altered their zoning regulations to allow it again.

While NU advocates higher densities than current suburbs, the resulting developments are still at a density considerably below that of true cities.

Rooftop Space

Few Americans are accustomed to using rooftops for any purpose, but in hot, dry regions, flat roofs are simply extensions of a family's living space. While solar collectors will probably be added to rooftops in sunnier regions during the coming decades, we should strive to retain access for other uses as well. In multifamily buildings, the family occupying the top floor should have access to at least a part of the roof, where they can establish a small garden and take the sun.

Rooftop balconies, Bologna, Italy, 1998

Small, Narrow Buildings

In order to permit a single family to occupy a building 9 meters deep and 4 stories high, the building must be relatively narrow. Most buildings are between 4 and 6 meters wide. Buildings this narrow are common in older urban areas. Some uses, however, require wider buildings. Restaurants, for instance, benefit from a frontage of 10 meters or so, although Amsterdam does boast some restaurants as narrow as 3 meters.

A building only 4 meters wide sounds very narrow, but when the building is four stories tall and 9 meters deep, it has about the same gross floor area as a smaller North American suburban house. The separation of the house into floors allows the arrangement of different uses on different floors, with a privacy gradient running from a fairly public first floor to a very private top floor. Larger or richer families may choose to occupy a wider and therefore larger building.

Hoisting Beams

The Dutch learned centuries ago that the provision of a hoisting beam at the top of every building provides an exceptionally convenient and efficient way to move goods and furniture into the upper stories of a building. A large-diameter pulley is hung temporarily from the beam, and a thick rope, easy to grasp, makes short work of moving even quite heavy items into upper stories. While the use of this arrangement is not essential, it eases the chore of moving into the upper floors of a building without an elevator.

VARIATIONS ON STANDARD BUILDINGS

We turn now to a consideration of several building types that do not meet the usual requirements but which may find useful application in some circumstances.

Single-Family Houses in a Carfree City

If walking times of up to 10 minutes are acceptable, then it becomes possible to build two-story single-family houses on lots 14 meters wide and 22 meters deep, with streets 10 meters wide. Porches about 2 meters deep would front directly on the street, with side lawns 2 meters wide (giving 4 meters clear between houses). The houses are thus

Narrow buildings, Amsterdam, 1999
During my tenure in Amsterdam, these two buildings were completely reconstructed. One of them was torn down to bricks and rebuilt. The facade of the other was carefully preserved in place and a new building constructed behind it. I can no longer recall which was which.

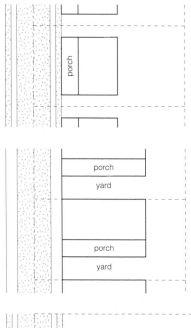

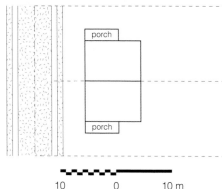

Top: Plot plan for single-family housing
Middle: Charleston side-porch house
Bottom: Duplex housing

10 meters wide and 7 meters deep. Each house has a back yard 12 by 14 meters. The density is 32 units to the hectare (13 units/acre). This borders on the limits of the single-family pattern. If the houses are oriented so the short dimension faces the street, then somewhat more space separates the adjacent houses, but the back yards are smaller.

The Side-Porch House

The Charleston, South Carolina, "side-porch house" is another approach to providing single-family housing in relatively dense areas. The building presents a narrow gable to the street, and a garden wall continues along the street frontage to the next house. A large porch is built on each floor along the side of the house, with the main entrance penetrating the wall underneath the porch. A narrow garden occupies the space between the porch and the next house. This pattern was exceptionally well suited to local needs and gives a relatively dense pattern of habitation. Many of these houses are very beautiful and much sought after.

Duplex Housing

In my opinion, duplexes are usually a better arrangement for low-density living than single-family houses on small lots. The larger mass of the building makes it more interesting (and, in the eyes of some, more prestigious), and the back yards are somewhat bigger. The common wall also reduces heating costs.

Having considered the layout of carfree cities from the largest elements to the smallest, we turn next to the matter of providing urban passenger transport without resorting to the use of cars.

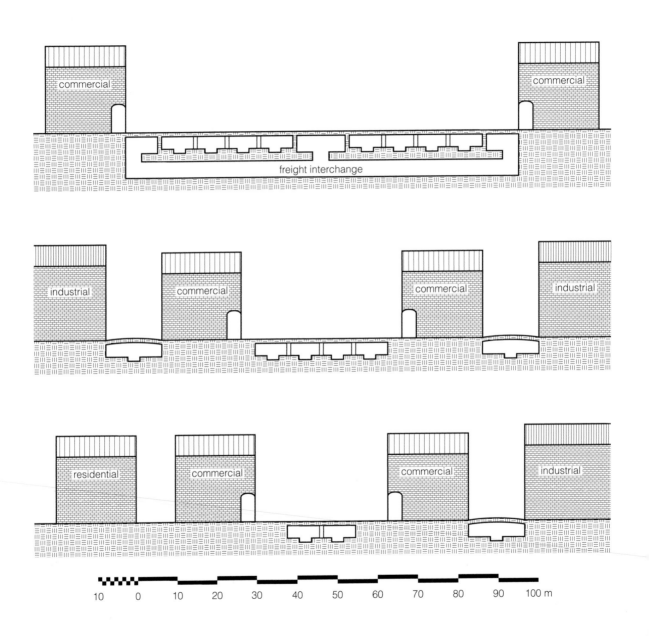

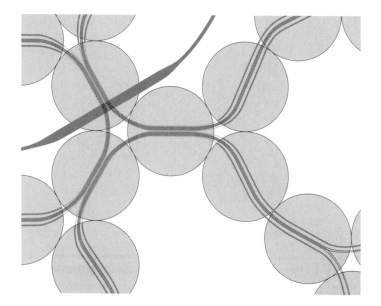

Downtown intercity rail station, 4-track metro lines, and metro-freight routes. The platforms of the train station are located on two levels, to save space.

Opposite: Profiles of the passenger and freight metro systems. The upper profile shows the layout of the passenger and metro-freight systems in the three downtown districts (where two of the lines are brought adjacent to each other for transfers). The middle profile shows the four-track metro and doubled metro-freight system in the 12 inner districts. The bottom profile shows the two-track metro and single metro-freight line in the 66 outer districts.

PASSENGER TRANSPORT

Superlative public transport is the only foundation upon which a carfree city can be built. Fortunately, existing rail technology easily fulfills the need, and we even have the luxury of a choice between two excellent systems: a heavy-rail underground system (metro) or a surface tram system. Another possibility is an improved bus system, as is used in Curitiba, Brazil. A long-term possibility is Personal Rapid Transit (PRT), discussed briefly in Better Public Transport. This chapter considers only passenger transport; freight delivery is taken up in the next chapter.

While the reference design for carfree cities might have been predicated entirely on bicycle transport, I have, in fact, assumed that public transport will provide *all* movement between districts. I have made this assumption because only a few regions enjoy sufficiently mild weather to permit year-round bicycling except by dedicated enthusiasts. In most climates, the transport system must be capable of meeting all transport needs during weather extremes. During fair weather, bicycling reduces the load on the transport system, is pleasant and healthy, and often provides the fastest door-to-door transport. For this reason, the needs of bicyclists remain a high design priority, notwithstanding the capability of the transit system to provide all passenger transport.

Journeys fall into three categories: within the district, between districts, and between the city and outlying areas. We will consider each of these in turn.

Venice, 1997

Handicapped access is a nightmare in Venice because of the frequent bridges with steps. Problems of this sort can be avoided when building new cities and retrofitting existing cities.

Transport Within the District

Walking is the most common means of transport within the district. No two doorsteps in a district lie more than a 10-minute walk apart. However, walking cannot meet all passenger transport needs within the district. For the longer distances, many people will prefer to bike. For the very young, the very old, and those with disabilities, an alternative way to get around is necessary. Various simple, inexpensive, non-intrusive vehicles can meet these needs:
- Large-wheeled pedal tricycles for those with poor balance
- Motorized wheelchairs
- Baby strollers
- Radio-dispatched pedicabs or slow, battery-powered taxis

The most difficult issue affecting transport within the district is the matter of right-of-way. While individual cities will make decisions based on local needs, the following two general principles assure safe, pleasant streets: pedestrians own the street, and bicyclists own the central boulevard. We take up each of these principles in turn.

Routine use of police squad cars is probably un-necessary: experience with police patrols mounted on bicycles has been good, and provisions for battery-boost during emergencies already exist.

Bicycle chaos, Amsterdam Central Station, 1999

Pedestrians Own the Street

One fundamental principle must be maintained: pedestrians take precedence over all other street users, no matter how inconvenient that may be for wheeled traffic. The only exceptions are emergency vehicles, of which there should be very few. All other street users must stay out of the way of pedestrians, including bicyclists, delivery vehicles, and carts. Because vehicle speeds are very low, any conflicts between street users should be resolved without bodily injury, even if some harsh words are exchanged. The narrow streets easily meet the demands imposed upon them, possibly excepting the narrowest streets, where bicyclists may be expected to dismount and walk for safety reasons. Bicyclists may also be expected to ride at slow speeds on most streets, out of consideration for other street users. Only emergency vehicles should ever travel faster than a reasonably fit runner can sprint.

We come now to a delicate issue: many of the problems with cars also apply to bicycles, albeit to a far lesser degree. One of the reasons that Venice is so relaxing is the complete absence of street traffic moving faster than a pedestrian. Only under these circumstances can people on foot truly let down their guard. Bicycles have the following problems in common with cars:

- Bicyclists require considerable street space
- Bike parking consumes a lot of space
- Bikes parked on the street are unattractive
- Bikes in poor repair can make enough noise to be irritating
- Bikes can be dangerous to both riders and pedestrians

In particular, bicycle parking near a metro or tram stop could become a problem. It may be easiest simply to discourage people from riding their bikes to the stop; otherwise, thousands of bicycle parking spaces may be required at each stop.

A few bicyclists adopt a holier-than-thou attitude that arises from their belief that they alone are not burdening the environment by their choice of transport. In a city without cars or trucks, this attitude should disappear by itself, and bicyclists should help to keep the streets safe for everyone, possibly with a minimal level of enforcement by bicycle-mounted police.

Bicyclists in Amsterdam now routinely ride on the sidewalks and expect pedestrians to stay out of their way. The cause is simple: too many reckless drivers in the street. This change, however, removes the last bastion of safe walking. Downtown Amsterdam lacks the space to solve this problem except by removing the cars.

Bicyclists Own the Boulevard

There is one place where bicyclists can ride fast: the central boulevard is their kingdom. Speed limits are unnecessary, and bike lanes provide sufficient capacity for heavy bicycle traffic. The required width may vary from city to city, depending on culture, weather, and topography, so the width of boulevard bike lanes must be adjusted to suit local conditions. Five meters in each direction is probably adequate in most cases and is the standard assumed in the reference design. In order to provide safe crossings of the boulevard, traffic signals may be necessary at some or all intersections. A median separates opposing traffic, making it possible to time the lights separately for each direction, so fast-moving bicyclists rarely have to stop. Bicyclists who fall behind the signal phase will encounter some red lights, but the duration of the red cycle need only be long enough to permit waiting pedestrians to cross the bike lane.

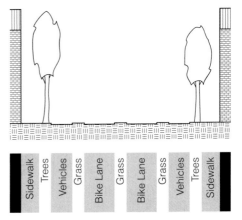

Boulevard cross-section and plan (metro)
Bicyclists will normally be the fastest-moving traffic, so the bike lanes are nearest the center of the boulevard, far from the sidewalks. The vehicle lanes provide a route for small battery-powered delivery vehicles and emergency service vehicles.

REQUIREMENTS FOR INTER-DISTRICT TRANSPORT

The need for passenger transport between districts imposes a variety of requirements on the design of a carfree city. I have assumed that the system must be capable of transporting one-third of the city's residents towards downtown during the morning peak hour. This might be a somewhat low

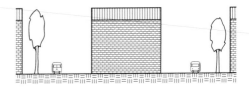

Divided central boulevard for trams

estimate but for the fact that many workplaces and schools are situated in the same district as the employee's or student's residence; these people do not require inter-district transport at rush hour. In addition, the substantial number of "reverse commuters," those whose commute does not take them in the direction of downtown, further relieves the system. Detailed computer simulation of travel patterns will be necessary to assure that the planned capacity is indeed adequate to the city's needs. If it turns out that more than a third of the population travels downtown during the peak hour, then a city of a million people definitely requires a metro instead of a tram system. A metro actually has the capacity to move two-thirds of the city's population in one hour, if built to the standards assumed in the reference design.

In particular, the boarding platforms in the stations are about 50% longer than the longest I have ever seen, permitting the operation of very long trains.

High Average Speed

Whatever system is installed, it must be fast. This requires acceleration as high as passengers can comfortably tolerate (0.22 G) and top speeds in the range of 100 km/hr. Appreciably higher speeds cannot be achieved because of the limit on acceleration and the short distances between stations. In the reference design, speeds in excess of 135 km/hr cannot be attained between two stops, and such a speed reduces maximum travel time by less than a minute as compared to a top speed of 100 km/hr; in cities with greater station-to-station distances, higher top speeds yield a noticeable advantage. The San Francisco Bay Area BART system has operated at speeds as high as 130 km/hr for decades, and even higher speeds present no special difficulties.

24-Hour Service

The tram or metro is the only transport system besides bicycling that provides rapid access to all parts of the city beyond reasonable walking distance, so it must operate around the clock. Part of the system can be taken out of service late at night for maintenance (or possibly for use in transporting freight), but all destinations must remain accessible. The closed-loop topology of the reference design makes it possible to shut down half the system while still providing service to all destinations; some trips are then only be possible via an indirect route, which in no case adds more than half an hour to normal trip times.

Short Waits

Waiting is a large component of total journey time when traveling by public transport. Passengers should never wait more than 4 minutes, except possibly late at night, when 8 minutes is probably acceptable. In the downtown districts, the 4-track metro reduces average waiting times to just one minute for destinations along the 4-track segment.

No Fare

Since almost everyone in the city can be expected to use the transport system, and since fare collection is a great bother for passengers and a large expense in itself, the system should not charge any fare. The savings on street maintenance in a carfree city probably exceed the operating costs of the transport system. However, the no-fare provision is not essential.

Economical Operation

Whatever system is adopted, it must be economical to construct and operate. Given that the route system required by the reference design is short and comprises just three, densely-exploited routes, the capital and operating costs of the system should be comparatively low. Only 60 metro trains (plus spares) are needed to provide service.

If rush-hour loads require headways shorter than every four minutes, then more trainsets will be required than the 60 mentioned here, up to a maximum of about 240. These figures are exclusive of spares, which are typically 10%.

Energy Efficiency

Sustainable development demands efficient use of energy. In the carfree city, short routes, dense utilization, and the inherent efficiency of rail transport should yield a passenger transport efficiency better than has heretofore been achieved.

INTER-DISTRICT TRANSPORT ALTERNATIVES

Having established the system requirements, we consider next the types of systems capable of meeting these requirements. The obvious choice is a conventional metro or tram system. Electric buses could also work if implemented with improvements, and the PRT option looms as a potential contender. We will take up each of these alternatives in turn.

Underground Metro

A standard underground heavy-rail metro is perfectly suited to the requirements of a carfree city. We have a century of experience with this technology. It is fast, reliable, and the safest mode of transport ever devised. From a strictly engineering standpoint, it is clearly the "best" way to provide passenger transport. Some people, however, dislike the metro because they find the underground location unpleasant or even threatening. Certainly, the view from a metro train leaves much to be desired.

A metro system provides the fastest passenger transport, with the possible exception of an extremely expensive PRT system. Typical door-to-door times for trips outside the district are around 15 minutes. No two points in the city are more than 35 minutes apart, assuming that trains run every 4 minutes (load variations can be compensated for by varying train lengths during the course of the day). The itinerary of the longest trip breaks down as follows:

Entrance to the Lexington Avenue subway
New York, 1999

The longest trip is between parking garages located in distant utility areas. Few people will ever need to make this trip.

Itinerary		Minutes
Walk to station		5
Wait for train	average	2
Ride to center		10
Change platforms		1
Wait for train	average	2
Ride to end		10
Walk to destination		5
Total		35

The maximum speed of the trains is 100 km/hr, well within contemporary limits. The required acceleration of 0.1875 G is quite high by most standards but is actually slightly less than the peak acceleration of a PCC streetcar from 1935. Assuming the stops are 760 meters apart, the metro can move from one station to the next in 43 seconds. Adding 12 seconds for the dwell time at the station gives a stop-to-stop time of 55 seconds and an average speed of 50 km/hr. This is around the upper limit for a transport system that makes frequent stops.

In practice, most station-to-station distances are somewhat more than 760 m because of curvature in the metro line. This increase has been taken into account in the timings given for all four systems.

While the construction of a heavy-rail metro in an existing city is very expensive, these costs can be controlled in a new city. The ability to combine the installation of water, sewer, power, communication, and transport infrastructure without having to work around installed infrastructure is an enormous simplification. The tunnels can be built using simple cut-and-fill techniques, work can proceed around the clock without disturbing residents, and extensive use of prefabricated concrete components simplifies and speeds the process. Falsework, the bane of urban construction projects, is eliminated when unrestricted cut-and-fill operations are possible, which presumes that groundwater intrusion is not a serious issue.

To put matters in perspective, the construction of a new metro in an existing city can be cheaper on a per-mile basis than the construction of a new urban highway. The metro capacity is about five times as great as the highway capacity.

Falsework is temporary structures built to prevent cave-ins and to support permanent structures until they have achieved full strength.

The cars are 25 meters long, with 20 rows of 4 seats each and 4 sets of doors on each side. Comprising 12 cars, such a train is 300 meters long, roughly the practical limiting length for a metro.

If it is known that this capacity is insufficient, a double-deck metro system would provide twice the capacity, albeit at higher cost. In extreme cases, a broader track gauge and wider car could be adopted; while there is no modern precedent, some early railroads used a much wider gauge than is now standard (England's Great Western was originally built to a gauge of 7' 1/4"). Above some size, however, the reference topology could not handle the demand: one of the alternative topologies would then have to be adopted.

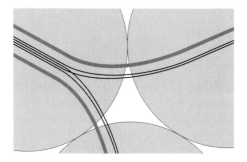

The metro lines become 4-track where the two branches join, so the downtown segments of the metro do not limit capacity. There are effectively 12 two-track metros (one in each of the 2 branches of each of the 6 lobes). The metro-freight lines are also shown.

Assume that a passenger departs from a point close to the rear of the train and that his destination is also close to where the rear of the train stops. If entrances are arranged at the rear ends of the platforms, then the passenger is spared 300 meters of walking (compared with a single entrance at the midpoint of the station), or about 4 minutes.

A single metro track can move more than 50,000 seated passengers per hour. This is derived as follows:

Minimum headway (minutes)	1	
Trains/hr	60	
Cars/train	12	
Seats/car	80	
Seated passengers/hr	60 x 12 x 80 =	57,600

This provides the capacity to move nearly 700,000 passengers from outer districts to the center during the peak hour. This capacity should suffice for a city of 2,000,000 people (especially given that some passengers travel from downtown to the outer districts), but may not be adequate for a larger city based on the reference topology.

It is worth noting that underground systems are basically immune to weather-related outages and delays. Trams and buses running on the surface can be put entirely out of action by a heavy snowfall, and autumn leaves on the rails will delay trams (traction is reduced).

The metro should be designed from the start as a no-fare system, because this allows several improvements while also reducing costs. Without fare collection, station entrances can be arranged solely with regard to the convenience of the passengers. If a fare must be collected, it is necessary either to install fare-collection equipment at each entrance or to require all passengers to pass through a central fare collection point, which increases the distances that many passengers must walk. Multiple entrances and exits also prevent congestion from developing at the single exit often provided on systems that collect fares. Fare collection is typically centralized on a mezzanine, where ticket vending machines, token sales booths, and an enforcement post are located.

With a no-fare system, this mezzanine level can be eliminated, saving passengers a flight of steps to reach the boarding platforms. While the elimination of the mezzanine is in itself a considerable savings, it leads indirectly to even greater savings, because the tunnels are at least four meters closer to the surface, reducing construction time and saving money, especially in existing cities. Construction at greater depths may also preclude the practical application of cut-and-fill techniques and force the boring of tunnels, still further increasing costs. Security is better at stations without mezzanines because some areas of the platforms are visible from the street, and most areas are within earshot of someone on the street above (in the absence of roaring car traffic).

A somewhat unusual platform arrangement speeds boarding and disembarking and helps to hold station dwell times down to the assumed 12 seconds. A center platform between the tracks is used exclusively by embarking passengers. The other two platforms, located on the outside of the tracks, are used by disembarking passengers. The downtown sections of the system are four tracks wide, and here boarding platforms are located between the two lines traveling in the same direction, with the disembarking platforms located outside. This arrangement allows people to catch whichever of the two trains may come along first, sometimes saving a passenger several minutes. The use of doors on both sides of the train reduces the required number of doors and makes more efficient use of them.

After decades of failed attempts, metro trains are now operating safely without drivers, greatly reducing personnel costs. Only a fully grade-separated system can operate without drivers because conflicts with other traffic cannot be permitted. Fully-automated systems are also free from strike-related outages.

The elimination of mezzanines is also a boon to wheelchair users and those pulling carts, because it is practical to arrange short, low-slope ramps between the street and the boarding platforms.

This arrangement is already in use at Shinjuku and two other rail stations in Tokyo.
Ishi Masaaki Shiraishi, personal communication

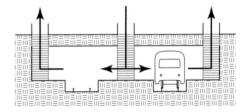

Platform arrangement for the 2-track section of the metro; the arrangement is doubled in the 4-track sections.

Lille, France, recently completed construction of a fully automated "light metro" system. Doors in the stations are synchronized with doors on the trains, and it is impossible to fall onto the tracks.

Platforms for regular and "fast" trams
Amsterdam, 1999

Obtrusive and expensive bi-level boarding platforms were built for the line 5 and line 51 extension.
The low-level platforms serve the conventional line
5 trams; the high-level platforms serve the line 51
fast trams. All in all, it makes for a lot of concrete.

This odd hybrid system has worked out poorly.
The trams are subject to the strict signaling controls
typical of a metro, but the tracks run on the surface
and have many grade crossings. In the eight years
since the opening, 8 people have been struck and
killed by trams, and an average of 17 have been
injured each year. Speeds have been reduced but
people are still struck while crossing the tracks.
This line was built on the surface as an economy
measure. The high-floor vehicles were essential
because they had to operate on existing sections of
the metro, also built with high-level platforms.
"Dodenlijn 51 naar Amstelveen moet ondergronds"
NRC Handelsblad, 2 September 1998

Tram

A tram system is also well suited to the requirements of the carfree city, provided that the population is not too large: the capacity of a tram system is about half that of a metro system. The electric tram is about as old as the electric metro train, and like the metro, it is a reliable, mature technology. The important advantages of tram systems are their much lower construction costs and the pleasant view enjoyed by the passengers. They are a bit slower than a metro because safety and noise considerations limit the speed of surface vehicles to about 50 km/hr. Surface vehicles will occasionally collide with other vehicles and pedestrians, so trams are not as safe as a metro. The danger has been found to be tolerable and can be reduced by separating the two tracks by several meters, so one tram does not conceal the approach of another. Better still is the division of the central boulevard into two streets, each one-way, separated by a row of buildings.

The slower speeds of a tram system are partially offset by reduced waiting time: trams must run more frequently to provide the necessary capacity. No two points in the reference design are more than 36.5 minutes apart, assuming that trams run once a minute. The itinerary of the longest trip breaks down as follows:

Itinerary	Minutes
Walk to station	5
Wait for tram	average 0.5
Ride to center	12.5
Change platforms	0.5
Wait for tram	average 0.5
Ride to end	12.5
Walk to destination	5
Total	36.5

The assumed maximum speed of 50 km/hr is well within contemporary limits. Here again, the required acceleration is 0.1875 G. Tram systems can be constructed for as little as $5,500,000 per kilometer if built entirely at grade.

A tram system can move more than 27,000 seated passengers per hour in each direction. This is derived as follows:

Minimum headway (minutes)	0.33	
Trams/hr	180	
Cars/tram	3	
Seats/car	50	
Seated passengers/hr	180 x 3 x 50 =	27,000

Based on 12 two-track tram lines, the system has enough capacity to move more than 300,000 passengers from outer districts to the center during the peak hour. This should suffice for a city of 1,000,000 people.

Trams (and all other public transport vehicles) work best when the floor level of the tram is at the same height as the boarding platform. This makes it much easier for the infirm to board, and permits baby strollers and bicycles to be brought rapidly aboard. With low-floor trams, inexpensive level-loading platforms can be constructed to ease and speed boarding, and these low platforms do not obstruct pedestrians crossing the street.

Trams normally run without complex signaling systems. The driver sees indications of switch (points) settings but often no other signals besides regular traffic lights. The driver must avoid collisions with all street traffic, including other trams. Metro systems, on the other hand, are built with interlocking signal systems and automatic enforcement of signal restrictions; collisions are in principle impossible and in practice extremely rare.

The San Diego Trolley and the Sacramento systems cost respectively $9,000,000 and $9,600,000 per mile, according to recent postings on the cons-spst-sprawl-trans list. These figures might be considerably reduced if fuel-cell-powered trams can be developed, as such trams would not require an expensive overhead power system

This is based on a car length of 15 m with 12.5 rows of seats and two sets of doors on each side. With three cars of 15 m length, a tram is 45 m long, as long as is desirable for an at-grade system.

Boarding platforms, Strasbourg, 1997
Just 36 cm high, these platforms permit fast, easy boarding. But notice how easily you could blunder into an oncoming tram hidden behind another tram. Separating the two tracks by a few meters is safer, but space is often a problem, as here. A properly-designed tram system offers smaller cities a practical way to install good, affordable public transit.

In Strasbourg the tracks dip underground in the city center, so service is unaffected by downtown traffic congestion. This strategy could be adopted in a carfree city, with the tracks running underground only in the inner parts of the city.

Buses

See page 101 for a discussion; the TransMilenio system in Bogotá, Columbia, is quite similar to the Curitiba system.

A sophisticated bus system, such as that in Curitiba, Brazil, could be made to serve the passenger transport needs of a carfree city. A bus system may even be preferable during the construction phase, but, except in small cities, the intrinsic disadvantages of buses outweigh their initial economies. Buses are uncomfortable due to their lurching ride and narrow seats, but on smoothly paved streets they can provide an acceptable level of service. Acceleration is low despite the relatively large engines employed, and the rough ride really does not allow for much higher rates of acceleration in any case.

There is a great deal of experience with buses, not all of it good. A generation of so-called "Advanced Design Buses" dating to 1977 was heavy, inefficient, unreliable, and expensive. Newer buses are better in most respects, and many of them are partially or even entirely low-floor designs.

Most buses are diesel powered and emit unhealthy, stinking exhaust. They are unreasonably noisy. Natural gas has been used experimentally as a replacement for diesel fuel in buses, and while this helps clean up the exhaust, the noise problem remains. However, electric trolley buses achieve better acceleration, produce far less noise, and completely eliminate local exhaust emissions. The overhead wiring is complex, expensive, and unsightly because electric buses require twin overhead conductors, whereas trams require just a single wire, using the rails to complete the circuit. Both diesel and electric buses can be made to work reasonably well, and their later replacement with a tram or metro system presents no special difficulty.

I lived at the top of a steep hill in San Francisco when new trolley buses replaced diesel buses. The change was wonderful. The diesel buses had lumbered up the hill, engines roaring; the trolley buses climbed the hill quickly and made almost no noise.

It is not out of the question to install overhead wires only at bus stops, where the bus would quickly recharge a small bank of batteries (or flywheel) before moving on to the next stop.

We would have to accept that a bus system would provide slower service than either of the rail-based alternatives. The numbers work out as follows:

Itinerary	Minutes
Walk to stop	5
Wait for bus	average 0.5
Ride to center	15
Walk to halt	0.5
Wait for bus	average 0.5
Ride to end	15
Walk to destination	5
Total	41.5

The assumed maximum speed of the buses is 50 km/hr and the acceleration 0.1 G. When stops are 760 meters apart, a bus can move from one stop to the next in 69 seconds. The limited number of doors increases dwell time to about 20 seconds, assuming the use of low-floor buses. The stop-to-stop time is 89 seconds, for an average speed of 31 km/hr. Of all the possible public transport systems, buses offer the lowest capital costs and the highest operating costs (each bus requires a driver, who transports no more than 70 seated passengers). The operating costs *alone* are reason enough to choose a tram system in a city with relatively high labor costs.

A bus system would provide capacity for 12,600 seated peak-hour riders in each direction, assuming that buses come every 20 seconds and that long articulated buses with 70 seats are used. This is derived as follows:

Minimum headway (minutes).	0.33	
Buses/hr	180	
Seats/bus	70	
Seated passengers/hr	180 x 70 =	12,600

In order to achieve 20 second headways in conjunction with 20 second dwell times, the bus stops must have room enough for at least two buses to stop simultaneously, one behind the other. Much higher capacities can be achieved by forcing some passengers to stand during rush hour. I reject this approach because it provides low-quality service.

This yields a total capacity of about 150,000 passengers from outer districts to the center during the peak hour, sufficient to support a population of about 500,000. It might be possible to shorten the headway to 10 seconds, doubling the peak capacity, but at this frequency, traffic congestion becomes a serious issue, and the sheer number of buses would burden homes and businesses located along the central boulevard.

Personal Rapid Transport

See page 103 for a discussion of PRT

Using the optimistic "People Pods" scenario, the maximum riding time between any two stations in the reference design would be less than 6 minutes. Assuming one never had to wait for a vehicle, the maximum transit time between any two doorsteps would be under 16 minutes. If it became possible to increase the number of stations, so that each neighborhood had 6 or 8 stops, even faster times become possible because of the reduced walking distances. This system is still speculative: it is an invention that has yet to be manufactured.

http://www.canosoarus.com/05MagLev/Pod01.htm

As noted earlier, PRT is a technology still under development, and costs and capacities do not yet compare favorably with conventional rail systems. This situation may change, and PRT may eventually offer equivalent capacities, affordable costs, private vehicles, and better speeds. PRT systems might then be applied to the reference design for carfree cities, possibly with some modifications. PRT systems do not offer any compelling advantage over conventional urban rail systems, except possibly speed. Some systems under development could in theory offer faster service than a metro because they provide for direct routing: the vehicle makes no intermediate stops, and the passenger never has to transfer. These systems, however, may have capacity limitations that preclude their use in larger cities.

PRT is not, in any case, necessary for the construction of carfree cities. Some day, it may offer even better service than a metro or tram, but we need not wait for this development before starting to build carfree cities.

Pros & Cons of Each System

The following table summarizes the pros and cons of various transport systems as applied to the reference design. The choice of a different topology or the application of the reference design to a larger population affects the analysis somewhat, but it should remain a useful guide.

	Metro	Tram	Bus	PRT
Location	underground	surface	surface	overhead
Construction cost	high	moderate	low	very high
Operating labor costs	low or nil	moderate	high	nil
Maintenance costs	low	low	moderate	?
Top speed (km/hr)	130+	50	50	160 ?
Acceleration (G)	.2	.2	.1	.5 ?
Shortest headway (sec)	60	20	20	2
Seated Passengers/vehicle	80	50	70	2-30
Capacity/direction/hr	57,600	27,000	12,600	20,000 ?
Maximum trip time	35	36.5	41	16
Safety	excellent	very good	good	?
Energy efficiency	excellent	excellent	moderate	?
Freedom from air pollution	excellent	excellent	poor	excellent
Absence of visual clutter	excellent	moderate	excellent	poor
Noise at street level	excellent	moderate	poor	?
Reliability & availability	excellent	excellent	good	?
Absence of weather delays	excellent	good	poor	?
Pedestrian safety	excellent	moderate	moderate	excellent
Ease of use	very good	excellent	good	very good
Comfort	excellent	excellent	poor	?
Pleasure of use	fair	excellent	moderate	excellent

The use of electric trolley buses instead of diesel buses improves most aspects of bus operation, except for the visual clutter of the overhead wires. Fuel-cell-powered buses, now under development, offer clean operation without overhead power.

Both trams and buses are capable of much higher speeds, but I have taken 50 km/hr as the maximum safe speed for surface transit in populated areas.

SPECIAL CIRCUMSTANCES

A number of unusual circumstances must be considered and solutions found for these special needs.

Personal Freight

As discussed earlier, people often need to carry small- and medium-sized goods with them, and one great advantage of a car is the ease with which this can be done. In carfree cities, provision must be made for people to move objects the size

See page 209 for a discussion

of a suitcase and preferably considerably larger. If the transport system is equipped with level-loading platforms (nearly essential in any case), then people can simply bring handcarts aboard the trains, providing an easy way to move baggage.

The US Interstate system was ostensibly built to permit the evacuation of cities during a nuclear threat, but the capacity of the system was never sufficient to quickly evacuate a large city.

Public Emergencies

A range of public emergencies must be considered. It is difficult to imagine all the possibilities, but the most pressing and difficult circumstance would be the total evacuation of a city. Most residents of a carfree city would have a bicycle, so most of the population could just bike into the countryside; long lines of people desperate to buy gasoline would not arise. It is a simple matter to attach a trailer to a bike, allowing evacuees to carry food, clothing, and a tent. The tram or metro system has enough capacity to move the entire population to the outer edge of the city in a few hours, where some could travel farther by car, and quite a few people could board intercity trains at the downtown station.

Electric taxi, Zermatt, Switzerland, 1998
Small taxis like this one can be used for personal emergencies. Even these taxis present problems: their speeds are high enough to be a threat, and the drivers are somewhat aggressive. Smaller, speed-regulated taxis could alleviate these problems.

Personal Emergencies

Alternative transport must be available for the rare occasions when someone is suddenly indisposed. Ordinary ambulances transport the seriously ill, but others who are suddenly taken sick need a ride home. Likewise, someone who has just learned of the death of a family member may not want to share his grief with the larger community. Relatively high per-trip costs are acceptable, and radio-dispatched pedicabs or slow battery-powered taxis fill this need.

Segregated First-Class Space

Some cultures provide high-status transport for the richest members of society, who may demand privacy and unusually posh accommodation. In Venice, luxury transport is provided by water taxis. In most cities, it is provided by chauffeur-driven limousines. Paris, however, offers first-class metro cars, and similar luxury can be offered wherever demand is sufficient to pay the full costs. On a fare-free system, the easiest method of fare collection is probably to offer monthly first-class passes. Fare enforcement can be provided by a conductor riding in the first class car.

Private Trains

At most times of the day, the capacity of the metro system exceeds the demand by a factor of perhaps four. While the needs of regular public trains carrying all passengers and stopping at every station must take priority, extra capacity could be sold in the form of private trains, perhaps using a Dutch "countdown auction" to sell each schedule slot. The possibility exists that the entire operating costs of the metro system could be paid for by charter fees. I think the approach should only be used in cities with a metro system, because with a surface system the extra traffic becomes an unnecessary burden for those living and working nearby.

A private train would run nonstop between any two stations on the line. Private trains could be of any length desired by the party buying the schedule slot. These private trains would take just as long as the public trains to travel between two given stations, because they cannot overtake public trains. They would, therefore, travel at a steady 50 km/hr and actually make more efficient use of energy than the public trains.

This arrangement could also serve for formal state occasions on which a motorcade is normally used today: the guest of honor would ride with his entourage in a private train. This approach should actually provide better security than a motorcade.

Regular trains need to run at 4-minute intervals all day long. The system can dispatch a train once a minute, so in three of the four minutes, a private train can be dispatched, except during rush hour.

At a countdown auction, the offer price starts at a level above what any buyer is expected to pay. As time passes, the price falls until someone buys. While a countdown auction is normally conducted in one minute, there is no reason the process could not be extended for months. Those who definitely wanted to secure a slot would buy early and pay a hefty price. Spontaneous buys just a few minutes before slot time might be quite cheap.

Opposite: road and rail connections between the utility areas and the external transport network. Metro and metro-freight storage yards are also shown.

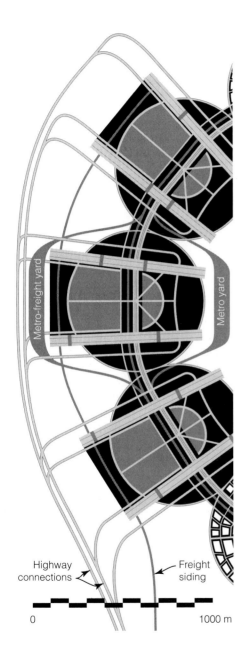

Metro-freight yard

Metro yard

Highway connections

Freight siding

0   1000 m

INTERCITY TRANSPORT

The question of transport from a carfree city to outlying areas and other cities must be considered. All of the usual transport modes are supported by the reference design.

Exuburban Commuters

Employees living outside a carfree city and commuting to jobs in the city may prefer to drive to work. The carfree arrangement actually eases their commutes, because they no longer have to slog through heavy inner-city traffic: they complete the last leg of their commute on a fast, efficient public transport system. Even for those who drive, total commute time should decline, and a variety of other transport modes can also offer service into the city. Any of the modes described below can be used to transport commuters into the city and to provide intercity service to both city residents and visitors from afar.

Intercity Trains

I believe that the intrinsic advantages of rail systems will lead in the coming decades to a renaissance in intercity rail travel. Intercity trains have long been important in Europe and Japan, and even in the USA they once provided most intercity transport. In many parts of the world, intercity rail traffic has continued to grow, although often at a slower pace than road and air traffic. Concerns about pollution and energy consumption have focused increased attention on rail travel, and high-speed rail systems have successfully lured passengers away from other modes. For instance, the Paris-Lyon market, once largely in the hands of the airlines, was substantially captured by the high-speed line, which offers equal or better door-to-door travel times. It seems clear that a carfree city should be planned to take as much advantage of intercity rail service as possible, so the rail infrastructure should be built with enough capacity to accommodate heavy volume.

The logical location for the intercity rail station is underground, in the very heart of the city, where two of the three metro/tram lines provide direct service. Rail tunnels leading to an underground station minimize the land consumed by intercity transport and greatly reduce the noise burden. A six-track railroad widening to a 12-track station on two levels should accommodate as much traffic as is likely to arise.

Buses

Bus terminals are located in some of the utility areas, close to the transport stops for easy accessibility. The utility areas are directly connected to the external highway network, permitting rapid access to superhighways without the usual trudge through city traffic. Buses are probably the easiest way to provide service to nearby towns.

Airport and Hotel Service

A city of 1,000,000 is large enough to support its own airport. Transport to the airport should be provided by a rail link from downtown. It goes without saying that the airport should be located far out of town to minimize the noise burden on the city.

In most cities, shuttle buses provide service between the airport and major hotels, permitting passengers and their baggage to travel together, directly to the hotel. In carfree cities, some hotels could be located in the immediate vicinity of the train station, and porters from these hotels could meet arriving passengers on the station platform. Guests at other hotels can transfer to the passenger transport system. It should not be difficult to arrange for through checking of baggage directly to the hotel, with bags delivered by train from the airport to a baggage depot at the train station and dispatched to the hotel using the freight system in the same way as other packages. A few hotels on the edges of the outermost districts could have direct road access to serve charter buses

Cars

Residents who make many trips outside the city may prefer to own a car, which they would park in one of the parking garages located in the utility areas. All locations within the garage are within a 5-minute walk of the transport stop in the utility area. Those who drive infrequently can save a great deal of money by joining a car-sharing organization or by renting a car when necessary. Parking fees at these garages should be set at a level high enough to cover the full costs of building and operating the garages. The capacity of the garages must be sufficient to accommodate the cars of both residents and those visiting the city by car.

The garages in the utility areas are connected directly to the highway system, which should be kept kilometers away from the city. The connections between the garages and the highway system should be arranged to keep traffic as far away from inhabited areas of the city as possible. Moderate speed limits help ensure that noise from cars on the access roads does not become a burden for residents of neighborhoods near the utility areas.

This concludes the discussion of passenger transport. We turn next to a more difficult problem: moving freight in a car- and truck-free city.

Multistory parking garage, Amsterdam, 1999
This is as attractive a parking garage as I have ever seen, which isn't saying much. In the carfree city, at least they are relegated to the utility areas.

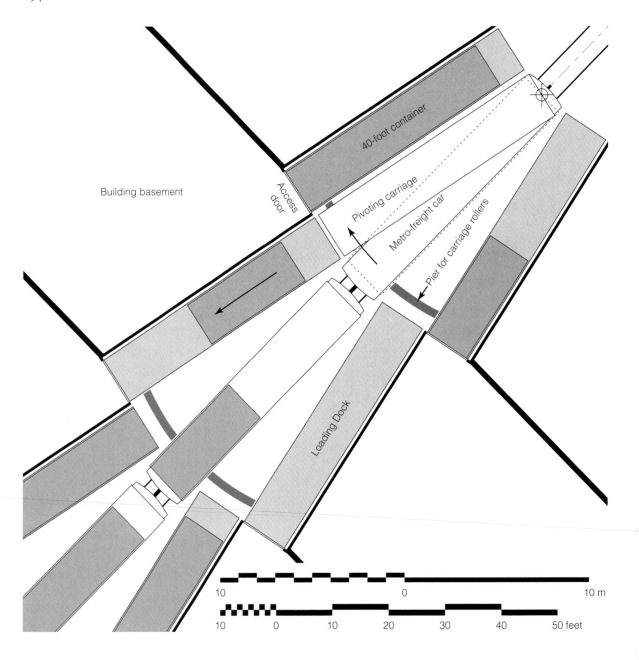

Building basement

40-foot container

Access door

Pivoting carriage

Metro-freight car

Pier for carriage rollers

Loading Dock

10   0   10 m

10   0   10   20   30   40   50 feet

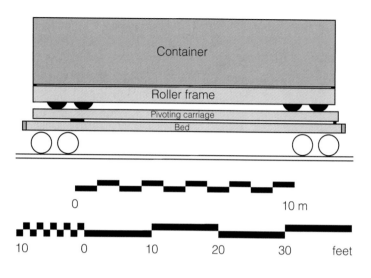

Metro-freighter, roller frame & container
A shipping container is latched to a self-propelled "roller frame" and loaded onto the pivoting carriage of a metro-freighter. When the metro-freighter is correctly aligned with the loading dock, the pivoting carriage swings out until it is aligned with the loading dock, and the roller frame is then driven off the metro-freighter and onto the dock.

Opposite: A metro-freight train is shown unloading a 20-foot container onto a loading dock adjacent to the basement of a building. Other, occupied and empty loading docks are also shown. Standardized shipping containers are dimensioned in feet.

Wherever reference is made to "battery-powered" vehicles, it is safe to assume that a fuel cell would be an acceptable substitute for the battery.

FREIGHT DELIVERY

The modern carfree city cannot reasonably be built without a practical method for delivering freight, and this need is the greatest challenge in the development of a carfree city. In Venice, freight is delivered by boat using the canal network. Freight only moves on the streets of Venice when porters use heavy-duty carts to deliver it from the nearest landing stage to its final destination. While this approach meets the freight requirements of Venice, the slow speed of waterborne transport, the small capacity of the boats, the extra handling, and the labor-intensive final delivery increase freight costs.

Carfree cities will only find widespread acceptance if provisions are made for quick, quiet, and inexpensive freight service. Slow, small, battery-powered electric delivery vans, common in the 1920s, could be revived for this purpose. Such vehicles could be limited to a maximum speed of 10 km/hr and would be quiet. However, given the considerable distances between the utility areas and the districts, the low capacity of these trucks, their slow speed, and the amount of street space they require, this approach would provide relatively expensive service while also imposing appreciable burdens on residents and other street users. Larger trucks would intrude even more on the streets. We need a solution that keeps heavy freight vehicles off the streets.

See page 215 for a description of utility areas

Labor-intensive freight delivery, Venice, 1997

Freight in a carfree city breaks down into three distinct classes, each with its own requirements. Freight moves:

- Externally, between city districts and the rest of the world
- Internally, between districts within the city
- Locally, within a single district

The adoption of a system I call "metro-freight" provides a means to move the first two classes of freight, which are the most difficult. Local shipments, within a district, can be handled by relatively simple means. Metro-freight is a rail-based system designed to provide fast service, high energy efficiency, low environmental impact, and relatively inexpensive delivery. While other approaches are also discussed, I believe that, in a city of a million people, only a dedicated freight system can provide 24-hour-a-day freight service without hindering passenger service or clogging the streets with truck traffic. A dedicated system is expensive to construct but is cheap to operate and imposes minimal external costs. Trucks only enter the streets of a carfree city under exceptional circumstances, thereby holding vehicular traffic to an irreducible minimum.

In the remainder of this chapter, it is the procedure for delivering inbound freight that is described. When freight is shipped out of a carfree city, the procedure is simply reversed.

We begin our examination of freight delivery by considering the advantages of containerized shipping. A detailed discussion of metro-freight follows.

CONTAINERIZED SHIPPING

"Break-bulk" freight consists of loose, crated shipments and requires the manual loading and stowing of each consignment in the hold of the freighter.

The metric equivalents are: 2.44 meters wide, 2.9 meters high, and 12.19 meters long (40-footer).

Container terminal, Vancouver, 1999

A yard crane is an overhead gantry (bridge) crane running on two widely-separated rails. Yard cranes are used to place containers in a storage yard once the much bigger ship cranes (visible in the photograph above) have unloaded them from the ship.

Malcom McLean pioneered standardized shipping containers in 1956. The reductions in handling, breakage, and theft are so compelling that this technique has all but replaced break-bulk sea freight; only bulk commodities such as oil and grain are not routinely containerized. Specialized containers for liquids, powders, grains, and refrigerated cargoes can be used when necessary. A ship that might once have taken weeks to unload can now be unloaded in a day, at a fraction of the cost. Standardized containers are 8 feet wide, 9.5 feet high, and up to 56 feet long. The most common sizes are 20, 40, and 45 feet long. Containers are tough and inexpensive, being fabricated in large numbers from cheap steel components, and can be stacked five-high.

Containers are fitted with universal hoisting and securing points on all eight corners. These fittings allow rapid, automatic attachment of a crane's lifting beam and also permit quick, rigid securing of containers to the deck of a ship, the bed of a rail car or truck chassis, and to other containers. The standardized attachment fittings, combined with universal sizing, permit fully automated handling in many situations.

Quite a few yard cranes at container handling facilities are already partially or fully automated. Complete automation is only feasible when the container is picked from or set on a precisely predictable location, so automation is effectively limited to operations involving known positions on the ground and locations aboard vehicles that can be reliably and repeatably positioned. Such precision is difficult to attain except with rail-mounted systems, and most automated yard cranes do indeed run on steel rails. Automation of ship unloading cranes is difficult, because the vessel constantly moves in three dimensions; likewise, the automated loading of containers onto trucks is problematic because fast, accurate positioning of manually-guided road vehicles is difficult.

Following the overwhelming success of seaborne containerized freight, the method is also being adopted for overland transport. Loaded containers are moved by road to the nearest intermodal facility, where they are set onto special rail cars for fast, cheap long-haul transport to another intermodal facility. Final delivery is usually by road.

Most bulk cargoes are now mechanically loaded and unloaded at low cost. In the carfree city, bulk cargo is loaded into containers at handling yards in the utility areas prior to final transport into the city. Most bulk cargoes are required by industries located in the utility areas, and this cargo can be delivered directly by rail or conventional truck. Companies making regular bulk shipments into a carfree city will find it expedient to containerize the cargo at their own facilities.

Air freight containers are unsuitable for use in an automated system. Their flimsy construction, absence of lifting points, and wide variety of sizes and shapes (designed to fit the holds of various airliners) do not lend them to automated handling. Air freight containers requiring delivery in a carfree city are loaded into a standardized container shell and delivered in the same way as any other container.

The advantages of containerized shipping are large, and we can expect the growth in this method to continue. Global standards for containers were adopted years ago, and huge investments have been made on the basis of these standards, so we can base the transport of freight in carfree cities on standardized shipping containers without fear of the system becoming obsolete or incompatible.

The many advantages of shipping in standardized shipping containers is ample reason to use them as the basis for almost

Europe is launching a new generation of freight trains that will operate at high speeds and with few intermediate stops. Lightweight aluminum "unit trains" will carry only standardized containers and will be uncoupled only for maintenance. Trains will operate as city-to-city "shuttle trains" without changing locomotives or passing through "classification yards" (where trains are broken apart and reassembled car by car). Container loading would be largely automated.

Disc brakes will replace the usual shoe brakes, reducing wheel wear and noise from both braking and the wheel irregularities formed by shoe brakes. Skirts would further reduce noise escaping from the wheels. The higher speeds simplify mixed passenger and freight operations, and so increase the capacity of existing track.

"Zeecontainers op de trein," *NRC Handelsblad*
6 February 1999

Alas, trucking interests have lobbied successfully in some jurisdictions for 102-inch widths, and some containers are now built to this size, making them incompatible with some systems. Legislation should be adopted to prohibit widths greater than 8 feet as soon as possible, as these wider containers are a hazard on the road.

all freight delivery in carfree cities, through the use of the system described in the following section.

METRO-FREIGHT

Metro-freight lines run in an open cut aligned parallel to the central boulevards and about 20 meters distant from them. The metro-freight system delivers standard shipping containers onto loading docks adjoining the basements of buildings abutting the metro-freight tracks. Even though only a limited number of buildings can have direct access to the metro-freight system, it delivers most freight directly to the consignee, because high-volume freight users tend to locate adjacent to the system, where they benefit from lower-cost, direct service.

District freight depots are sited near the center of each district, along the metro-freight line. Freight destined to buildings not abutting the metro-freight line is delivered to the nearest depot, from which it is then forwarded to its final destination using the means discussed later in this chapter. Freight users whose premises do not abut the freight system must pay somewhat more for deliveries, which take slightly longer, but the level of service should match the current practice of delivering freight by truck.

Specialized rail cars, "metro-freighters," deliver containers to loading docks along the metro-freight line, where they are unloaded onto the docks. The container doors (always found on the end of the container) open into the basement of the building to which the delivery is made, permitting easy unloading directly into the basement, with the container floor and basement floor at the same height.

As discussed later in this chapter, intermodal facilities in the utility areas are arranged to handle the transfer of

A big advantage of basement delivery is that freight delivery, a utility function, does not clutter up the street and the ground floors of buildings.

A combination of higher occupancy taxes and land prices for sites on the metro-freight line will encourage economically-efficient location decisions.

Special arrangements may be required to serve the three downtown districts, which might not have their own district depots. Freight destined for downtown could be delivered via depots in the adjoining districts.

The use of standardized shipping containers and the provision of a dedicated, grade-separated rail right-of-way makes it possible to automate the metro-freight system. When the volume of freight is sufficient, the costs of automation are quickly repaid, and customers enjoy faster service.

containers between the external global freight network and the internal metro-freight system. Three container interchange facilities, one in each of the downtown districts, permit the exchange of freight among the three metro-freight lines.

The ultimate capacity of the proposed system is enormous. Oddly enough, this little affects the basic system design: the construction of the right-of-way is the largest cost, and the anticipated volume of freight does not affect this cost. Bringing the system up to its ultimate capacity requires only the expansion of the intermodal facilities, the construction of additional loading docks, and the acquisition of more rolling stock. Capacity problems are only likely to arise in cities already far too large for the reference topology to support the required level of passenger transport, indicating the need for a more complex topology.

Delivery by metro-freight conveys several advantages compared to conventional trucking:

- Low operating costs
- Energy-efficient operation
- Modest land requirements
- Full compatibility with standardized shipping containers
- Low externalized costs such as noise

Metro-Freight Right-of-Way

Metro-freight vehicles based on metro technology operate in an open cut running parallel to the central boulevard and separated from it by a row of commercial buildings 20 meters deep. Larger retail stores are located between the boulevard and the freight line, with light industry and the freight depot located on the opposite side of the line. This arrangement permits the location of larger stores along the central boulevard, with its high public exposure.

By "global freight network," I mean the existing worldwide freight system, which includes rail, road, water, and air transport.

The theoretical ultimate capacity of the system is over 10,000,000 containers per year. By comparison, Singapore, the world's busiest container port, handles 15,000,000 containers a year.

Figures for Singapore from "The 20-Ton Packet," *Wired,* October 1999

See City Topology for a discussion

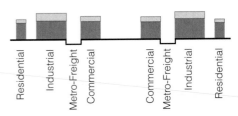

Building profiles in the inner districts, showing the dual freight lines, stores, factories, and residences.

The metro-freight line is located outside of the central boulevard in the outer districts, and on both sides of the central boulevard in the inner districts. This arrangement averts the need for the freight line to cross the passenger line. The closed-loop topology allows a single freight track to provide service, with metro-freighters running in one direction only. This adds somewhat to the mileage containers must be carried, but the cost of this additional transport is small compared to the costs of constructing a bidirectional system. The downtown interchange facilities reduce the extra mileage that containers are carried.

The metro-freighters operate in a cut 14 meters wide (including the angled loading docks on both sides of the track). The cut is deep enough to permit loaded metro-freighters to pass beneath street-level bridges. This requires a cut 5 meters deep, perhaps less if low-floor metro-freight vehicles can be developed.

Each of the outer districts has only 1500 linear meters of direct access to the freight system, so only a limited number of businesses in a district have direct access to the freight system. Each loading dock occupies 14 linear meters of space on one side of the freight line, allowing room for 106 freight docks in each district. The inner districts have twice as much access because of the doubled freight lines, running on both sides of the central boulevard in these districts.

The system must not be accessible to passersby because of the third-rail power supply, but there is no reason for anyone to enter the tracks except for maintenance personnel familiar with the necessary safety measures.

Metro-Freight Operations

Every container entering the metro-freight system is first set onto a "roller frame" by a yard crane in one of the utility

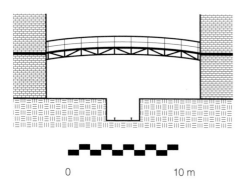

0   10 m

Cross-section of the metro-freight right-of-way, showing the track, buildings and basements, and a bridge carrying a street over the right-of-way.

areas. These roller frames, shown in the illustration at the beginning of this chapter, are the same size as the base of the container to be carried and about a meter high. They are latched onto the bottom of the container using the standard attachment points on the containers. Built into the roller frames are motor-driven wheels fitted with pneumatic tires, batteries, and control equipment. They are self-propelled at speeds no higher than a normal walking speed and can be controlled either by automated equipment aboard the metro-freighters or by a tow arm inserted into either end of the roller frame. An operator can move a loaded roller frame through the streets of the city simply by manipulating hand controls on the tow arm.

Loaded roller frames are set onto metro-freighters, which are based on metro technology, with steel wheels running on steel rails. The metro-freight cars are coupled into trains. The lead car has a driver's cab ahead of a bed somewhat longer than the longest containers to be transported. Pivoted above the bed is a carriage upon which containers resting on roller frames are set. The self-propelled metro-freight cars draw power from a third rail and need travel no faster than about 70 km/hr.

When a metro-freighter reaches the correct loading dock, it is stopped in precise alignment with the dock. The pivoting carriage on which the loaded roller frame rests is then swung out and aligned with the loading dock. Automated equipment installed on each metro-freighter controls the operation of the loaded roller frame and unloads it onto the loading dock. The loading dock is a simple structure with a smooth, flat surface the length of the longest container used on the system (48 feet is probably sufficient, but this point requires careful consideration, as it becomes a permanent limitation for the entire system).

Overhead power is not suitable for metro-freight because the wires would prevent access by yard cranes in the utility areas. It would be possible to use overhead power in the districts and third-rail power in the utility areas; this hybrid arrangement is in common use. If overhead power had to be used throughout the system, changes to the utility areas would permit the loading of metro-freighters from the end or side, rather than from above. The application of roller frames makes this fairly simple to do.

A freight interchange facility incorporates a trolleying crane that lifts a container-plus-roller-frame combination off a metro-freighter and moves sideways until the combination is directly above a shaft. The combination is then lowered down the shaft and onto the bed of a rail-mounted transfer car that moves underneath the rail tunnels and across to the bottom of another shaft. Another trolleying crane then hoists the combination up and onto the bed of a waiting metro-freighter.

The freight interchange facilities require the metro-freight lines to dip underground in the downtown districts, so downtown buildings cannot have direct metro-freight access. However, a district freight depot could be incorporated into the interchange facility, permitting the delivery of packages of any size. Downtown is not, in any case, a sensible location for businesses with heavy freight requirements.

Downtown Interchange Facilities

The construction of container interchanges in the three downtown districts permits the exchange of containers between the metro-freight lines, thereby minimizing the distance that containers have to be moved. These underground facilities will require some specialized handling equipment. So far as I am aware, nothing like this has ever been built, but the necessary equipment would be adapted from existing technology. Package sorting facilities can be included in the interchanges to facilitate the movement of small freight within the city. A detailed analysis of freight flow patterns will reveal the most advantageous arrangement.

ALTERNATIVES TO METRO-FREIGHT

I believe that metro-freight has compelling advantages, but several alternative approaches are briefly considered here.

Freight Delivery Over Passenger Metro Tracks

There appears to be no precedent for the transport of freight by metro except for the distribution of tokens and money by special trains on the New York subway. The big problem with this arrangement is the difficulty of off-loading the containers: the container docks need to occupy the same locations as the passenger boarding platforms. Also, freight traffic would probably delay passenger traffic. I ultimately abandoned this approach as too limiting and complex.

Freight Trams Sharing Passenger Tram Tracks

A surface tram system could use excess capacity to move freight on special trams. In Porto around 1900, freight trams carried coal and fish over the same tracks used for passenger service. This approach suffers from two drawbacks:

- Freight service would either run only at night or be likely to delay passenger service while the freight tram unloaded. This problem can be solved simply by providing sidings where the freight trams can unload.
- Direct delivery to the recipient cannot be achieved, and all freight would require additional handling between arrival in the district and final delivery to the consignee.

Dutch engineer T. van Popta has proposed a neat solution to both these problems. A special tram running on ordinary tracks would approach its destination as closely as possible. It would then leave the tracks and run on rubber tires using battery power to its final destination. When the tram returned to the tracks, the batteries would be recharged using overhead power. The concept is unproven, but there do not appear to be any fundamental difficulties. If the tram can enter and leave the tracks quickly, it might even share the tracks with passenger trams. This approach is worth careful study, because it offers a practical solution for freight delivery in existing cities being converted to the carfree model.

Overhead Systems

Just as with people movers, it would be possible to construct an overhead freight system. While this might be cheaper in existing cities, it is unsightly, noisy, and best avoided.

Trucking

It would be possible to deliver freight by truck, but trucks are even more noxious than cars. Their noise, vibration, stink, and danger are ample reason to keep them off city streets. The streets of the reference design are probably not wide enough to carry the volume of traffic that would be necessary to provide freight service by truck. In a few highly specialized cases, it may be necessary to allow heavy trucks into the city, but the usual diesel tractor should be replaced by a battery tug to limit speed, noise, and air pollution.

Underground Tube Systems

Underground pipeline systems may some day deliver freight directly into most buildings. Packages the size of a suitcase might be delivered automatically using technology based on airport baggage systems or pneumatic-tube systems. Such systems could be a useful adjunct to a heavy freight system but would not supplant it because of the need to move heavy and bulky articles. In addition, many wholesalers will prefer to receive freight in full containers with unbroken seals.

Paris installed a pneumatic postal delivery system beginning as early as 1866, and the system eventually connected all the post offices in the inner city.

EXTERNAL FREIGHT

In this section, we consider the movement of freight between a district in a carfree city and the global freight system. Later sections consider the movement of freight between two districts and within a single district.

Incoming freight normally arrives in containers, which are stored in a utility area for as long as necessary and delivered to the consignee at his convenience. Three delivery conditions must be accommodated:

- Delivery of full containers to metro-freight loading docks
- Delivery of containers to locations off the metro-freight line
- Delivery of packages, wherever the recipient is located.

Direct Container Delivery

The intermodal terminals can support all the usual external freight modes: rail, truck, barge, or ship. Containers are automatically or semiautomatically unloaded from the delivering vehicle and automatically stacked in a storage yard. When a consignee with direct metro-freight service requests

Intermodal terminals are discussed later in this chapter, in the section Utility Areas.

delivery of a container, a yard crane retrieves it from the storage yard, mounts it on a roller frame, and loads it onto a metro-freighter for delivery to the consignee's loading dock.

Off-Line Container Delivery

When a full container must be delivered to a location without direct metro-freight access, it is first delivered to the district freight depot, where a tow arm is inserted into the roller frame on which the container rests. An operator then pilots the container up the long ramp that passes through the district depot, onto the street, and directly to the consignee. A container destined for an address on a street narrower than about 8 meters is instead delivered to the nearest wide street, in no case more than 75 meters from the door, from which point the freight is unloaded and hand-trucked to its final destination. Businesses that occasionally receive full containers will tend to locate on the broader streets to simplify delivery, but full containers are ordinarily delivered to addresses with direct metro-freight service, so delivery by tug should occur relatively infrequently. The difficulties of turning corners on narrow streets may restrict street delivery to containers no longer than 20 feet.

Package Delivery

Packages and loose freight are consolidated at facilities in the outlying utility areas into containers destined for each district freight depot, from which they are delivered in the manner described later in Local Delivery.

Delivery wagon, Brig, Switzerland, 1998
This simple battery-powered wagon is used by the Swiss post office to deliver packages within Brig's carfree central business district.

INTERNAL FREIGHT

Freight must also move internally, within a carfree city. Some of this freight moves between one district and another, and some of it moves locally, within the same district. The movement of freight between districts is considered in this section, with local delivery taken up in the next section.

When moving freight between districts, the metro-freight system generally offers the best means, but other methods may occasionally be expedient, particularly when the two districts are close to one another. Within a district, the use of metro-freight only makes sense if the shipper and the consignee are both directly served by metro-freight.

Freight Between Districts

When a large shipment is moved from one district to another, it is generally easiest and cheapest to use the metro-freight system, particularly when both the shipper and the consignee have direct metro-freight service. In that case, the shipper requests an empty container at his loading dock. Once the container has been loaded, the metro-freight system simply moves the container to the loading dock of the consignee. When the shipment must move from a location on one lobe to a location on another lobe, use of the downtown freight interchange considerably shortens the distance that the container must be transported.

Absent the freight interchanges, containers would have to be moved by conventional rail between the utility areas in two different lobes. In most cases, this would considerably lengthen the distance the container would travel.

If either the shipper or the consignee are located off the metro-freight system, a number of options arise. The freight can, of course, simply be loaded into a container atop a roller frame, towed to the district depot, shipped by metro-freight to the depot in the consignee's district, and finally moved to the consignee's doorstep. In cases involving large volumes of freight, this is probably the best and cheapest way to move the shipment.

When the districts are near one another, it would be possible simply to tow a loaded container from one district to the other, although this is slow, cumbersome, and adds an undesirable burden to street traffic. I propose that this be permitted only when the two districts are adjacent to one another, in which case the total distance the container is moved over the streets is about the same as when it is moved to and from the district depots. In other cases involving full containers, it makes sense to use the metro-freight system.

Freight bikes often provide the cheapest and easiest means to move shipments up to about 400 kilograms, provided that the terrain is fairly flat. When long distances are involved, the freight depot's package delivery service may offer a better solution. In this case, freight bikes move the shipment to and from the freight depots, and the package delivery system moves the shipment between the depots.

LOCAL DELIVERY

This section considers the movement of freight within a district, whether that freight originates within the same district or elsewhere.

The Return of Delivery Bikes

Freight bikes, in one form or another, have been in use throughout the world for about a century. In the carfree city, most small freight is moved by freight bikes, especially final deliveries from the district freight depot to the recipient. Following a long hiatus, the development of pedal-powered delivery vehicles has resumed in the industrialized nations. While pedicabs have long been used to transport both passengers and freight in Asia, this method had largely fallen out of use in the USA and Europe until recently. In Amsterdam, however, freight bikes never entirely disappeared, and the last few years have seen the first new vehicles produced in some time. These bikes are reasonably easy to pedal.

Bakfietsen, Amsterdam, 1999
The "bakfiets" is an Amsterdam classic. These low-geared freight bikes are still in common use today.

Heavy Freight Movement Within a District

When heavy freight must be moved within a district, the same options are available as when moving freight between districts, but the use of the metro-freight system is only practical when both the shipper and the consignee have direct metro-freight service. In this case, the container is simply moved from one loading dock to another by a metro-freighter.

A large and heavy shipment within a district could be loaded into a container and towed to another address within the district. In the case of shipments composed of cartons, it may sometimes be cheaper and simpler just to make repeated trips with a freight bike. The local freight depot should always be prepared to take responsibility for forwarding any of these shipments.

Personal Freight

People often need to carry small- and medium-sized goods with them, and one great advantage of cars is the ease with which this can be done. Provision must be made for people to move objects the size of a suitcase and preferably considerably larger. The simplest solution is the use of hand carts. In New York City, where most apartment buildings are provided with elevators, groceries are usually hauled in lightweight, collapsible carts that require little storage space. The carts are large enough to haul a week's groceries for a small family. Large wheels make them fairly easy to drag up over curbs and other low obstacles. In a carfree city, such carts, supplemented by a range of larger carts, allow people to roll quite large and heavy objects onto the metro trains or trams.

The district depot must offer a range of small pushcarts and freight bikes available for rental. Most consumers use pushcarts to haul their purchases the short distance from local

Postal pushcart, Brig, Switzerland, 1998
This aluminum pushcart is used to deliver mail. Big wheels and light weight make it easy to push.

Roll-on boarding requires platforms at the same height as vehicle floors as well as narrow gaps between vehicles and platforms. This is difficult to arrange with buses, even using the advances made in Curitiba, because of the wider platform-floor gap. Roll-on boarding is in any case essential to provide good mobility for those confined to wheelchairs.

stores to their homes. Local delivery services transport goods for residents who cannot or do not wish to handle this chore themselves. Delivery of larger items, such as furniture, is arranged via the local freight depot or directly from stores located adjacent to the metro-freight line. Carts are also suitable for moving baggage from homes and offices to vehicles parked in the utility area.

Urgent Freight

It might be possible to arrange for passenger metro trains to haul a freight car at the back of the train where bicycles and pushcarts could be loaded and unloaded quickly enough not to interfere with the regular operation of the train, thereby providing a solution for small freight requiring immediate carriage.

Electric Service Vehicles

Many tradesmen require immediate access to a heavier assortment of tools and parts than can readily be moved by human power alone, so cart-sized battery-powered vehicles are permitted where their use is shown to be essential. The technology has existed for years: these vehicles are little more than modified electric golf carts. However, the convenience offered by these vehicles would exert a constant pressure to bring ever more of them onto the streets, and, despite their limited size and speed, they still impose a burden on other street users. The best way to limit their use is to tax them heavily, probably on the basis of length, width, and annual mileage driven. Height needs to be restricted to about 1.4 meters, so that pedestrians can see over them. Speed must not exceed 10 or at most 15 km/hr to ensure the safety of pedestrians and cyclists and to assure the continued livability of the carfree city. Speed limits must be enforced by making

Battery-powered utility vehicle

The relatively slow electric taxis in Zermatt, Switzerland, still run too fast for the comfort of pedestrians.

it impossible for these vehicles to travel faster than the permitted speed; long experience has shown that drivers cannot be relied upon to limit their own speed.

Electric vehicles are required for several essential functions, including:

- Substitute tractors for specialized trucks entering the city
- Local delivery from the freight depot
- Street cleaning & trash collection
- Tradesmen transporting tools & materials

There is no reason why these vehicles should not be moved between districts using the metro-freight system: they fit easily into 20-foot shipping containers. To move one of these vehicles from one district to another, the owner simply drives it to the district depot and up a ramp into a waiting container, which is then shipped to the desired district in the usual manner. If the mileage fee for driving on the streets is high enough, there is a strong disincentive to use surface streets to move between one district and another, thereby holding street traffic to an irreducible minimum.

Building Construction

The delivery of building materials presents a difficult problem. The last few decades have seen the extensive deployment of specialized, self-unloading trucks for bulky and heavy materials such as gypsum board, cinder block, brick, and lumber. These trucks are often capable of hoisting their loads directly into upper stories of buildings under construction, with considerable labor savings. If each new district were built from the center out, then the block under construction would always lie on the outside edge of the district, permitting direct access by delivery trucks. These trucks could use the low-capacity road network (needed in any case for emergencies and bicycles) to deliver materials directly to the construction site, which they would approach without travelling over the streets in occupied sections of the district. After the completion of the initial round of construction, materials for renovation would be loaded into standard containers and delivered by the metro-freight and freight depot systems.

Concrete is a special case, and some provision must be made for the delivery of ready-mix concrete. At present, this is only done by specialized trucks, and it would probably be necessary to permit them to drive directly to construction sites. The wider radial streets in each district permit access by these vehicles, although in some cases they may be unable to reach the construction site directly. Concrete is now routinely pumped through hoses, a technique that provides a solution for sites located on narrow streets.

There is often no substitute for the use of a crane, and they must sometimes be allowed into a district. Cranes unable to access a site directly can reach over other buildings if necessary. Cranes with long booms are in common use, and many newer models are both self-propelled and self-erecting.

An alternative is on-site mixing using a purpose-designed double 10-foot container. At the site, a 10-foot container filled with cement, sand, and aggregate would be stacked on top of another 10-foot container with a built-in mixer. The mix constituents would flow by gravity from the upper container into the mixer. Water and power would be taken from local connections. On-site mixing of cement mortar is already commonplace.

Moving House

When a family moves into a carfree city, they simply pack their belongings into a shipping container modified by the addition of the securing slats normally found in moving vans. The loaded container is delivered by rail or road to a utility area in the carfree city. The metro-freight system then delivers the container to the district freight depot, from which point it is towed to the residence and unloaded.

Local moves could be handled in the same way. However, many people in Amsterdam still move house using freight bicycles, which is a perfectly reasonable solution if distances are not too great.

It must be admitted that the Dutch can do anything on a bike. You haven't really seen serious bicycling until you've seen someone ride past with an unframed full-length mirror tucked under one arm.

Trash collection, Venice, 1997

Trash

Trash collection is always a troublesome point. One of two basic approaches can be adopted. Residents could be expected to bring their trash to a collection facility integrated into the district freight depot that is found near the center of each district. Alternatively, sacks could be set out in front of the building on designated days. Battery-powered trash trucks are already a common sight in Amsterdam, and trucks like these could collect the trash and deliver it to the district trash facility.

Whatever means is chosen for collection, the district trash facility consolidates wastes into specialized containers for transport to waste disposal and recycling facilities. Much waste would probably be burned in high-temperature incinerators located in the utility areas. Recycling can easily be supported; all that is necessary is to keep the waste streams separated and to move wastes in dedicated containers suitable to the type of waste. Reprocessing facilities can be located in the districts, in the utility areas, or in another city; the containerized shipments are easy to handle whatever the ultimate destination.

Empty Containers

When a business has received a containerized shipment, the container may not immediately be required for an outgoing shipment from that location. The metro-freight system can collect an empty container and roller frame that are tying up a loading dock needed for another incoming shipment. Empty containers are stored in the intermodal storage yards in the utility areas. Likewise, when a business needs an empty container for an outgoing shipment, it is mounted on a roller frame in the storage yard and delivered by the metro-freight system to the point of need.

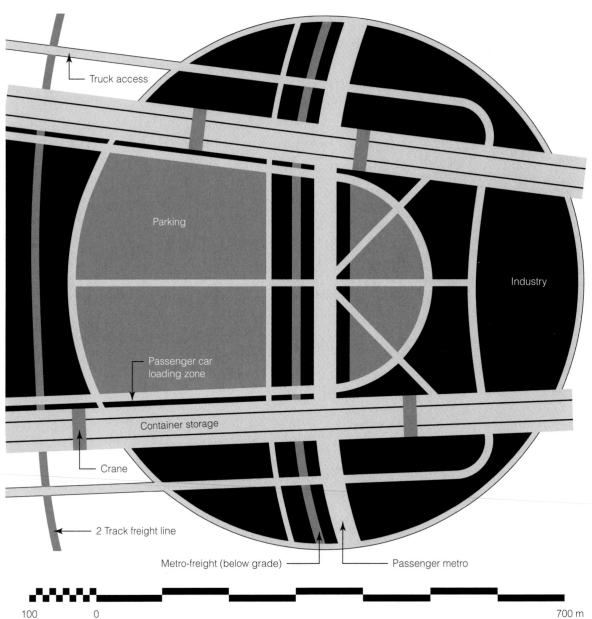

Truck access

Parking

Passenger car
loading zone

Industry

Container storage

Crane

2 Track freight line

Metro-freight (below grade)   Passenger metro

100   0   700 m

UTILITY AREAS

A prototype utility area already exists in Zermatt, Switzerland, a health spa and ski resort. Cars may not enter the town. Visitors park several kilometers away and take the train into town. Residents and truckers may drive directly to a utility area at the north edge of town, where residents park their cars in underground garages and freight is trans-shipped to small electric delivery vehicles.

Car-sharing provides convenient access to a car without the expense and bother of owning one. See The Commons for information on car sharing:

http://ecoplan.org/carshare/cs_index.htm

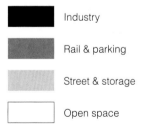

⬛	Industry
▩	Rail & parking
▨	Street & storage
☐	Open space

Above: Key to drawing opposite
Opposite: A typical utility area

Utility areas provide a location for all activities that do not mix well with residences. Thus, while offices and light industry can generally be mixed with residences, heavy industry, parking garages, and freight handling facilities must be relegated to areas some distance removed from inhabited areas. The demands imposed on the utility areas will vary from city to city and from lobe to lobe, so a flexible approach to their design is required. The utility areas are essential to the metro-freight system, because this is where freight is transshipped between external freight and metro-freight.

The nature of a city's economy affects the number of utility areas required; the three utility areas per lobe shown in the reference design is an arbitrary number that is probably adequate to the needs of a nonindustrial city. To a degree, the number of utility areas required depends upon the willingness of the city's residents to join car-sharing programs instead of owning their own cars, as this determines the space requirements for parking garages. Likewise, the intensiveness of freight transport determines the space required for container storage and intermodal transfer. We consider now the various functions that are sited in utility areas.

Intermodal Terminals

Intermodal terminals are facilities where shipping containers are transferred from one mode to another, for example from rail to road. The reference design shows every utility area equipped with an intermodal facility, but it is possible that fewer storage yards and yard cranes would be required than I have assumed. The exact requirements can only be determined on the basis of sophisticated computer simulations.

Each intermodal terminal includes a storage yard where

containers can be stacked, an overhead gantry crane that can reach all areas of the yard, and direct access to all freight modes that must be served, including rail, road, and water. In some cases, the yard crane can remove containers directly from the vehicle; in the case of ships, however, an intermediate "ship crane" must be used to unload containers to a point from which the yard crane can retrieve them.

Ship cranes are the towering cranes visible in the photograph on page 197.

Yard cranes can readily be automated, so the stacking and retrieval can be accomplished with surprising speed. These cranes are also used to load the metro-freight trains, which requires the coordinated automation of both systems, but this is not in principle a difficult task.

Heavy Industry

Industries with heavy freight needs are also likely to be those industries that are not compatible with residential uses. Steel mills, for example, have large freight requirements and generate noxious emissions; such industries are located in the utility areas, where they can be provided with direct access to conventional freight services, including rail, road, and barge.

Warehousing

The storage yard can be used as a warehouse by individuals and businesses. The goods to be stored are loaded into a container which is then moved by metro-freight to a utility area for storage. A drawback to this approach is that the container probably must be returned to the owner prior to adding or removing goods from storage. It might be possible to build an in-storage access facility in the utility areas: the container would be picked out of storage by a yard crane and brought to a point within the yard where safe access to the container could be arranged. This point needs further consideration.

Bulk Cargoes

Bulk cargoes delivered to the utility areas by water, road, or rail require containerization prior to delivery inside the city. Most shippers will containerize bulk goods themselves, given that it is a simple matter to place a suitable container on a truck chassis or rail car for loading at the shipper's own facility. In rare cases where the shipper is only equipped to load barges and ships, this may prove problematic, and mechanized bulk cargo handling equipment might have to be installed in one utility area.

Food Distribution

Wholesale food markets, warehouses, and distribution facilities are located in the utility areas, where they have quick connections to both the global freight network and the metro-freight system.

Proximity to the Transport Stop

In utility areas, as in the districts, those uses that involve the greatest number of people are located as close to the transport stop as possible. Parking garages are kept close to the transport stop, except for long-term parking by city residents who own a car but use it infrequently.

Functions that involve few or no members of the public and only a few employees are located farther from the transport stop. Examples of such activities are:
- Container storage yards & intermodal transfer facilities
- Metro or tram operations & maintenance facilities
- Trash & recycling operations

A few land-intensive functions are probably best located entirely outside the city and accessed from the utility areas by bicycle, bus, or car. Examples of such uses are:
- Water purification & sewage treatment

The parking fees in the more distant garages would be lower than the fees in garages near the transport stop, as is common practice at airports today.

In Europe, several enterprises now offer bikes for free use. Their frames are unique, so there is little point in stealing them. They are equipped with solid rubber tires, eliminating flats. The bikes carry advertisements by those who underwrite the costs of the program. In Copenhagen, these free bikes have been so popular that a large increase in their number is planned. Boulder, Colorado, has adopted a similar "green bike" program. Arrangements like this provide a solution to the need for transport to locations outside the utility areas.

- Long-term storage for boats, mobile homes, etc.
- Plant nurseries

The governing principle in all of these arrangements is to minimize the aggregated time spent traveling from transit stops to functions located in utility areas

Package Delivery

All freight, except for full containers destined for a single consignee, must be sorted and handled in the utility areas prior to delivery within a carfree city. Most of this freight is refrigerator-sized or smaller, so it is easy to handle. Whatever method is used to deliver packages, they must always be sorted, often several times between shipment and final delivery. Modern package delivery systems apply bar codes to every package entering the system, which allows the sorting chore to be automated. A package sorting facility is needed in at least one utility area in every lobe.

As packages arrive at the consolidation facility, they are sorted by destination district. Once or twice a day, all the packages destined for a particular district are loaded into a container and shipped by metro-freight to the local district depot for final delivery.

Packages being delivered within the city are collected at the district depots and shipped by container to the nearest package consolidation facility, where they are sorted for shipment to the appropriate district depot.

Personal-Freight Transshipment Area

Provisions must be made for people to move light freight and baggage from their home or office to vehicles parked in the utility areas. Two separate provisions must be made.

When the freight in question fits onto a small hand cart, the owner can simply roll it aboard a metro or tram and ride

It might also be feasible to run a package express train through each of the lobes once an hour. These trains would look very much like conventional metro trains, with floors at platform level. The district freight depots could be provided with platforms to make it easy to roll carts on and off the train. The train would call at each district depot, where express packages would be loaded and unloaded. Such a system could provide two-hour express service at moderate prices.

Opposite: road and rail connections between the utility areas and the external route network. The highway connections are elevated above grade in order to keep the surface clear for pedestrians and the rail freight track that must be crossed.

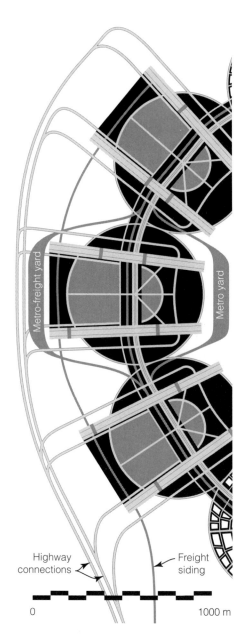

Metro-freight yard

Metro yard

Highway connections

Freight siding

0   1000 m

to the utility area. Once off the train, he rolls the cart directly to his car in the parking garage.

In the case of larger quantities, or when the driver does not wish to be bothered with this chore, the district freight depot collects the baggage and delivers it to a temporary storage area in the utility area. When the driver is ready to load his freight, he collects his car from the parking garage and drives to a loading zone in a personal-freight transshipment area where the goods are then loaded into the car.

This is perhaps the largest compromise with convenience in a carfree city, and this facility must be arranged to make it as fast and convenient as possible for drivers to collect their freight. The time required to collect the freight from the point of origin and deliver it to the loading zone must be kept as short as possible.

The use of package express metro-freighters for this chore could speed the process. Once an hour, this special metro-freighter would travel through the lobe and collect the accumulated shipments, probably still loaded on the carts used to pick them up at the doorstep. They would be transported to the personal-freight transshipment area, where they would be available for loading within a few minutes of their arrival. This would be a fairly labor-intensive operation, and therefore moderately expensive; most people would probably choose to handle their baggage themselves, reducing the elapsed time and also saving money.

Road & Rail Connections

The utility areas must be connected to the external transport network. Road connections are certainly required. Careful analysis is needed to assure that the capacity of the road is sufficient, but I expect that a 4-lane divided highway connecting each lobe with the highway network would suffice. A rail connection between the lobes and the external rail network is not absolutely essential: all containers could be delivered by road, but the advantages of rail shipment argue strongly for a rail freight connection between each lobe and the external rail network. A single track is probably adequate in most cases, although allowance for two tracks has been made in the design of the utility areas.

Ship channels can also be dredged into cities located near the sea or major waterways. All that is necessary is to bring ships or barges alongside the utility areas so that ship unloading cranes can deliver containers to the yard cranes for handling.

Marshalling Yards

Metro and tram systems require marshalling yards where trains and cars not in use are stored on sidings. As trains are required, they are assembled from cars and put into service. Similarly, at the end of rush-hour, some trains are taken out of service and stored in the yards. Two yards must be provided, one for passenger equipment and another for the metro-freighters. These yards are fairly large and not especially attractive, and for this reason they are located near the utility areas, to keep them as far as possible from the inhabited districts. Marshalling yards must also include maintenance sheds for the rolling stock.

This concludes the presentation of the reference design for carfree cities. Part III turns to the matter of implementing this design, with necessary alterations, in the real world.

Prague, c.1900

Campo San Vitale
Venice, 1997

PART III

GOING CARFREE

SUPPORT FOR CARFREE CITIES
Considers how the necessary popular and policy support can
be developed.

PLANNING CARFREE CITIES
Examines tools we can use to plan carfree cities and takes up
the matter of converting existing cities to the carfree model.

SOME MODEST PROPOSALS
Proposes several ways to get started with the first modern,
large-scale carfree developments.

AFTERWORD: MAKING MAGIC
Sets forth the need for magical places to help make our lives
richer and fuller.

San Marco
Venice, 1997

Large carfree area in Freiburg, Germany, 1998

SUPPORT FOR CARFREE CITIES

Developing a wide base of support for carfree cities may turn out to be less difficult than one might expect. One American tourist sitting at a Venetian sidewalk café recently remarked to his companion: "We ought to have cafés like this in Los Angeles. [pause] Oh, no. That wouldn't work. All the cars." People love carfree areas and are, at least subconsciously, aware of the damage cars do to city life. The public takes such great delight in the carfree environment of Venice that it is all but impossible to find a hotel room without a prior reservation except in the depths of winter, and sometimes not even then. Some of the most expensive resorts, such as Zermatt, are essentially carfree. Switzerland, probably the richest land in the world, has carfree areas in most of its cities. Residents and visitors alike flock to these areas.

I think there is already broad support for carfree areas, and the only thing holding us back from rapid progress towards completely carfree cities is that people simply can't imagine getting along without a car. We simply need to show them how. Once the practicality of carfree cities has been demonstrated, a groundswell of support may arise rather quickly.

I expect that events in the coming decade will make carfree cities even more desirable. One or another of the many looming environmental crises may suddenly force the issue, and we need to develop the carfree city to the point where it can be implemented quickly in the case of sudden need. We should begin the necessary research and development work and build some prototypes. These prototypes will prove (or disprove) the feasibility of urban life without automobiles. The demonstration projects will attract widespread attention and initiate a public discussion of the idea.

In this chapter we consider a number of objections to carfree cities and ways to meet these objections. We will also consider how to build the public support and policy infrastructure necessary to implement carfree cities.

Resistance to Carfree Cities

Many objections will doubtless be raised against carfree cities. Several objections that will certainly arise are considered below.

"I Won't Live in a Carfree City"

Many people will say that they don't want to live in a carfree city. Of course, if the city in question is new, those people need only decide not to move there. The question of converting existing neighborhoods into carfree areas is more difficult. It will be necessary to reach broad agreement on the need for and desirability of the conversion before it can be allowed to proceed. While the car would be accommodated at garages in the utility areas, some people will doubtless

Yosemite Valley, c.1987
Even in the USA, the idea that drivers and their cars have limitless rights of access is being challenged. The National Park Service has adopted measures to reduce car use in its parks, and there is a chance that cars will be entirely removed from beautiful Yosemite Valley. This introduction to carfree areas would put the idea before millions of Americans.

insist that they must have a car at their doorstep. Every effort should be made to accommodate the needs of these people without admitting their cars into the area. In the end, however, some people will undoubtedly decide to leave rather than give up their cars. If there is broad support for the conversion, then the few who decide to move away should have no difficulty arranging the profitable sale of their residences: if the planning work has been done correctly, more people will want to move into the area than will want to leave.

Autophilia

Americans are in the throes of a love affair with their cars and will not give them up for anything, or so runs the conventional wisdom. Many people seem to use their cars to project an image of themselves, even though most of these images are false: unless you live in the wilds of Alaska, you probably don't need a Land Rover to pick up a liter of milk. In nations across the world, driving a big, shiny new car is a major indicator of success: you are what you drive.

I think, however, that the costs of cars are beginning to weigh on Americans, and that many would be awfully glad of a little peace and quiet. Recognition of the costs of automobility is growing, and people are losing their patience with traffic jams. The surging popularity of the New Urbanism signals the dawning American realization that something was lost when cars took over the city and that the time has come to take it back. Ironically, the New Urbanism is largely a return to early 20th century US patterns of town and city building, in the years just before cars changed everything.

We will have to stop regarding car ownership as *the* badge of prosperity and modernity. Westerners must do this first; the rest of the world may then begin to reevaluate the balance sheet for urban automobility.

Bairro Alto, Lisbon, 1999
A narrow street overrun and ruined by cars

People Hate Public Transport

As already discussed, people won't use public transport unless it is of extremely high quality. Frequent service, on-time performance, efficient route systems, comfortable vehicles, easy use, and assured personal safety are essential. Zürich, Switzerland, offers high quality public transport, and the proportion of journeys to work using public transport increased from 67.5% in 1980 to 76.1% in 1990, following a rigorous program of further improvements in the quality of service. In this, perhaps the world's richest city, 90% of commuters to downtown take public transport. Few cities offer the level of service found in Zürich, but the means are within the grasp of any reasonably densely populated city.

See page 96

"Canberra at the Crossroads: A way out of the Transport Mess," Conservation Council of the SE Region and Canberra, October 1997

Overcrowding and Congestion

During the intensive industrialization of the 19th century, dense urban areas became equated with squalor. Extreme overcrowding in the dark, airless "dumb-bell tenements" of New York City yielded what was perhaps the most frightful urban housing of the era, ridden with disease, filth, crime, and poverty. Huge numbers of poor immigrants settled in New York during this period, with large families often crowded into a single room. Disease, especially tuberculosis, spread rapidly in the filth and extreme crowding.

Those accustomed to suburban living may find the proposed densities too high, and it is certainly true that not everyone wants to live in a dense urban core. Congestion, density, and overcrowding are not the same things, however. The perceived congestion of modern cities is largely a result of motorized transport. On a summer afternoon, there may be more people per square kilometer in Venice than anywhere else in the world, yet it does not feel oppressively crowded. Once streets are dedicated to human uses, very

See Hall, page 36, for a description

"Planners and citizens, particularly in North America, often assume that moderate and high-density land use are synonymous with crime and unhealthy conditions. Yet there is no scientific evidence of a link between these social problems and density *per se*. For example, a recent report on the world's 100 largest cities found that Hong Kong–the most densely populated city, with 403 people per hectare–has fewer murders per capita than all but 11 of the other 99 cities. Hong Kong's infant mortality rate, 7 deaths per 1,000 live births, is lower than that of all but 5 other cities...."

"Shaping Cities: The Environmental and Human Dimensions," Marcia D. Lowe, Worldwatch Paper 105, page 22 high densities are no longer unpleasant and offer rich social opportunities.

In historical terms, the density proposed in the reference design is not at all unusual. While many families with children prefer suburban life because of the perceived disadvantages of city life, many of these objections collapse once the danger, congestion, noise, and pollution caused by cars are eliminated. In addition, the presence of truly rural areas adjacent to a carfree city would provide an outdoor environment superior to that of the suburbs.

Carfree cities will definitely require greater density than contemporary suburbs, but I certainly do not propose a return to overcrowded, disease-ridden cities. Modern carfree cities can provide ample living and working space for everyone at densities below those of modern-day central Paris.

Mixed Uses

Many planners still hold to the doctrine of the separation of uses. This doctrine is expressed in the USA through zoning ordinances that, with few exceptions, permit only a single class of use in any given area. While the reference design for carfree cities could easily be modified to permit the separation of uses, I am quite certain that a city with integrated uses would be a better place to live. It is, of course, possible to try both approaches, in different parts of the same city.

In the case of mixed uses, safeguards are required to protect residents from noxious uses. A somewhat higher level of noise can be tolerated during business hours, but most people will want reasonable quiet during evenings and weekends. Noise and odors from restaurant kitchens must be tightly controlled. Some uses, such as small woodworking shops, present fire hazards, which can be minimized by sawdust evacuation systems (now required for health reasons in most jurisdictions), and noise can be controlled by keeping the doors closed. By contrast, sawmills would be located only in utility areas because they make a great deal of noise almost continuously. (In practice, sawmills would probably locate closer to the standing timber.) Printing shops require special attention to ventilation because many inks and solvents release toxic vapors. Most problems of this kind can be solved by careful attention to detail and through cooperation with neighbors. The carfree city can be expected to develop close-knit neighborhoods where problems can be worked out cooperatively. Ultimately, however, those businesses that cannot coexist with residences and offices will have to relocate to the utility areas, where their activities would not impinge upon the "quiet enjoyment" of their neighbors.

Noise

The invention of electronically amplified music has severely taxed the ability of people to live in close proximity to one another. It seems difficult to manage this problem, although a strong sense of community would certainly help. Dutch police have the authority simply to seize the offending equipment after repeated offenses. I live in a dense area in Amsterdam, and I was pleasantly surprised to discover how few problems there were with neighbors: everyone understands that we live close together, and people keep their dogs under control and their music at moderate levels. Everyone tolerates an exception on the national holiday celebrating the queens' birthdays: the entire city takes on a festive air, and people play loud, live music outdoors, which is prohibited at all other times. It's one of the most enjoyable days of the year.

Much more research must be done to find better means of acoustically insulating dwellings. Independent side bearing walls help to prevent building-to-building transmission,

Noise problems are now becoming acute even in low-density Los Angeles. People have become so inconsiderate of their neighbors that they now hold outdoor parties with extremely loud amplified music. Some of these sound systems can rattle windows at distances of a kilometer. Escaping the dense city for suburban densities no longer offers a respite when people behave in such utterly anti-social ways.

Richard Risemberg, personal communication

Side bearing walls support the upper floors in row houses. In many districts, a single, shared wall supports floors in two adjacent houses.

raising construction costs somewhat. Floor-to-floor transmission is a more difficult problem but can be solved by building thicker floor structures in which the ceiling of one apartment is not directly attached to the floor of the apartment above. The traditional narrow four-story canal houses in Amsterdam provide an answer, as proposed in the chapter on buildings. These houses are small enough to be occupied by a single family, an approach that eliminates the problem of noisy upstairs neighbors. Each family also has its own small patch of garden behind the house.

Shipping in Standard Containers

For a variety of reasons, much freight is not yet moved in standardized shipping containers, but the growth in containerized shipping seems set to continue. Those shipping into and out of a city using metro-freight would be forced to use standardized containers for everything larger or heavier than a large refrigerator. The advantages of standard containers are so compelling that their use will probably become almost universal in the years ahead, but their exclusive use can be restrictive under some circumstances. The need to use shipping containers instead of moving vans is one example, but with minor accommodations, moving in a carfree city need be no more difficult than anywhere else.

The carfree city offers excellent freight service despite the requirement to use shipping containers. Businesses are quite flexible in the face of transport limitations, and package express companies have managed to cope with deliveries in Venice, although the methods are unorthodox in comparison to their usual mode of operations. The metro-freight system should be economical enough to give most businesses in a carfree city a competitive advantage over businesses that depend entirely on trucking for their freight service.

DHL delivery boat, Amsterdam, 1999
This express company recently began delivering parcels in the center of Amsterdam by boat. Bicycle couriers deliver the packages from the boat to the recipient's doorstop. The system seems to be working out well for both the city and DHL.

Carfree Activism

The earliest known movement for a completely carfree city was the Alternativ Stad in Stockholm. This group, founded in 1965, called for a complete ban on cars in Stockholm, which has one of the world's best metro systems. Postwar development in this city was centered around stations on the newly-expanded metro network. In the event of another major disruption in oil supply, Stockholm will probably weather the storm better than any other large city except possibly Tokyo.

Hall, 312

There are active anti-car movements in most of the richer nations of the world. The current generation of activists is generally quite effective and knows how to organize actions that receive a great deal of publicity in the mass media, without making too many people angry. Perhaps the most important lesson that activists have learned is the importance of fun and humor. The demonstrations organized by European Youth for Action (EYFA) in Lyon in October 1997 were a good example. The group organized several street actions that certainly did inconvenience some motorists. However, large numbers of passersby joined the organizers in dancing in the street, and almost nobody got angry. The media gave the conference a considerable amount of attention, and even the Paris newspaper *Le Monde* found this provincial conference worthy of coverage. People in many cities seem to be quite receptive to the notion of bringing car use under control.

Critical Mass, the pro-bicycle group that organizes disruptive mass bicycle rides in cities, has generally done fairly well in garnering public support, notwithstanding a few unpleasant incidents.

Opinions of EU citizens regarding traffic:

Traffic is "hardly bearable" or "unbearable"	69%
Traffic can be improved by restricting cars	71%
Establish more pedestrian zones downtown	75%
Extend public transport to ease traffic	80%
Give priority to public transport over cars	84%
Give priority to pedestrians over cars	85%

"Assessments of Mobility"
International Union of Public Transport and
Socialdata GmbH, München
(no date, probably about 1995)

Progress Towards Carfree Cities

We have already made some progress toward carfree cities, even though this has not been an explicit goal of the projects that have accomplished this. Carfree areas have now been established in many European cities. Even in that bastion of automobility, the USA, many cities have implemented carfree districts in downtown areas. One fairly large carfree residential development has been completed, with at least two more under construction. Finally, circumstances forced Cuba to curtail automobile use suddenly and dramatically.

Carfree Centers

Large, successful carfree areas have been established in several European city centers, including:

The Grote Markt in Groningen, 1997

- The Strøget, an extensive area in Copenhagen
- The Grote Markt area, Groningen, the Netherlands
- Most of the center of Freiburg, Germany
- Almost all of Zermatt, Switzerland

Most German and Swiss towns of any size have at least a small carfree area in the commercial center. These areas are almost always in the oldest parts of the city, where the streets are narrow and where many stores, theaters, cafés, and restaurants are located. These areas are popular and draw good crowds at most times of the day.

It must be admitted that not every carfree area has met with success. In most cases, retail sales in carfree areas have increased, but in some cases they have fallen. Of the roughly 200 carfree malls instituted in the USA between 1970 and about 1998, some 100 were subsequently reopened to regular traffic. This is a distinct contrast to the European experience, where initial resistance from merchants has usually given way to strong support once the project was implemented. Most failures have been associated with poor public transport arrangements. In particular, transit malls based on diesel buses have failed quite frequently: the noise and stink of the buses has destroyed the ambiance of the area.

Warren, 64-65

This should come as no surprise: we must implement top-quality public transport before attempting to move cars out of an area. Buses are not pleasant either for their passengers or for pedestrians on an otherwise carfree street.

Several Small Carfree Initiatives

Europe has already seen the development of a number of carfree projects, some of them quite large. The more notable efforts are described below.

A carfree residential development was completed in 1998 on the site of a disused waterworks near the end of an existing tram line in Amsterdam's Westerpark neighborhood. Some 600 residential units were built in this 6 hectare project, and the demand for apartments far exceeded the number available. The architecture is uninspiring (to be charitable), some of the buildings are many stories too high, and the green areas are chopped up by miles of chain-link fence, but the project clearly demonstrated that carfree housing can be commercially feasible.

The Green Party in Vienna has worked for years to build a carfree neighborhood. The project was stymied for a long time by a law requiring one parking space for each new apartment, but an exemption was finally obtained. The site includes only a few parking spaces, for car sharing and visitors. Construction of 250 apartments began in 1997, with full occupancy of the self-governing community expected in 1999. The future tenants participated in the design, and they invested the money saved on parking garages in solar energy, gray-water recycling, roof-gardens, a sauna, an Internet cafe, play areas for children, a party roof, and a bicycle garage.

The Forum Vauban project is a sustainable development project in the Vauban district of Freiburg, Germany. A major university town, Freiburg already has a large, nearly carfree

Carfree housing, Amsterdam, 1997
Part of a 600-unit carfree project in the Westerpark district. I predict a great future for the architect as a prison designer.

See Jan Scheurer's site on carfree housing efforts:
http://wwwistp.murdoch.edu.au/istp/research/carfree.html

Kärnthnerring, Vienna, c.1900

center. Upon completion in 2005, the project will accommodate 5000 residents and 600 employees, with the first phase scheduled for completion in 1999. The project was driven by a desire to create a sustainable district in which car traffic was kept to a minimum; the residential areas are carfree.

As of June 2002, the project was not complete. A few problems had arisen because some residents were abusing the privilege of bringing their car up to their door to load and unload. This will probably be resolved in the course of community meetings. The project seems otherwise to be a success.

The Saarlandstraße project in Barmbek, an inner suburb of Hamburg, Germany, is a carfree development with good metro service. Some 220 apartments in low-rise buildings are being built around courtyards. The project's initiators founded an association to plan and construct it in cooperation with the future residents, and over 1,400 families have formally expressed an interest in living in the project. The first 120 units were scheduled for completion in 1999.

And One Large Accident

With the collapse of the USSR, Cuba lost most of its sources of foreign exchange. The country was forced to cut its oil imports dramatically, and gasoline was rationed beginning in 1992. Havana imported 1.2 million bicycles from China to substitute for automobility, and 30% of all trips are now by bicycle. Car use in Cuba plummeted, and Havana made major changes to its streets, to accommodate fewer cars and many more bicycles. Havana may now be the world's most sustainable city. As one resident said, "We should have done this 20 years ago." While not truly a carfree initiative, this experience does indicate that rapid shifts from cars to bikes are possible, at least under duress.

Trans-mission, Summer 1992

Rapid Urbanization

The world is becoming urban at a staggering rate. Most of the world's population was still rural and agrarian just 100 years ago. Some day soon, a peasant with his life savings tucked into his pocket will arrive in the shanty town of one of the world's megacities. Unbeknownst to him, he will tip the world balance between rural and urban: the world's population is about to become more than half urban. Every day, about 100,000 peasants abandon the countryside and depart for the city. Most of them end up in one of the shanty towns that surround most large cities in the developing world. Conditions in these shanty towns range from poor to horrible, although the social structures in these largely carfree areas may function better than is commonly supposed.

Trouble in the World's Megacities

Most huge cities are unwieldy and function poorly. One has only to think of the favelas of São Paulo, the frightful over-crowding of Shanghai, the killing air pollution of Mexico City, or the poverty, filth, and disease of Calcutta to find examples of how not to arrange cities. One cannot really fault the governments of these cities for their failure to solve problems unknown until modern times, but it certainly is time to seek solutions, beginning with the development of transport systems that do not pollute.

Tokyo: One Megacity That Works

The largest city in the world is the Tokyo-Yokohama agglomeration, boasting about 27 million inhabitants, a size it could never have attained with road-based transport: there was simply not enough land available to build the necessary highway system. Although very crowded, Tokyo is a city that still works fairly well and does not suffer from the worst problems afflicting other megacities. One reason is that most people in Tokyo take public transport to work. Japan prob-

Iriya District, Tokyo, 1998
This street is not carfree, but traffic is low and no on-street parking clutters the narrow pavement. Notice the delivery bicycle in the foreground.

ably has the world's best rail system and people use it intensively. Tokyo would be a living nightmare if it had adopted auto-centric transportation in the manner of Los Angeles or Phoenix.

Despite high levels of car ownership, Tokyo has maintained and expanded its rail-based urban transport system, and outlying development is arranged at densities high enough to provide ample passenger traffic, so rail systems remain workable. Car traffic is heavy in Tokyo, but most people commute to work by rail because it is faster.

Coping with Continuing Urbanization

Many thinkers on sustainability believe that we must encourage migrants to remain in their villages, but unless a way is found to bring the social, cultural, and economic opportunities of cities to villages, the likelihood of stemming the tide of migration seems slim. This is especially true given the declining number of farmers needed to till the soil. The problem is particularly acute in China, where countless millions who once worked the land are moving to urban areas, most of which are located in prime agricultural regions. China does not have arable land to squander on sprawling auto-centric cities, but the carfree model offers China a means to greatly improve the quality of life without converting too much farmland to urban uses.

We must, therefore, prepare for the continued migration of rural people to the city. In order to accommodate swelling populations, we will either have to continually expand existing cities or begin to build some completely new cities. Given that the world's existing megacities have become almost unmanageable, I believe there is some advantage to building a number of new, smaller cities, which should be arranged from the beginning as carfree cities.

BUILDING NEW CITIES

Rather than continuing to pack ever more people into existing megacities, we should build new cities near large cities experiencing rapid growth. If these new cities were developed on a more modest scale than the nearby mega-cities and linked to them by rail, we could improve life for a great many people while also reducing the burden on the ecosystem.

Precedents for New Cities

There are a surprising number of precedents for cities designed as a whole and built on previously rural sites, although the results generally have left a lot to be desired. The following list of new cities (and their populations) is by no means exhaustive but does give an idea of the range of variety that exists:

- Milton Keynes, United Kingdom (150,000)
- Canberra (300,000)
- Washington, D.C. (550,000, excluding suburbs)
- Chandigarh (650,000)
- Brasília (1,800,000 in the entire capital district)
- New Delhi (10,100,000)

With the exception of Washington, all of these cities were established in the 20th century. We turn now to a brief consideration of each of them.

Houten, the Netherlands, 1997
This new town of 32,000 is much denser than a US suburb, so the cars are especially obtrusive, because most open space is taken up by parking.

Milton Keynes

Milton Keynes is really an ordinary auto-centric town. Roads are arranged in a rough grid pattern, and the density is low despite some medium-rise buildings. Most transport is by car, although there is a bus system. I found no areas with any sense of vitality when I visited in 1987.

Canberra

Canberra, the capital city of Australia, has a population of 300,000. It is a low-density city based on automobile transport with all the usual problems. The city is now in the throes of a debate regarding the transportation future of the region. Freeway proponents and public transport advocates are jockeying for control of transport policy, so far without a clear outcome.

Washington, D.C.

In Washington, most transport is by private car, despite the construction of an excellent metro system. The city is laid out in a confusing pattern with a grid of streets and intersecting diagonal avenues, a pattern that is not particularly conducive to the smooth flow of traffic, and traffic congestion became a serious issue as early as 1927. The city has exploded beyond its original boundaries and is encompassed by sprawling suburbs and ringed by a beltway that suffers from monumental traffic jams. The population of the surrounding suburbs now greatly exceeds the population of the city itself. Most residents of this capital city live in poverty.

Chandigarh

The city of Chandigarh was designed soon after the partition of India, and the plan was essentially the product of Le Corbusier, working in his favored city-in-the-park style. Chandigarh was supposed to provide local services within walking distance in each of the nearly 50 "sectors" that were constructed. Peter Hall comments:

> … Corbusier found his patron in a post-colonial government steeped in the autocratic traditions of the British Raj. He produced for them an exercise in the City

Getting There, between pages 192 and 193

Beautiful decked in the trappings of modern architecture, a latter-day New Delhi. There was a grid of fast traffic roads, already used in plans for Marseilles and Bogotá, to cater for a level of car ownership even lower than the Paris of 1925, which was low enough. The relationship between streets and buildings is totally European, and is laid down without regard for the fierce north-Indian climate or for Indian ways of life. There is a total failure to produce built forms that could aid social organization or social integration; the sections fail to function as neighbourhoods. The city is heavily segregated by income and civil service rank, recalling *La Ville contemporaine;* there are different densities for different social groups, resulting in a planned class segregation.

Hall, 214

Corbusier appears never to have understood that his auto-centric urban plans would not work once cars became commonplace: the space devoted to roads is totally inadequate. This does not yet appear to be a serious problem in Chandigarh because private cars remain rare in India, and most urban transport is provided by bus. The photographs I have seen of Chandigarh show a city built without any understanding of the importance of positive open space, a city of monumental buildings, each isolated on its own parcel of land, without any thought to the development of a coherent whole.

Brasília
Brasília is an expansive city designed mainly for cars, characterized by superblocks surrounded by vast swaths of superhighway. Constructed between 1957 and 1960, it became the sterile capital of Brazil. Rich people forced by circum-

stances to live in the city flee it at the weekends for a slice of real life in one of Brazil's authentic cities. The city is ringed by shantytowns, some at a great distance from downtown.

New Delhi

Hall, 183-192

In 1911, King George V announced that India's capital would be relocated from Calcutta to Delhi. It was to be a monumental capital, designed by British planners. Vestiges of Indian architecture were applied to a European plan. A grand boulevard linked the two centers of power: the viceroy's residence and the secretariat. The streets were laid out on a hexagonal grid with traffic circles at the intersections. Today New Delhi's traffic is snarled despite low levels of private car ownership.

Locations for New Cities

Rural areas still commonly exist reasonably close to large cities, and these sites could be developed as new cities. For example, I have identified five possible sites for a new carfree city within 100 km of the Randstad (the large conurbation in the densest part of the Netherlands), including one site that is actually right in the center of the region. The Montezuma Hills, located about 65 km from San Francisco, provides another example of a suitable site relatively close to a major metropolis.

Building a new city in the sparsely-populated "green heart" of the Netherlands is a controversial notion that violates a sacred Dutch cow. Retaining a large green area in the midst of the big cities is an appealing idea, but most of this area is in private hands and is nearly inaccessible to city dwellers: it does not function as usable green space. Poor soil conditions once precluded development, but modern foundation technology would allow construction of a carfree city at this site, which would enjoy superb connections with the other big Dutch cities and would make the beauty of this area accessible to many more people. The new city should be designed to complement this lovely landscape.

One danger must be avoided: the new cities must become genuine urban centers, with their own employment and cultural institutions. They must not become merely bedroom communities for existing cities: this simply exacerbates the problem with excessively long commutes. The establishment of a large government installation, a major university, or a research facility can provide the economic basis for reasonably rapid development of a new city.

POLICY SUPPORT

The development of carfree cities will require public policy support. If carfree cities are to manage their own destinies, changes in zoning regulations (now commonly legislated at a regional or national level) are essential. National governments will also need to delegate regulatory authority in several other matters that have traditionally been their purview or that of regional governments.

Because carfree cities would be such a break with current practice, most jurisdictions will require legislative changes before they can proceed. This is not as daunting as it may seem. Already, the New Urbanism has booked a number of successes in getting street standards and zoning ordinances changed to permit NU development to proceed. The following policy initiatives are required.

Montezuma Hills, near San Francisco, c.1989
This tract of marginal farmland could accommodate a large carfree city. Apart from a few gas wells and farmhouses, the area is uninhabited. Some soil instability and the moderately hilly terrain are the only impediments. An existing rail right-of-way links the site to Sacramento and Oakland.

Regulation

The city must have the authority to completely regulate all types of traffic on its streets and to prevent the entry of automobiles. In most jurisdictions, such controls are in the hands of larger political divisions less interested in resolving local problems. This must change.

The city must also have the authority to regulate the use of the greenbelt surrounding the city. While much or even all of the land could remain in productive use, the uses must be compatible with proximity to a major city. Thus, clear-cutting of forests would be unacceptable for aesthetic and ecological reasons, but managed productive forests, accessible for day use, would be a desirable addition. Farmland should remain in agricultural use, but heavy concentrations of livestock would be phased into field crops, fruit, and vegetables.

Speculation

Ideally, the city should own all the land on which development will occur. As the value of this land increases due to the expenditure of public funds on infrastructure, the city could recover its investment as land is sold for development. If speculators are permitted to buy this land, they will reap the benefits that arise from the large expenditure of public funds for infrastructure construction. I do not believe that private gain resulting from public expenditures is in the public interest.

Community Land Trusts

For a thorough treatment, see *The Community Land Trust Handbook* (from the Institute for Community Economics).

The community land trust is a vehicle that was created to preserve agricultural areas near cities. Before land trusts were developed, many farmers were forced to sell their farms when the land was reassessed on the basis of its development potential; the resultant tax increases destroyed its economic viability as farmland.

In Marin County, north of San Francisco, the dairy industry was threatened with extinction because so many dairy farms had been sold for subdivision that the local milkshed was becoming too small to support the necessary infrastructure. Farmers in the county banded together and established a community land trust. They then donated to this nonprofit organization the development rights to their land (for which they received substantial income tax credits). Because the development rights were then the property of a nonprofit trust, those rights were no longer subject to any taxation, and the dairy industry in the county was saved. These farms are, in principle, protected in perpetuity. Community land trusts could also be applied to other ends, including the permanent protection of the greenbelt that is proposed to surround a carfree city.

The "severability," or unbundling, of the various rights that inhere in a parcel of land is an essential precondition to the application of this approach. It appears that this is a reasonably well established precedent in US jurisprudence.

FUNDING

Who is going to pay for the necessary research and development and the construction of infrastructure? The first carfree city will probably require government funding. The scope of the research required, the cost of building prototype districts, and the long period before any payoff can be expected will probably exceed the means of for-profit organizations. There is, however, some possibility that a major developer will recognize the need for carfree cities in Florida and Arizona to serve the rapidly increasing number of elderly people who can no longer drive safely.

See page 281 for a further discussion

THE LYON PROTOCOL

The implementation of large carfree areas in existing cities will be one of the most difficult and contentious changes ever attempted. It cannot reasonably be imposed from above: people will have to be convinced of the need for carfree areas and of the desirability of living in them once they are implemented. This will require a long, painstaking process in which the needs and fears and hopes of all users of the area must be respected. Only a plan based on deep insight, a plan developed in full cooperation with the people affected, stands a chance of acceptance. Only a plan that provides good answers to all objections can win the support of the vast majority of residents and businesses alike.

This matter was taken up at the "Towards Carfree Cities" conference in Lyon, France, during October 1997. The "Lyon Protocol," one of the fruits of this conference, describes a method for building a consensus to remove cars and trucks from large urban districts. A summary of its most important points is given below.

The Design and Implementation of Large Car-Free Districts in Existing Cities

The complete protocol can be consulted on-line at: http://www.carfree.com/lyon.html

The protocol addressed the question of how a large carfree area could be created in the center of Lyon, which suffers greatly from the effects of heavy traffic. A number of essential steps in an iterative process were defined:

- Identify all interested parties both inside and outside the area under consideration.
- Engage governmental authorities from the beginning of the work.
- Gather all necessary data available for the area under study: transport patterns, economic activity, and demography.
- Develop a preliminary concept, including the boundaries of the carfree area, transport changes, and measures to ease the transition. Phasing must also be addressed at this time.
- Enlist the media to help publicize the proposal and develop interest by those who would be affected by the changes.
- Iterate the process until general agreement is reached on basic goals and the means to achieve those goals.
- When the process is well advanced, hold a week-long design charette to allow all interested parties an opportunity to participate directly in the planning of the changes.
- If all the preceding work has been properly executed, there should then exist widespread support for the implementation of a workable scheme to convert the area in question into a carfree district over a period of several years.

A charette is an intensive design workshop in which a specific design problem is attacked by all interested parties over the course of a few days. Rapid changes in the design are common, and innovative solutions are often adopted.

We consider next the planning tools that will be needed to help create workable, livable carfree districts and cities, whether in new or existing cities.

Schuhgasse, Hildesheim, c.1900

The first maquette (scale model), built in 1997 at a scale of 1:500, depicts 31.9% of a carfree district. The actual footprint of the buildings is 47.3%, whereas the target value was 37.5%. This area would thus reach a FAR of 1.5 if built to an average height of only 3.17 stories.

See: http://www.carfree.com/calc.html

PLANNING CARFREE CITIES

Even though the reference design for carfree cities is developed in some detail, it is not a blueprint for constructing a carfree city. A great many details still require attention, and the feasibility of the design must be demonstrated at a level of sophistication that far exceeds the simplified spreadsheet models on which I have been forced to rely.

This chapter considers the steps required before construction of carfree cities can begin. The need for simulations, urban planning techniques useful in the design of carfree areas, the construction of prototype neighborhoods, the possibility of compromises with the reference design, and the conversion of existing cities are discussed in this chapter.

SIMULATIONS & CALCULATIONS

A variety of simulations and calculations are required to assure that a carfree area will function as intended. The two most important are considered below.

Calculating Density & Land Uses

Detailed calculations of the floor area required by every kind of urban use must be completed, including functions that will be sited in utility areas. The reference design is based on simplistic per-capita allocations of gross floor area. More accurate calculations based on net floor area are needed to verify the preliminary calculations of densities, populations, FARs, and land uses as given in this book.

Simulating Transport Systems

In the course of developing the reference design, I relied on simplified spreadsheet analyses of the capacity and time-to-destination for both the passenger and freight system. This preliminary work must be verified using sophisticated computer simulations. The simulation should be capable of calculating energy consumption, pollution, capital costs, and operating expenses. It might also calculate these same values for an auto-centric city with the same population and economic base, giving a vivid picture of the improvements resulting from the carfree approach.

A Brief History of Urban Planning

Urban planning has a long, troubled history, and the public has rightly become suspicious of architects and planners offering new ways to shelter mankind.

Urban planning probably began with the rigid street grids imposed on Roman cities. Human nature, however, appears to resist simplistic geometry, and by medieval times, the grids in many Roman cities had morphed into irregular, organic tangles that are bad for cars but good for people. From the 17th century onwards, the Cartesian quest for certainty and order led once again to formal, regular geometry.

Great apse, Arcosanti, New Mexico, 1989
Paolo Soleri has been building this new town in the New Mexico desert for several decades. While it only reaches a height of a few stories, the view from the rooftops at sunset is breathtaking. Soleri is the inventor of "arcologies," cities-in-a-single-structure that might rise a kilometer above the ground and that would occupy tiny amounts of land. However, cost and engineering difficulties may never permit their construction, and I wonder about the healthiness of living so far removed from the ground.

Those interested in an excellent history of urban planning since about 1880 are referred to Peter Hall's *Cities of Tomorrow*. For the longer view, see Edmund N. Bacon's *Design of Cities*, which encompasses virtually the entire history of urban design.

Bijlmer district, Amsterdam, 1999
Based on Corbusier's towers-in-a-park design, this district only reaches a FAR of about 1.2 even though the buildings are 11 stories tall. Serious social problems in these buildings have led to their gradual demolition and replacement with 3- to 6-story row houses at roughly the same FAR.

This district formerly had almost no surface automobile traffic. However, the elevated roads created dark, scary spaces where criminal types hung out. During the redevelopment, the elevated streets are being replaced by grade-level streets, and the area is no longer carfree.

In the late 19th century, the Garden Cities movement of Ebenezer Howard presaged the modern separation of uses, which makes it necessary to travel longer distances to reach routine destinations. Howard did his work at a time when factories often blighted residential neighborhoods. However, when he relegated factories to their own districts, he also proposed that each use ought to have its own section of town. The result is commercial and industrial areas, devoid of residences, that become ghost towns after quitting time. All of these changes did grave damage to street life.

But much worse was soon to come:

[Corbusier] was not deterred: "The design of cities was too important to be left to the citizens." He developed his principles of planning most fully in *La Ville contemporaine* (1922) and *La Ville radiuse* (1933). The key was the famous paradox: we must decongest the centres of our cities by increasing their density. In addition, we must improve circulation and increase the amount of open space. The paradox could be resolved by building high on a small part of the total ground area. This demanded, as Corbusier put it in characteristic capital letters: "WE MUST BUILD ON A CLEAR SITE! The city of today is dying because it is not constructed geometrically." The needs of traffic also demanded total demolition: "Statistics show us that business is conducted in the centre. This means that wide avenues must be driven through the centres of our towns. *Therefore the existing centres must come down.* To save itself, every great city must rebuild its centre." This was the first suggestion of its kind; thirty years later, it was to be taken up with a vengeance. But, as Anthony has pointed out, there is no recognition anywhere in it of the problem of garaging all these cars, or of the environmental problems that would result from their noise and emissions; they are simply ignored."

Hall, 207-209

With Le Corbusier we reached the ultimate expression of rectilinear geometry. Everything in the city was to be laid out with no tool more complex than a right triangle. Many of the areas planned in accordance with Le Corbusier's Radiant City design have worked out so badly in practice that they have been demolished, beginning in 1972 with the dynamiting of the Pruitt-Igoe housing project in St. Louis.

Early morning, Siena, Italy, 1998
Given a chance, Corbusier would doubtless have levelled this comfortable bit of urbanity.

The most recent practice, beginning in the early 1970s with the work of Rod Hackney, involves local citizens directly in the design of and sometimes even the execution of urban redevelopment work. Hackney renovated a district in Macclesfield, England, for a third of the cost and in a third of the time required by the usual practice of demolition and replacement. With this change, local control over local areas was finally recognized as an essential ingredient in building good neighborhoods.

Hall, 269-272

Current thinking tends to stress the rehabilitation of existing areas in preference to demolition and replacement by newly-planned areas. Given the terrible planning failures of the past, this more conservative approach is now widely supported. It has the further advantage that it does not destroy functioning neighborhoods.

Planning appears to work best as an incremental process lasting decades or centuries, in which changes build on existing work, guided by a vision of what is desired for the future. Clearly, most of the best existing urban areas evolved over a period of centuries, each generation fixing past errors and searching for ways to meet changing needs. As we shall see, Christopher Alexander's experiment based on the use of

See page 256 in this chapter

A completely pedestrian version of Richard Register's high-density ecocity

Richard Register and I have discussed the matter of FAR and building heights. He does not support the four-story limit: with taller buildings, humans would occupy a minimum of land. Register has developed some exceptionally attractive plans for tall buildings, and arrangements such as he proposes can certainly be achieved within the context of carfree cities. He believes that taller buildings with "ecological features" address the realities of a high-population world and that "without exploring the third dimension, our architecture will lack imagination and the sheer pleasure of a new ecological aesthetic."

drawings and maquettes offers a method for rapid but incremental planning: it is not necessary to wait for each building to be constructed before deciding what to do about the next one, because the spatial relationships can be visualized.

The basic processes of urban planning and building design require no special adaptation for the carfree city, except that the fundamental requirements established by the design standards must be achieved. As long as the necessary FAR is attained with a radial street pattern centered on the transport stop, any reasonable approach to urban planning should yield a workable district.

Designing Carfree Areas

Recent books from Christopher Alexander and Léon Krier offer planning tools that are highly suited to the design of carfree cities. We will consider several of these works here.

Both Alexander and Krier have attempted to develop a theoretical understanding of the ways in which great urban areas were developed in the past. They do not apologize for their abandonment of modernism, which both believe to have led to grave deterioration in the quality of public spaces. We begin with Alexander's *A Pattern Language* because it is arguably the most important 20th-century planning tool.

A Pattern Language

In *A Pattern Language,* Christopher Alexander and his associates defined 253 patterns of human habitation that help meet fundamental human needs. The first patterns deal with human organization on the largest scales: the placement of cities and towns in the countryside. Later patterns deal with successively smaller elements, and the last patterns consider the smallest details of individual rooms. This important book is generally known to planners and is beginning to influence actual planning and development.

A Pattern Language has sometimes been criticized by those who believe that it was intended as a cookbook that would magically result in good designs. Alexander only attempted to codify patterns that are useful in thinking about the design of the human environment. It was never his intention that people should apply the patterns without deep thought about their relevance to the problem at hand.

While the entire corpus of *A Pattern Language* is relevant to carfree cities (saving aside a few experimental construction techniques and some patterns relating to transport in general and cars in particular), several patterns had especially great influence on my thinking. Each section below begins with the pattern name (followed by the pattern's identifying number). The pattern itself is then quoted, followed by comments on its application to carfree cities. Illustrations are included by courtesy of Oxford University Press.

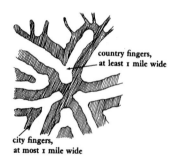

City Country Fingers
Alexander (1977), 25

City Country Fingers (3)

This pattern states: "Keep interlocking fingers of farmland and urban land, even at the center of a metropolis. The urban fingers should never be more than 1 mile wide, while the farmland fingers should never be less than 1 mile wide." The reference design essentially supports both conditions.

Scattered Work (9)

"Use zoning laws, neighborhood planning, tax incentives, and any other means available to scatter workplaces throughout the city. Prohibit large concentrations of work, without family life around them. Prohibit large concentrations of family life, without workplaces around them." The

Alexander (1977), 56

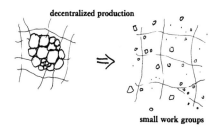

Scattered Work
Alexander (1977), 56

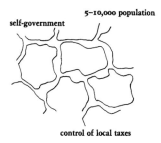

Community of 7000
Alexander (1977), 73-74

Four-story buildings, Amsterdam, 1999
Statement of pattern: Alexander (1977), 119

reference design fully respects this pattern, which reflects the earlier work of Jane Jacobs, who calls for an end to zoning regulations that require the separation of uses. Mixed uses lead to interesting, vibrant, and healthy neighborhoods. This pattern is not intrinsic to the carfree city, but I believe that it makes any city a better place to live.

Community of 7000 (12)

"Decentralize city governments in a way that gives local control to communities of 5,000 to 10,000 persons. As nearly as possible, use natural geographic and historical boundaries to mark these communities. Give each community the power to initiate, decide, and execute the affairs that concern it closely: land use, housing, maintenance, streets, parks, police, schooling, welfare, neighborhood services." The reference design calls for districts of 12,000. Each district separates naturally into two parts along the central boulevard, and the areas on either side of the boulevard can be treated as separate communities with populations of about 6,000. The question of how to arrange governmental jurisdictions is a difficult matter. We must avoid, on the one hand, excessive fragmentation of authority, and, on the other hand, unresponsive central bureaucracies.

Four-Story Limit (21)

"In any urban area, no matter how dense, keep the majority of the buildings four stories high or less. It is possible that certain buildings should exceed this limit, but they should never be buildings for human habitation." I do not entirely agree with Alexander on this point, although the reference design is indeed based on a maximum building height of four stories. Many very fine older neighborhoods in European cities have entire blocks built six stories high, without apparent ill effect. Routine construction of buildings higher than this should probably be avoided.

This is, to say the least, a controversial point. People who want taller buildings can have them.

Accessible Green (60)

"Build open public green within three minutes' walk—about 750 feet—of every house and workplace. This means that the greens need to be uniformly scattered at 1500 foot intervals, throughout the city. Make the greens at least 150 feet across, and at least 60,000 square feet in area." The basis for this pattern is research indicating that people do not routinely use green areas unless they lie within a three-minute walk. This research was conducted in cities with cars; I think that the walk can be stretched to five minutes if it is pleasant, safe, and unimpeded by cars. The open green areas shown in the reference design for carfree cities are very much larger than Alexander's minimum. The interior courtyards (which in many cases will probably be private spaces and thus "accessible green" only for residents) at the center of each block are nearly half the size prescribed by Alexander.

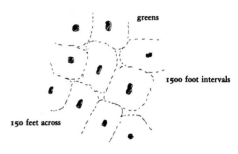

Accessible Green
Alexander (1977), 308-309

Small Public Squares (61)

"Make a public square much smaller than you would at first imagine; usually no more than 45 to 60 feet across, never more than 70 feet across. This applies only to its width in the short direction. In the long direction it can certainly be longer." In new towns, one sometimes sees vast squares with few people in them. This displays an ignorance of the function of squares: bringing people together, not keeping them apart. The reference design calls for a great many small squares, as narrow as 8 meters (about 26 feet), but the three downtown districts each have squares much larger than this pattern would allow. I believe Alexander has erred slightly here. Piazza San Marco in Venice is about 70 by 180 meters, or

Small Public Squares
Alexander (1977), 313

Central square, Houten, the Netherlands, 1998

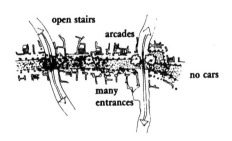

Pedestrian Street
Alexander (1977), 490-491

City of arcades: Bologna, Italy, 1998

three times as wide as Alexander's maximum. A few large squares near the heart of a city contribute to the public life of a city. Beijing's vast Tienanmen Square is one of the city's most famous landmarks. Despite heavy traffic, London's Trafalger Square forms a vibrant central feature, and it, too, is far longer than 70 feet in both directions. Squares certainly can be too large, however. The Dutch new town of Houten has a population of 32,000 and a huge downtown square. There never appears to be anywhere near enough foot traffic to make this place come alive. On the other hand, Amsterdam's vital Leidseplein is quite small and sometimes too crowded. The key point is to determine the size of a square on the basis of the foot traffic that will pass through it.

Pedestrian Street (100)
"Arrange buildings so that they form pedestrian streets with many entrances and open stairs directly from the upper stories to the street, so that even movement between rooms is outdoors, not just movement between buildings." Alexander cautions that the pattern will not work unless the area is small enough to be filled with pedestrians. This is one of the reasons that a carfree city should have a FAR of 1.5 and mixed uses: this combination will produce a considerable amount of foot traffic most of the time. The whole of a carfree city would be built largely in accordance with this pattern, although the outside stairs are not well suited to cold or snowy climates, and I have omitted them. Note also that the pedestrian street works best when it is quite narrow, which is the prime reason that the streets in the reference design average only 7 meters wide. The small buildings proposed in the reference design also provide the many entrances called for by the pattern. Arcades make a very satisfactory addition to cities with hot or wet climates.

Positive Outdoor Space (106)

"Make all the outdoor spaces which surround and lie between your buildings positive. Give each one some degree of enclosure; surround each space with wings of buildings, trees, hedges, fences, arcades, and trellised walks, until it becomes an entity with a positive quality and does not spill out indefinitely around corners." The reference design supports this pattern in two ways. The buildings surrounding the interior courtyards create positive outdoor spaces, as does the continuous wall of buildings bordering the streets and squares. Ideally, the interior and exterior spaces should be linked by a *sottoportego.*

Transform this. . . . . .to this.

Positive Outdoor Space
Alexander (1977), 521-522

Connected Buildings (108)

"Connect your building up, wherever possible, to the existing buildings round about. Do not keep set backs between buildings; instead, try to form new buildings as continuation of the older buildings." The reference design for carfree cities fully supports this pattern, which is essential if a high FAR is to be achieved. The pattern is closely related to "Positive Outdoor Space" and just as important.

connections

Connected Buildings
Alexander (1977), 534

A New Theory of Urban Design

Christopher Alexander published another highly significant work ten years after *A Pattern Language* appeared. This new book, *A New Theory of Urban Design,* proposed an entirely new approach to urban development. The method resulted from efforts to create the kind of satisfying designs so often seen in older districts around the world. The principal objective of the method is to create urban areas that are:

• Whole and coherent
• Unique to the site and its requirements

Alexander (1987), 23

Maquette from *A New Theory of Urban Designs*
Alexander (1987), 176-177

Alexander (1987). The rules are stated and explored in Chapter 3 of that work (31-99). For a discussion of the difficulties of applying the rules, see: 30, 50, 60-63, 99, 243-244.

- Developed incrementally
- Polycentric

Polycentrism requires that each center be a part of a larger organization and comprises smaller organizations. All areas must belong to this hierarchy: no developed area may fall outside this hierarchical organization. Alexander describes these areas outside the hierarchy as "negative space," because they make no contribution to the development of wholeness, and in fact impede the attainment of this quality.

The fundamental ideas are expressed in seven specific development rules intended to foster the achievement of wholeness. While these rules are fairly simple to express, Alexander's students had considerable difficulty in grasping and implementing them. Only long experience in applying the rules, coupled with Alexander's commentary on the failed attempts, finally helped his students to achieve the deep understanding of the rules that is a prerequisite to achieving their aims. Superficial attempts to apply these rules are unlikely to yield good results.

One of the greatest advantages of Alexander's technique in comparison to conventional approaches is that it permits fairly rapid design of an area: it is no longer necessary to wait for one building to be constructed before designing the next one. Historically, most urban areas were developed over a span of centuries, and each remodeling, restoration, or extension could be planned on the basis of field observations of the existing spaces and their strong and weak points. Alexander's students drew paper plans and built maquettes; these tools were adequate to the task of developing plans for a 30-acre (12 hectare) site on the waterfront near the Bay Bridge in San Francisco. By Alexander's own evaluation, the experiment was largely successful, notwithstanding a number of problems. In particular, Alexander believed that the effort failed to achieve the deep unity that had been sought, although the results appear to be far better than those characteristic of most contemporary urban planning and design. The plan was never realized.

Alexander has thus given us a method of urban planning that allows the employment of traditional planning methods, but at a much faster tempo than had been possible using traditional approaches. This method is admirably suited to the task of designing and building new carfree cities.

Architecture: Choice or Fate

Léon Krier is a contrarian among modern architects. He was chosen by the Prince of Wales to design Poundbury, a new community on one of the Prince's estates. Developed in accordance with Krier's ideas, this old-style town is attractive and highly livable. Krier begins his book with this impassioned plea for a return to older values in urban design:

> If, one day, for some mysterious reason, all the buildings, settlements, suburbs and structures built after 1945— especially those commonly called "modern"—vanished from the face of the earth, would we mourn their loss? Would the disappearance of prefabricated tower blocks, mass housing estates, commercial strips, business parks, motorway junctions, modular university campuses, schools, and new towns, damage the identity of our favourite cities and landscapes?
>
> If, on the other had, some parallel phenomenon destroyed in one fell swoop the whole of our pre-World War II architectural heritage, namely all "historic" buildings, hamlets, villages, and cities, what would be the significance of such an event?

In terms of real estate volume, both heritages are approximately equal; comparing them globally as alternatives allows us to appreciate the fundamental differences in their nature: their specific symbolic, aesthetic, civilising and emotional qualities, their power of attraction, identification and repulsion. Has so-called "modern" architecture, with its insatiable drive for autonomy, its cultivation of the *tabula rasa* approach and celebration of change and revolution, really liberated us from our "historic" past? Or has it made us more dependent?

Krier, 13

Krier has developed an approach to building in the classical style but with a modern twist. His buildings are at once familiar and original. He has grasped the fundamental principles that distinguish an urban area that works from one that does not, and these principles are codified in *Architecture: Choice or Fate* in a clear, approachable manner.

CONSTRUCTION OF MAQUETTES

An alternative to physical maquettes is 3-D virtual reality simulations of the city. Anyone with Internet access could wander through the virtual streets.

Early in the research and development phase it may be useful to construct a maquette showing an entire carfree city. The prototype maquette shown at the beginning of this chapter was built at a scale of 1:500, a suitable scale for this use. A maquette that depicted the entire reference design at this scale would be about 32 meters square; while a large project, there are precedents for maquettes of this size and scope.

Prototype Maquette

I lacked the resources to taper the houses so that they would fit tightly against one another, as would surely be done in practice. In calculating the maquette's footprint, I assumed that all the narrow gaps between the buildings would in reality be occupied by buildings.

I made a number of errors in the construction of the first maquette, and it is worth examining each of them and the effects they would have had if a district had been built as depicted by the maquette.

In the first place, the district is too dense. The maquette was constructed by eye, and subsequent calculations of the density show that while the targeted building footprint was 37.5% of the area inside the district, this was considerably exceeded: the building footprint came out to 47.3%. If an actual district were constructed with such a high footprint, the buildings would only need to average a little over three stories in order to reach the FAR of 1.5 assumed in the reference design. This could, in fact, be as good an arrangement as the reference district, although there is, of course, less green area.

Another discrepancy is that most of the buildings are considerably deeper than called for in the reference design, so building interiors would be rather dark. Some buildings are double the depth assumed in the reference design.

The maquette shows many squares, and most of them are too large. The total area occupied by streets and squares is greater than is now proposed in the reference design. I only recently came to fully appreciate the need for very small squares.

The maquette also differs from the reference design in that the central boulevard is divided by a row of buildings; the reference design shows a single boulevard twice as wide. The arrangement used in the maquette would be preferable if trams were used instead of a metro; a single one-way tram line would run through each of the two narrower boulevards, thereby eliminating the danger of one tram concealing another tram approaching from the opposite direction; this would reduce the number of pedestrians struck by trams.

In the maquette, many of the streets are both tapered and curved, and this pattern can be seen in the drawing of the reference district and reference block designs. The streets in the older parts of Venice are rarely of constant width for

Giudecca district, Venice, 1997
This is one of the newer neighborhoods of Venice. Streets in this area were laid out on a rigid rectilinear plan, and, to my eye, the result is considerably less pleasing than the narrow, irregular streets of San Marco. Storefronts would help.

more than a short distance, and long, straight streets are fairly unusual. Only the quaysides along the lagoon are wide and relatively straight. I have only recently become thoroughly convinced of the desirability of irregular streets, and even the Venetians seem to have lost their understanding of this point.

CARFREE PROTOTYPES

As with any new undertaking, it will be useful to proceed slowly and to begin with small pilot projects before moving on to the construction of a full prototype city. Some of the features in the reference design are not yet proven, and their implementation will be easier in a new city specifically designed to accommodate them; this is particularly true of the utility areas and the freight transport system.

Planning Controls

One of the most important reasons to build prototype districts is to find a satisfactory way to create districts with their own distinct characters. The problem of building to a common theme without imposing authoritarian controls is difficult. The best approach is probably to designate the character of each district (on the basis of preferences expressed by prospective inhabitants) and then to establish a community council to implement it. Control over open space development, architectural style, signage, use permits, etc., could be given to a community council. Such a council would enjoy far-reaching powers but would be directly accountable to the district. Given the small size of the districts, the possibility exists for direct democratic administration. It would also be possible to establish different characters for each of the two communities that are located in each district; in this case, each community should have its own council.

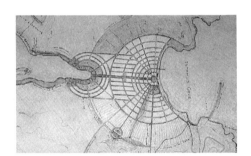

Proposed Carfree Two Harbors, Catalina Island Michael E. Arth of Santa Barbara, California, developed this proposal for a carfree town on an island near Los Angeles. Arth is the founder of the New Pedestrianism, an urban planning effort to more effectively separate cars from pedestrians and bicyclists. He designs and promotes various types of pedestrian-oriented communities.

From *The Labors of Hercules: Modern Solutions to 12 Herculean Problems*, Michael E. Arth (Santa Barbara: Golden Apples Publishing, 2000) (used with permission of the author)

Demonstrating Livability

Many people will not accept a carfree environment as a good place to live without first seeing a demonstration of what a carfree city would look like and how it would work. Venice really ought to be proof enough, but it differs sufficiently from the reference design that some people may not accept it as a generalizable proof of the livability of dense, medium-rise neighborhoods.

The world's most livable city? Venice, 1997

Compared to the reference design, the streets in Venice are quite narrow and the interior courtyards are very much smaller. Quite a few buildings in Venice are five stories high, but there are also many lower buildings, including even a few single-story buildings. The FAR of the San Marco district in Venice appears to be nearly double that proposed for the reference design. San Marco is the oldest part of the city, and it appears to be significantly denser than other areas of the city. Interestingly enough, San Marco is also the most attractive part of the city, and some of the streets are very narrow indeed. I have not dared to propose such densities in the reference district, but one of the lobes of the reference design was drawn at densities that approach those of Venice. It is worth keeping in mind that many important streets in Venice are barely 4 meters wide, and the widest street, the Strada Nuova, is just 9 meters wide.

The newest areas of Venice appear to be the least dense, with streets wider than in San Marco. Large areas of Giudecca and eastern Venice near the naval shipyard appear to have taken on their current form within the past century or so. There is little foot traffic on these streets, and they seem less inviting than the older, narrower, more crowded streets in the older parts of the city.

Living at High Density

One of the most serious concerns about living in high-density neighborhoods is the loss of privacy. In Venice, most windows are fitted with external wooden shutters, and these are normally closed by the occupants after dark. During the day, most windows are covered by thin gauze curtains that admit lots of light and air but provide excellent visual privacy.

In the more than three weeks I have spent in Venice, I

never heard a stereo turned up too loud. Such consideration is necessary if people are going to get along in high density areas, but as noted earlier, in Los Angeles, people have become so inconsiderate of their neighbors that they hold outdoor parties with music loud enough to disturb entire districts. At some level, society must intervene to stop selfish people from making life miserable for everyone else.

It is well to remember that some of the most desirable residential areas of Manhattan are built at a density that far exceeds the density proposed in the reference design for carfree cities, and that residents of these neighborhoods still have to cope with heavy car traffic in the relatively narrow streets. Some of the older areas of Philadelphia and Boston are built at densities that approximate those proposed for the carfree city.

In any case, it seems wise to build a prototype carfree neighborhood in the style proposed for the carfree city: four-story buildings, narrow streets, and fairly large interior courtyards. An area of just a few blocks is sufficiently large to show what denser living is like and to confront the problems that must be solved. An area of this size could simply be built as infill housing in almost any reasonably large city with decent public transport.

Infill is new construction in an existing urban area

Hand truck delivery, Venice, 1997
Prototype areas might get their freight in this way

A Test with Peripheral Parking
A carfree neighborhood with several thousand residents is sufficiently large to serve as a test bed for carfree living. This would be an area of perhaps 25 small blocks or about 300 meters on a side. A project of this size could be undertaken in an urban area in urgent need of redevelopment, and some of the candidate districts are large enough that peripheral parking could readily be arranged. This is a big enough project to test the proposals for local freight distribution.

Prototype Districts with Tram Service

At some point, it will be necessary to make a test of the full carfree concept. This will require the construction of several districts each roughly the size of the reference district. The test will also require the construction of a tram line connecting the new carfree area to an existing urban center. There should be no particular difficulty using standard passenger trams to provide transport between the existing urban area at one end of the line and a newly-constructed utility area at the other end of the line. The utility area would include all of the usual functions, including parking, freight storage and handling, and heavy industry.

An area of this size is also large enough to conduct a test of the metro-freight concepts, possibly using modified trams running on the surface and sharing the right-of-way with regular passenger trams. It might prove difficult or impossible to move full-size standard shipping containers on a normal tram system, in which case freight would have to be broken down in the utility area and consolidated into smaller containers that would fit aboard a specially-modified freight tram. Standard air-freight containers, while not ideal, might serve this purpose. The use of specialized freight trams with off-rail capabilities, such as proposed by van Popta, offers another solution. A final approach would involve the construction of sidings along the tram route, where freight trams could unload off line, without delaying passenger trams.

A freight consolidation facility would be built in the utility area at the end of the line. Inbound freight would be sorted by destination district and loaded into containers for delivery to each district depot, just as proposed in the reference design. Final delivery would be as proposed in Freight Delivery. Because of the small scale of this operation, costs would be somewhat higher than in a full-scale city.

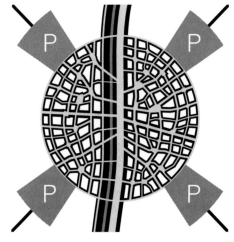

Carfree district with peripheral parking

See page 204

Building the First Lobe

The first full-scale lobe need not be built as part of a completely new city. Rather, a large addition to an existing city could be built using the carfree model, provided that fast transport could be offered between the new lobe and the existing city core. The city should already have a good public transport network in place, so that residents of the carfree addition will have ready access to all parts of the city. A fast-growing city of 300,000 to 1,000,000 with a large undeveloped area reasonably close to the city center is the most suitable site. This project is close to being a full-scale test of the carfree concept; only the termination of the passenger and freight lines at the center of the existing city is at variance with the reference design, and this would have but slight effect on the operations of the transport systems.

Site for Full-Scale Trial

A greenfield site is one on which buildings have not previously been erected.

A full-scale trial of the carfree city might best be conducted in open country, on a greenfield site. Only 250 sq-km are required, and many such sites are available. While a carfree city might be integrated into an existing built-up area, the problems that must be solved are perhaps too complex for the first full-scale trial.

DESIGN COMPROMISES

Especially when converting existing cities to the carfree model, it may be expedient to make some compromises with the reference design.

People Movers

See page 101 for a discussion of people movers

People-mover technology is already sufficiently advanced that it could provide ancillary transport from district centers to outlying neighborhoods. This would permit the construction of a larger inhabited area (possibly at lower density) than provided for in the reference design. The addition of satellite districts (usually on the outside of a lobe) would increase travel time and require an extra transfer for trips outside the district, but the compromise is not large and offers considerable flexibility. This arrangement may prove especially useful in the conversion of existing cities.

Lower Density

Living at high density is probably the most important objection that will be raised to carfree cities. However, if people will accept walking times of up to 10 minutes (or bike rides of just a few minutes), it is possible to build at densities only 25% of those proposed in the reference design. I believe that, in the absence of car and truck traffic, a denser city is a better, more interesting place to live.

A range of densities could be accommodated in the same city: the outer districts could be less dense than the central districts. See the drawing of the tapered lobe on page 136 for an example of how this might work out in practice.

Peripheral Parking

As mentioned in the discussion of prototypes, parking lots could be arranged at the perimeter of the districts, thereby allowing quick automobile access. The disadvantage is that it fills the green space near the districts with vast parking lots, hideous concrete parking structures, or expensive underground garages. It also generates traffic on the access roads and tends to encourage automobile usage. It would even be possible to construct houses with individual garages and direct road access along the perimeter of a district. This compromise is best avoided whenever possible.

0   800 m

Adding 400-meter satellites to a district
A single track, with a passing siding at the middle stop, can provide service at 4-minute intervals.

Something similar to this was done during the construction of the new university at Louvain la Neuve in Belgium. The pedestrian areas were raised above the streets and parking.

Unhappy compromise, Bologna, Italy, 1998
Clearly, this small square still works: people use it. Without the pair of Darth Vader SUVs, we could see the lovely building behind. Would we really miss the cars parked inside the arcade?

Underground Streets

With some relatively minor changes in the district topology, it would be possible to put narrow, one-way access lanes in the basements of long rows of buildings, together with quite a lot of parking. This form enables the construction of a district without surface traffic but with a significant capacity for automobile movement and parking. The costs would be high, and the environmental problems associated with cars are not addressed except for noise, which should be fairly well contained. Finally, every person driving through the basement is one less person walking on the street, which diminishes the liveliness of the streets.

One Compromise to Avoid

From the car driver's point of view, the best place for car parking would be the center of a district, close to most functions. Unless this garage and its access roads were built completely underground, this compromise would largely destroy the quality of life that the carfree district is intended to create. For proof of this, one has only to look at the beautiful Italian squares ruined by their use as parking lots.

REDEVELOPING EXISTING CITIES

The conversion of existing cities to the carfree model is a great challenge. If vast demolition work is acceptable, the conversion becomes simple, but it is unreasonable to assume that cities will simply demolish most of the built environment and begin again. This raises the question of how existing cities can be transformed into carfree cities during the course of several decades.

The following sections present proposed rearrangements of several widely-divergent urban areas as carfree cities.

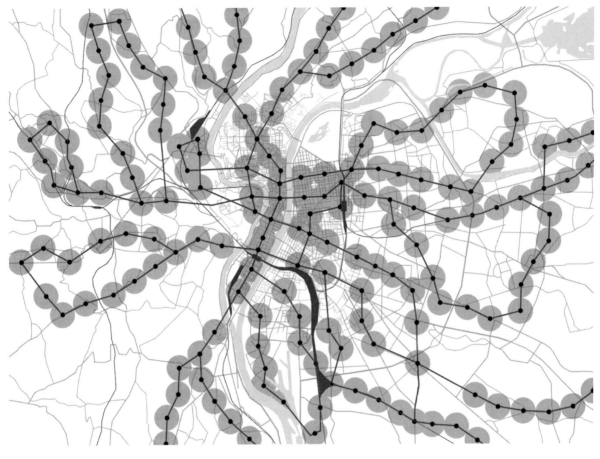

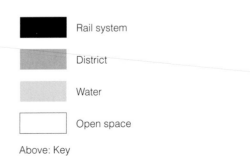

Rail system

District

Water

Open space

Above: Key

LYON

Premier arrondisement, Lyon, 1999

Opposite: Carfree districts superimposed on a simplified map of existing streets in Lyon. Full use was made of the four existing metro lines, which already provide excellent service in the dense downtown area. At the time, we lacked the tools to draw curved metro lines; in practice, the sharp corners would be rounded.

In the fall of 1997, I attended an anti-car conference in Lyon, France, (population 1.25 million) and presented a plan for a carfree Lyon, developed without any firsthand field observations. As was to be expected, there were some conflicts between what was proposed and what was physically possible, but the plan remains interesting enough to consider here. This drawing is in any case the first public presentation of a plan in which the concepts of the reference design were applied to redevelopment of an existing metropolitan area.

Inhabited since Roman times, Lyon is located at the confluence of the Rhône and Saône Rivers. The original settlement was west of the rivers, and the city has since expanded to the east. The 17th and 18th century additions filled most of the peninsula between the two rivers.

Steep hills rise in the western and northern parts of the city. Funiculars provide public transport from the riverbank to the western hilltops. One of the four metro lines runs north up the peninsula and is, as far as I know, the only rack-driven metro in the world. Despite the precipitous grades, it operates in much the same manner as any other metro.

The construction of several new metro lines and the extension of several others was proposed. An attempt was made to site the utility areas in existing industrial sections of the city and to maintain all of the older districts as urban areas with few changes. In newer parts of the city, those areas near metro stops would slowly be rebuilt at higher densities, while more distant areas would revert to open-space uses. Although there appears to be little waterborne freight delivery, large areas of the city are within easy reach of the riverbanks, and these areas could receive freight by water. Conventional metro-freight would, however, serve the entire city.

AMSTERDAM

Leidseplein, Amsterdam, 1999
The flat Dutch countryside encourages bicycling.
The Dutch have such a remarkable, living tradition
of bicycling that bike parking becomes an issue.

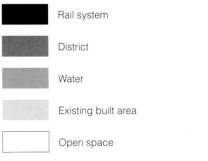

Rail system

District

Water

Existing built area

Open space

Above: Key
Opposite: Amsterdam redeveloped as a carfree
city. New metro and tram lines would be built to
complement the existing system. Some center-city
areas not within easy walking distance of a transit
stop would be served by people movers, but most
areas more than 400 meters from a transport halt
would gradually become park land.

Like most cities in the industrialized nations, the geographic extent of Amsterdam has increased remarkably since 1945, despite a population decline. The causes are many, but the most important are the demand for more floor area per person and the large amount of room that has been devoted to accommodating cars and trucks in the newer districts.

Amsterdam has a metro system, and plans for an extension through the city center are already far advanced. Trams, however, provide service in most of the city. The plan for a carfree Amsterdam is based on the assumption that, in addition to the metro extension in progress, a number of new tram routes would also be constructed.

The existing downtown was entirely platted and largely constructed by 1700. The city has never resolved the conflict between cars and other uses in this historic area of canals and narrow streets. Some canals were filled and paved over to provide car parking, but protests in the 1950s brought a halt to this practice. The city has for years had an official policy of reducing center-city automobile usage, and on-street parking is slowly being replaced by hugely expensive underground and underwater garages. All of this has had little effect on traffic in the inner city; the impacts of this traffic are large in the narrow streets laid out before anyone had even conceived of an automobile.

The first experiments with modern waterborne freight delivery have already begun, and freight in the center of a carfree Amsterdam could almost certainly be delivered by boat, using the extensive canal system. Other arrangements would be required in the newer areas of the city; some combination of metro-freight and freight trams operating on surface tracks could provide the necessary freight transport.

Washington Square North, New York, 1999
Four-story townhouses overlooking Washington
Square Park in Manhattan's Greenwich Village.

Metro with station

New tram line

• • • • • • Freight tram

Above: Key
Opposite: Manhattan redeveloped as a carfree city

Manhattan

Manhattan is already a carfree city, or nearly so, if you consider only the statistics. Notwithstanding Manhattan's brutal street traffic, most movement of passengers is by subway and train: without its rail systems, Manhattan could not function at all. There are two difficulties with subway service in Manhattan: the East Side needs another north-south line, and crosstown service is poor except for a few cases where subways already provide service.

In order to provide better passenger transport, I propose simply to remove cars from the streets of Manhattan while maintaining and expanding crosstown bus service during the construction of crosstown tram lines. Manhattan has major cross streets at roughly 10-block intervals (about 0.8 km), and tram lines would be built from river to river along all the major cross streets; since the subways stations are almost always located at the major cross streets, this arrangement permits easy transfers between trams and subways. Construction of the 2nd Avenue Subway has resumed after a lapse of decades. When completed, this subway would provide the needed service improvements on the East Side. These changes would provide the whole of Manhattan with excellent public transport, at which time all surface bus routes would be discontinued.

Freight service would be provided by freight trams running river-to-river in loops along minor cross streets, eastbound on one street and westbound on the adjacent street. Freight terminals would be built along the riverfront, where containers would be unloaded from barges and transferred to the freight trams for delivery to district depots along the route. Barges would be loaded with containers at existing container terminal facilities at Port Newark and Port Elizabeth, not far from Manhattan.

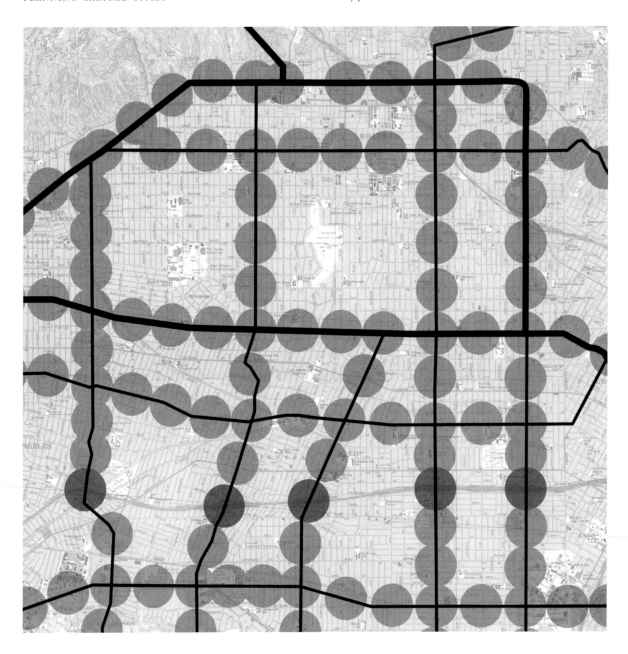

REDEVELOPING THE AMERICAN NIGHTMARE

Los Angeles seen from the Hollywood Hills, 1999

Metro

Light rail

Utility area

District

Above: Key

Opposite: The ultimate challenge: LA morphed into a carfree city. (Much of the area on the map is shown in the photograph above.)

The construction of additional north-south tram lines would permit more of the area to remain in urban uses, with, of course, less green space.

The greatest challenge in the development of carfree cities is the conversion of vast auto-centric cities in the USA. Cities such as Los Angeles and Phoenix sprawl out over huge areas and lack clear centers. Buses provide most public transport (although Los Angeles has restored some commuter rail service and is building a metro). These cities are the antithesis of the carfree model, and their redevelopment will be difficult, slow, and expensive. Once agreement has been reached regarding the need for the change, the first step will be the development of an urban plan based on the carfree model.

Auto-centric cities will shrink considerably, but not uniformly. In order to establish green areas near the city, large tracts now occupied by sprawling outer suburbs must return to open-space uses. Some areas near the center of the city will also be converted into open space adjacent to the inner-city districts. It will therefore be necessary to greatly increase the density in the remaining areas. As this is done, dwellings in designated open space areas will gradually be demolished.

The most important and time-consuming task will be the construction of the passenger transport and metro-freight systems, and work on these projects should receive priority. The passenger transport system must be operational before redevelopment can begin, because cars will have to be removed in order to permit the required street narrowing and density increases.

Densities can be increased and street widths greatly reduced by constructing rows of four-story buildings in the centers of existing streets more than 15 meters wide (virtually all streets, thus). The end result is two narrow streets and a row of buildings where there was once a single wide street. Streets wider than about 30 meters can actually become two streets with two rows of new buildings opening on an interior courtyard, in accordance with the arrangement of the reference block.

"Mother-in-law" units can also be constructed behind existing buildings, putting the large back yards to use. In the course of time, the old one- and two-story buildings will be demolished and replaced with four-story buildings. In many cases, two buildings will fit on the site of what formerly was just a single building. In this way, the necessary density can be developed gradually and without first having to raze the entire neighborhood. This approach keeps the neighborhoods intact during the redevelopment, although the level of construction work may disturb residents.

Economic Dislocations

Unfortunately, the US economy is largely founded on the assumption that suburban sprawl is the only viable development model. Huge sums have been invested in the infrastructure, and much of this may eventually have to be abandoned; the value of the houses could fall to nearly zero.

If the depopulation of the suburbs must proceed rapidly (in the event of a crisis involving fuel supplies or global warming), then many houses will become worth less than the outstanding amount of the mortgage, leading to a banking crisis. The only way to mitigate this problem is to begin now to discourage the construction of new suburban houses by increasing the minimum down payment from 10% to 25% or more of the purchase price. At the same time, the dense redevelopment of downtown brownfield sites must be encouraged. Economic dislocations may still occur even if these measures are adopted; the important question is whether they come suddenly and unexpectedly or more gradually and predictably. Planning ahead is important.

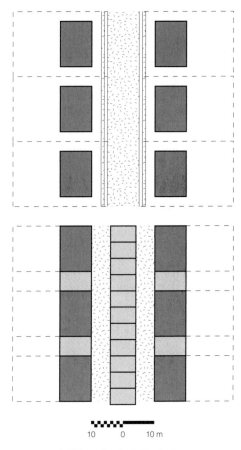

10   0   10 m

Infill housing for US suburbs
Upper drawing: existing condition
Lower drawing: infill buildings added

A brownfield site is an empty or derelict site that was formerly part of the city's fabric. US inner cities have many such vacant or underutilized sites.

The most severe problems will affect the outermost ring of suburban towns, which still carry huge bonded indebtedness undertaken to build the necessary infrastructure. These areas may become largely or entirely depopulated, in which case the bonds will become worthless: as people move away, the burden of repaying the bonds will fall on steadily fewer residents, and the town will eventually default on its debt. I see no solution to this problem: the investments were fundamentally unsound. Given that sprawling suburbs were permitted and even encouraged by governments at all levels, it seems reasonable that the costs of this mistake be shared by the USA as a whole.

The high energy efficiency of rail-based transport systems should improve the competitive position of those cities that make the change. The advantage will only increase as fuel prices climb. Cities that resist the change may find themselves left behind.

There is one silver lining: a large source of public revenue will arise as streets in the redeveloping areas are converted to building sites that will fetch a good price, offsetting some of the losses.

Clearly, we should stop building suburban sprawl as quickly as possible and concentrate our efforts on denser urban redevelopment. Fortunately, the political tide in the USA seems to be turning swiftly against sprawl development and in favor of real urban neighborhoods closer to downtown.

Historic Preservation

We should make certain to preserve characteristic examples of suburban development so that future generations can wonder at the unsustainable manner in which their forebears chose to live for a few brief generations. Several blocks of each type of suburban development will be quite enough. A few strip malls and shopping centers ought to receive preservation status, to squat forever amid fields of asphalt.

We turn next to some proposals to launch the change to carfree cities in earnest.

Chiesa di S. Pietro in Banchi, Genoa, c.1900

Carnival, Venice, 1997

SOME MODEST PROPOSALS

The need for carfree cities may come upon us rather more suddenly than we might expect, as was the case in Havana, Cuba, in the 1990s. A sudden change in the availability of petroleum, unexpected grave news about the state of the planet's ecology, or some other calamity could force rapid and widespread adoption of carfree cities. We should complete the development of the methods for designing and implementing carfree cities in advance of this need. Given that the need is largely prospective, governments and nonprofit foundations are the likely sources of funding for the work.

This chapter proposes several sponsors and locations for the first new carfree city. These proposals are only modest in the context of the scope of the task: the redevelopment of the world's auto-centric cities as carfree cities will be a far larger undertaking than the construction of the US Interstate highway system, up to now the largest construction project in history. This task will require the commitment of enormous

Recent reports indicate that the CO_2 cycle is one of the major regulating mechanisms that is responsible for the relative long-term stability of the Earth's climate. We have now made a large "adjustment" in this system, and there is every possibility that this will have major effects on the global climate.

resources, so it is essential that the development work be careful, thorough, and correct. We cannot afford to make another serious mistake with the form of our cities. For this reason, a full-scale prototype carfree city should be constructed as soon as possible: we will need practical experience before applying the carfree concept on a global scale.

EuroCity

Installations of the government of the European Union are scattered across several nations in northern Europe. While the major legislative and executive functions are centralized in Brussels, important installations are also found in France, Germany, and Luxembourg.

Denmark, Sweden, the Netherlands, Germany, Switzerland, and Luxembourg are arguably the world's leaders in environmental research and sustainable development. Major commitments have been made to sustainable energy, habitat and species preservation, and reduced urban pollution. Public transport in these nations is at a standard exceeded only in Singapore and Japan (Amsterdam is a noteworthy exception to the otherwise-excellent public transport in the Netherlands). This region, with its top-flight infrastructure and a long tradition of environmental awareness, is an excellent region in which to build a prototype carfree city. The tests can begin on a small scale, in conjunction with a variety of other environmental initiatives.

I therefore propose that the EU establish a long-term project to build a new city in northern Europe that would function as the headquarters for the EU's Directorates General concerned with transport, sustainable development, and environmental protection. These installations would also provide a substantial and durable economic foundation

EuroCity in the Markermeer
This proposal amounts to the construction of a second Venice. Like the original, it would be surrounded by water.

The Markerwaard was to be the fourth and last of the great polders in the IJsselmeer (created in the 1930s, when the Afsluitdijk turned the Zuider Zee into a lake). The first three polders were diked, drained, and inhabited decades ago. The Markerwaard was cancelled because of opposition by environmental groups, who objected to the draining of so much of the remaining area of the IJsselmeer. The proposal for EuroCity involves an entirely different land reclamation technique, one now being used to build the IJburg district in the IJmeer, near Amsterdam. EuroCity would preserve nearly all of the lake's surface area while considerably lengthening its shoreline and creating new habitats.

Given that a large rise in sea level would overwhelm the Afsluitdijk and flood the IJsselmeer, the bureaucrats living in the city would have a personal incentive to assure that global warming and sea level rise were controlled.

The metro-freight line could be replaced by a canal, allowing waterborne freight delivery. This region of Europe is well served by barge canals, and the necessary infrastructure is already largely in place.

for a new city. Once a willing host nation and a suitable site are found, work on prototype neighborhoods, districts, and lobes can begin. The ultimate goal would be the development of a city with a population of at least 250,000, a real city in its own right, with the EU installations as one of it main economic activities.

SUNBELT RETIREMENT CITIES IN THE USA

While I generally oppose the development of cities in ways that tend to accentuate divisions based on age, race, or wealth, the time is ripe to build some carfree retirement areas in the southern states of the USA. For decades, these states have been flooded by retirees fleeing cold northern winters, and nothing seems likely to stanch the flow. Vast areas of the desert around Phoenix have been turned into low-density suburbs. In Florida, sprawling suburbs have been built from one end of the state to the other, often with serious environmental consequences. Water supplies in some parts of the state are now in a critical condition, despite ample rainfall. Irrigation of lawns surrounding single-family houses has exacerbated the problems with water supplies.

As the transplanted retirees grow old, their frailties eventually make it too dangerous for most of them to continue driving safely. Since life in these sprawling suburbs is built around transport by private car, the incentive to continue driving after it is safe to do so becomes very large: to lose one's driving license is to become a second-class citizen. These suburban environments preclude the establishment of an effective public transport network, and driving is usually the only way to get anywhere. Daily necessities are rarely within walking distance, so those who can no longer drive become dependent for their mobility on others who can.

As the baby boomers begin to retire in large numbers after 2010, we can expect to see some action to solve this problem. This generation is large, active, and accustomed to having things its way. Baby boomers are likely to demand solutions that permit them to live dignified lives after they have had to give up driving. I believe that a market exists in the southern states for carfree developments. A fairly large project would be able to sustain an adequate base of services to permit residents to meet their daily needs without driving. If built at fairly high densities (but perhaps at densities lower than the reference design), carfree districts could help millions of elderly people to live independent lives in their last years. Denser habitation would also offer a social boon to the elderly, making it much easier to meet people and enjoy an active social life. I think this is a commercial opportunity for a major developer bold enough to take up the challenge.

Some US real estate developers have started nibbling around the edges of carfree cities. Several retirement communities already permit residents to use golf carts for transport within the community, and Palm Desert, California, permits their use throughout the town.

LAND-GRANT CITIES IN THE USA

The USA has a long history of making grants of federal land to achieve public policy objectives. The settlement of the US frontier was driven largely by land grants to enterprises that built transcontinental railroads and to families who home-steaded farms in the West. Later, the government granted land to many states for the construction of universities.

The land grant approach could be used to solve a vexing public problem: the shortage of decent low-cost housing. While there is widespread agreement in the USA that more low-cost housing is urgently needed, little is being done to meet this need. Many large-scale public housing projects were constructed in the USA in the postwar era, but this work came to an abrupt halt during the 1970s, following the widespread realization that these projects almost always turned into ghettos that were at least as bad as the substandard housing they had replaced. Since that time, little has been done to preserve and expand the stock of inexpensive housing. The increase in homelessness in the USA was in part caused by the rising cost of housing in relation to income: many individuals and families earning very low wages were simply priced out of the housing market, including even rental units. The New Urbanism proposes the creation of a permanent stock of relatively inexpensive rental units by permitting "granny flats" above garages and encouraging the construction of apartments above retail stores. These approaches are expressly prohibited by most zoning ordinances, but exceptions are now being made in some cities. These measures will help, but the need for affordable housing is larger than these measures are likely to satisfy.

Another problem must be considered: the wealth of many families is largely in the houses they own. Anything that might threaten to diminish the value of suburban real estate is thus a real threat to the welfare of these families and will meet with strong objection. The homeless, on the other hand, are a smaller and less powerful group whose members rarely vote. The construction of land-grant cities, at a distance removed from existing metropolitan areas, offers an opportunity to provide a permanent stock of less expensive housing while avoiding a direct threat to the market value of houses in existing suburban areas.

The USA owns many huge tracts of land and could dedicate a suitable parcel to the development of a carfree city. "Citysteaders" would be granted land in the same way as the homesteaders who pushed the US frontiers west, although these grants would be for small plots instead of the 160 acres (65 hectares) granted homesteading farmers. As with the earlier grants to homesteaders, citysteaders could claim land subject to the condition that they build a house on it and live there for several years in order to validate their claim. The grant conditions would require the construction of a house that fit with the general tone of the city and the district in which it was located. Given the economies of infrastructure development within a dense, compact city, the per-capita infrastructure costs should be considerably below the current norm. Carfree cities also help low-income families by averting the need to own and maintain a car.

It would be possible to combine the land grant approach with the community land trust concept. The rights to speculative gains on the land would be held by a nonprofit corporation. When an owner sold his house, he would not be permitted to realize any gain on the land, which would be valued at zero in perpetuity. Owners would thus be permitted to sell only the improvements they had built on the land. This would create a stock of owner-occupied housing that would remain within means of the working poor.

See page 243 for a discussion of community land trusts.

In any case, such a city would require an economic base. The establishment of a major university, research center, or government data-processing facility could provide a sufficient foundation for the establishment of a city; once it reached a critical size, economic development should continue without outside stimulus. The competitive position of carfree cities should be sufficiently favorable to attract private investment in new enterprises.

Leading by Example

We are confronted with a moral dilemma. The developed nations have no right to deny developing nations the use of the technologies, resources, and patterns of development on which economic life in the developed nations was founded.

In particular, the intensive use of cars in Western nations sets a destructive example for the developing world. It is not realistic to expect that most adults in a world with more than 6 billion inhabitants can own a car and use it routinely.

The developed nations must take the lead in abandoning car use in cities. Once the developing nations see the economic efficiencies of this approach and witness the resulting improvement in the quality of life, these nations should be eager to adopt this approach themselves. No one living in Mexico City needs to be told that air pollution is a serious problem. No one living in São Paulo needs another reminder of the severity of traffic congestion in a large auto-centric city. These societies are merely attempting to imitate what they see as the successes of the rich nations. The sooner the rich nations admit that widespread car ownership is expensive but not an indication of true wealth, the sooner the rest of the world will be ready to consider alternatives.

If car ownership and usage in China rose to American levels, China's oil consumption would rise to 80 million barrels a day, exceeding the current *global* production of 67 million barrels a day.
Press release from the Worldwatch Institute
25 February 1999

Urban Renaissance in North America

In many metropolitan regions in the USA, a new trend is emerging: people want to live in cities again. Demand for housing in cities and older, denser, inner suburbs is increasing. Quite a few people have had enough of sprawl, endless commutes, and places that are not communities at all. The popularity of the New Urbanism is another expression of this desire. People once again want to live in communities that are not arranged solely for the convenience of drivers. That this trend should arise in the USA, that bastion of automobility, indicates that urban car usage is poised to decline.

"Denver Stands Out in Mini-Trend Toward Downtown Living," *New York Times,* 29 December 1998

It is also worth noting that the demographic picture in the USA is changing: there are fewer traditional families and more single-parent families and people living alone. The aging of the baby boomers will give further impetus to this trend. These households are not well served by conventional single-family housing.

Having considered the theoretical and practical aspects of carfree cities, we turn now to one final matter: the importance of creating magical places.

Untere Bahnhofstrasse, Zürich, c.1900

Sundown, Parma, Italy, 1998

AFTERWORD

MAKING MAGIC

Many people have never experienced a magical place, and they are the poorer for it. Most such places are magical only some of the time: they require the right conjunction of light, weather, and congregation to come alive. You can feel it when it happens. The creation of such magic is one of the highest achievements of mankind.

Friends of mine built a gorgeous house high in the hills above Oakland, with a sweeping view of San Francisco Bay. The garden was perfectly integrated with the house, and the whole place was magical at night. It burned in the big fire several years ago. Those who knew the place will never forget it.

Other magical places I have experienced include Venice at almost any time, Stonehenge before the enclosing chain-link fence, the 1964 New York World's Fair at night, punting on the River Cam at Cambridge University, the town of Horta in the Azores at dawn, the seaman's memorial at Halifax, Nova Scotia, emerging out of the night fog, central Paris before it was overrun by cars, much of Bermuda, evenings in the Balinese town of Ubud, summer evenings at Tivoli Gardens in Copenhagen, and Obidos (a fortified mediaeval town in Portugal) at dusk. One thing many of these places have in common is water. Another is that the buildings are old, often really old. Finally, many of these places are at their best in the evening.

Magical places are characterized by human scale, rich detail, beautiful setting, harmonious sounds, and evocative scents. They require an appreciative public to come alive: people involve themselves in the magic, helping to sustain it.

Magic is what Disney tried to create. It's not for nothing that they call it a "magic kingdom." We should take up the creation of magic as a shared civic responsibility. To leave a magical place for future generations is admirable. To do so without thought of profit is noble.

Few of the places we have built in the 20th century are ever magical, and many are downright repulsive. If we bring this magic back into our lives, we will be a happier people. The task lies within our grasp: we need but the will to achieve it. Should this book lead to the genesis of a single magical place, it will have more than repaid the effort of its creation.

Riva degli Schiavoni, Venice, c.1900

Bridge of Sighs, Venice, c.1900

Freiburg, Germany, 1998

APPENDICES

THE BICYCLE CITY

THE AUTO-CENTRIC CARFREE CITY

BIBLIOGRAPHY

ILLUSTRATIONS

INDEX

CONVERSION TABLES

THE AUTHOR

RESOURCES AT CARFREE.COM

Carfree.com home page	http://www.carfree.com/
Carfree Times (bimonthly)	http://www.carfree.com/cft/
City Design	http://www.carfree.com/design/
Discussion Forum	http://www.carfree.com/forum/
Internet Links	http://www.carfree.com/links.html
Spreadsheet (Excel 7)	http://www.carfree.com/calc.html
Metro Operating Costs	http://www.carfree.com/metro.html
The Lyon Protocol	http://www.carfree.com/lyon.html
Cumulated Errata	http://www.carfree.com/errata.html

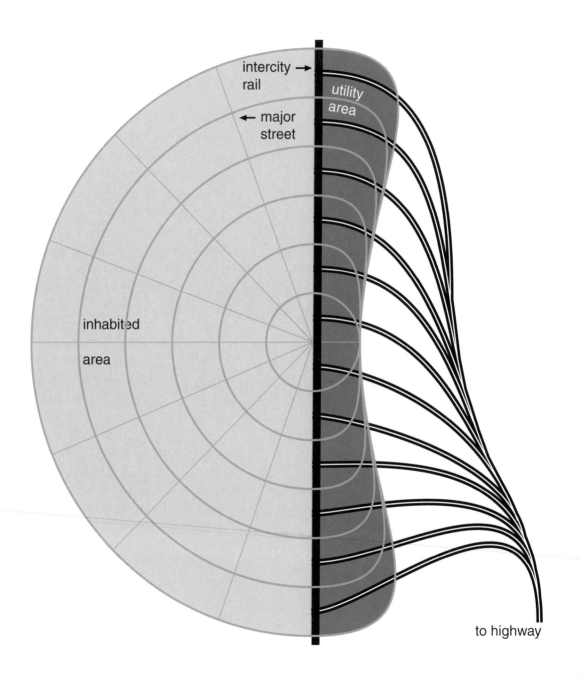

intercity rail →

← major street

utility area

inhabited

area

to highway

THE BICYCLE CITY

The much-touted Segway self-balancing electric scooter is a possible alternative, although it offers no real advantages over the "electric donkey" and costs far more. Both the Segway and the electric donkey must, in any case, be treated as bicycles and kept out of pedestrian areas.

Opposite: It's not my first choice, but I would be happy to live in such a city. The built-up area of the city is about the same as that of the reference design. The radial streets are mainly for pedestrians. The circumferential streets are wider and designed to carry heavy bicycle traffic; they cross over the intercity passenger and rail line, which would run in a cut or tunnel.

A million people live in an area about 10 km north-south and 5 km east-west. East of the vertical line are the utility areas and interfaces to the highway and rail systems.

Small parks would be provided every 500 meters or so, but this design lacks the rapid access to large open green areas such as is provided by the reference design for carfree cities.

Some of my bicycle-advocate friends cannot understand why I lay so much emphasis on rail-based transit (and metros in particular). The reason is simple: not everybody wants to bike everywhere they go. For those who want a city oriented around bicycles, I offer the design opposite.

One could bike across the city in less than an hour. A fit pedestrian could walk from the center of the city to its western edge in an hour. I propose the use what I call "electric donkeys" for those who must travel long distances and are not fit enough to do this using their own strength. Narrow-track tricycles (which are more stable than a bicycle) would be equipped with pedals for power, but a small motor and battery would also be fitted, making it possible for the rider to reach speeds of, say, 12 km/hr under battery power alone, rising to about 20 km/hr with pedal assist. The maximum range of this vehicle need not exceed 20 kilometers (the length of the longest possible round trip within the city). Preliminary calculations indicate that the required battery is half the size of a standard lead-acid car battery.

Most freight would be transshipped in the utility areas to bicycles for final delivery. It would doubtless be necessary to permit a little truck traffic in the inhabited part of the city, but careful design could keep this to a low level; uses with heavy freight requirements would locate in the utility area.

Such a city probably offers the most easily sustained transport arrangement for a million people that can be devised, using as it does principally human energy for transport. The reference design requires more energy for its operation, but the amount is probably comfortably within the limits of renewable supplies that will be developed. I believe that the reference design offers a better quality of life than this design.

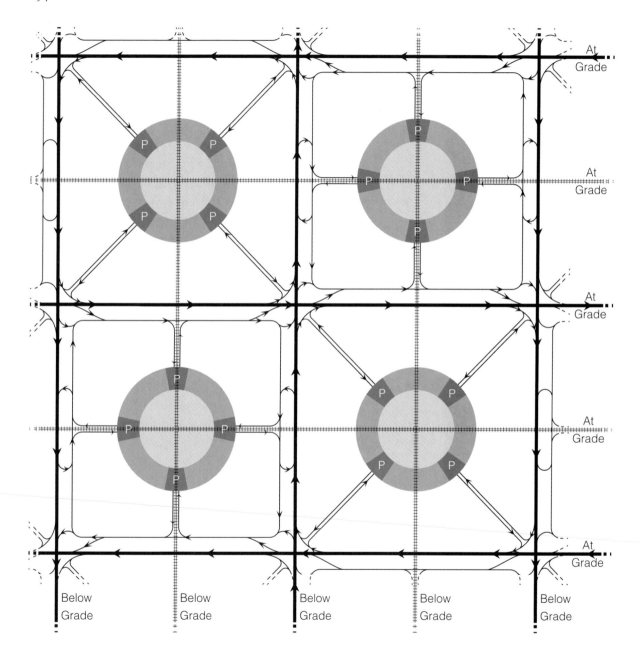

At Grade

At Grade

At Grade

At Grade

At Grade

Below Grade

Below Grade

Below Grade

Below Grade

Below Grade

THE AUTO-CENTRIC CARFREE CITY

Some Americans will expound, "They will take my car from me when they pry my cold, dead hands from the wheel." I have no intention of prying anyone's hands, dead or alive, loose from anything, so I offer this compromise design for a city with a population of one million on a site only a little larger than that proposed in the reference design for carfree cities. The design is, of course, predicated on a solution to the pollution and energy problems that now threaten the continued use of cars in cities. I will not be surprised if the necessary solutions are indeed found.

The principal problem with the existing highway system, from the users' standpoint, is that it routinely subjects them to congestion delays. Nothing much can be done about this because the cost of adding highway capacity has become unthinkable. Simple cloverleaf intersections can be used up to about 3 lanes in each direction. When 4- and 5-lane highways intersect, the usual cloverleaf lacks sufficient capacity to handle the traffic, and it must be replaced by a giant 6-layer intersection that can cost nearly a billion dollars. It has become almost impossible to expand roads beyond about 5 lanes wide in each direction because of the frightful costs.

Highway engineers have always tried to keep the travelling lanes of the two directions as close to each other as possible, and usually they are as close as clearances permit. If, however, we separate the two directions by a distance of 2.4 km, then we can build a city like the one illustrated on the facing page. The freeways can be as wide as necessary, and the cost of the interchanges is very low and little affected by increasing the design capacity. I hope that nobody will ever build such a city, but it would certainly represent an improvement on Los Angeles.

Opposite: Plan of part of a carfree auto-centric city
The design assumes a carfree district based on the reference district. The carfree area is surrounded by a doughnut 220 meters thick (where cars are permitted), giving a total district diameter of 1200 meters. If the population of the carfree heart is 12,000 and the population of the outer district is 8,000, then the total district population is 20,000.

A city of a million people therefore requires about 49 districts arranged in a square 7 by 7. Assuming that the driver can maintain 100 km/hr for the entire distance and that parking takes no time at all, the maximum travel time by car between the centers of the most distant districts is about 34 minutes, including two walks of 7 minutes each between the parking garage and the center of the district. The same journey by metro and tram takes 25 minutes.

Nancy, France, 1997

BIBLIOGRAPHY

PRINT

Alexander, Christopher. *The Timeless Way of Building* (New York: Oxford University Press, 1979). The first book in the long series by Alexander. This one lays out the basic theoretical framework.

Alexander, Christopher *et al. A Pattern Language: Towns, Buildings, Construction* (New York: Oxford University Press, 1977). A ground-breaking work magnificently prepared by Oxford. In my opinion the most important book on architecture and urban design in the 20th century.

Alexander, Christopher *et al. A New Theory of Urban Design* (New York: Oxford University Press, 1987). Describes an organic approach to urban development. A group of Alexander's students redeveloped the area at the foot of the San Francisco Bay Bridge, in maquette. The approach amounts to a return to centuries-old practices of urban development, albeit with a large increase in tempo. These techniques should be applied in the development of city districts, including carfree cities.

Alexander, Christopher *et al. The Production of Houses* (New York: Oxford University Press, 1985). Outlines a method for producing unique houses, designed by their owners, at costs not exceeding those for comparable mass-produced houses.

Appleyard, Donald *et al. Livable Streets* (Berkeley: University of California Press, 1981). This is the definitive work describing the effects of traffic on community life. Essential.

Bacon, Edmund N. *Design of Cities* (New York: Penguin Books, revised edition, 1974). An interesting look at the urban form from ancient to modern times. The drawing of Michelangelo's renovation of the Capitoline Hill is as brilliant as Michelangelo's work on this wonderful square. Deserves a better printing.

Callenbach, Ernst. *Ecotopia: The Notebooks and Reports of William Weston* (Berkeley: Banyan Tree Books, 1975). Utopian fiction.

Calthorpe, Peter. *The Next American Metropolis: Ecology, Community, and the American Dream* (New York: Princeton Architectural Press, 1993). Peter Calthorpe is in the vanguard of the New Urbanism. The book presents both the theory of the New Urbanism and a number of typical projects, most of which have yet to be built.

Page 290

In order to address a criticism made by one reviewer regarding the retouching of the photographs in this book, I have inserted the original scans of the most extensively retouched photographs here. The retouched image can be found on the page given.

Ching, Francis D.K. *Architecture: Form, Space & Order* (New York: Van Nostrand Reinhold, 1979). A beautiful explication of the logic underlying a variety of urban and architectural forms. Beautifully hand-drawn and lettered by Ching himself.

Crawford, J.H. "Carfree Cities: A Blueprint for Sustainability" in *World Architectural Review,* 2000:01 (no. 70).

Durning, Alan Thein. *The Car and the City* (Seattle: Northwest Environment Watch, April 1996). A slim volume that examines the problems caused by urban cars and proposes some solutions.

Fathy, Hassan. *Architecture for the Poor: An Experiment in Rural Egypt* (Chicago: University of Chicago Press, 1973). An excellent account of an attempt, ultimately thwarted by the government that had initiated it, to use traditional forms and methods in developing new communities for Egypt's growing population. The illustrations of the work show the simple brilliance of the indigenous forms and the practicality of mud construction in the desert.

Fouchier, Vincent. "Mesuring [sic] the Density: But Which Density??" paper presented at the Norwegian Ministry of Environment, Workshop on "Density and Green Structure," Oslo, 25-27 January 1996. The density figures given on page 10 of this paper (and cited here on page 36) were taken from *Dense Cité,* M.O.S. and I.N.S.E.E., 1990 or 1995 (dates conflict within the source and may refer to different editions).

Fouchier, Vincent. *Les densités urbaines et le développement durable. Le cas de l'Île-de-France et des villes nouvelles* (Edition du SGVN, Secretariat General du Groupe Central des Ville Nouvelles, 1997). Fouchier has studied density in the Paris region and the relationships among density, transport, and energy use.

Fowler, Edmund P. *Building Cities That Work* (Montreal: McGill-Queen's University Press, 1992). Examines postwar failures in city building and analyzes the problems. Good examination of economic costs in particular.

Freund, Peter and George Martin. *The Ecology of the Automobile* (Montréal: Black Rose Books, 1993). Takes a broad look at the phenomenon of the automobile, including psychological and social factors.

de Geus, Marius. *Ecological Utopias: Envisioning the Sustainable Society* (Utrecht: International Books, 1999). A detailed examination of the history of ecological utopias and their relevance to the modern condition.

Page 109

Page 279

Page 2

Page 43

Goddard, Stephen B. *Getting There: The Epic Struggle between Road and Rail in the American Century* (New York: Basic Books, 1994). An excellent scholarly work, clearly written, describing the death of US rail transit at the hands of the Road Gang. Goddard is a lawyer, so there is some emphasis on legal aspects. Includes an interesting discussion of how the road interests, led by GM, broke the law in their efforts to destroy rail passenger transport and how they in essence got away with it.

Hale, Jonathan. *The Old Way of Seeing: How Architecture Lost Its Magic (And How to Get It Back)* (Boston: Houghton Mifflin Company, 1994). Brilliant if tentative look at how modern civilization lost a gift that was once nearly universal: the ability to design beautiful things. Desperately needs further followup.

Hall, Peter. *Cities of Tomorrow: An Intellectual History of Urban Planning and Design in the Twentieth Century* (Oxford: Blackwell, 1988). The title says it all. A detailed and scholarly examination.

Institute for Community Economics. *The Community Land Trust Handbook* (Emmaus, Pennsylvania: Rodale Press, 1982). The community land trust is a vehicle for preserving open space and providing tax relief to farmers. This book is a complete manual on how to set up a community land trust. Aimed at the USA, but the principles should be applicable elsewhere.

Jacobs, Allan B. *Great Streets* (Cambridge: MIT Press, 1993). A simply marvelous compendium of great streets from around the world. Beautifully illustrated, with dimensions.

Jacobs, Jane. *Cities and the Wealth of Nations: Principles of Economic Life* (New York: Vintage Books, 1985). An interesting look at how city economies drive national economies and why some cities fare better than others.

Jacobs, Jane. *The Death and Life of Great American Cities* (New York: Vintage Books, 1992, first published 1961). A highly critical look at how misguided urban planning destroyed many American city centers in the 1950s. A seminal work.

Jackson, Kenneth T. *Crabgrass Frontier: The Suburbanization of the United States* (New York: Oxford University Press, 1985). Examines the genesis of the modern North American suburb.

Kashin, Seymour and Harre Demoro. *An American Original: The PCC Car* (Glendale, California: Interurban Press, 1986). A mine of information about PCC streetcars, including a vital chapter describing the human factors engineering that went into the design of the PCC car in the 1930s.

Katz, Peter. *The New Urbanism: Toward an Architecture of Community* (New York: McGraw-Hill, 1994). An excellent discussion of the concepts of the new urbanism. A lavish coffee-table book and also a useful source.

Kay, Jane Holtz. *Asphalt Nation: How the Automobile Took Over America and How We Can Take It Back* (New York: Crown Publishers, 1997). Takes a comprehensive look at all the problems caused by automobility in the USA and considers ways to reduce car dependency.

Kostof, Spiro. *The City Shaped: Urban Patterns and Meanings Through History* (London: Thames and Hudson, 1991). The title says it all. This book and its companion (see below) were lavishly and beautifully produced.

Kostof, Spiro. *The City Assembled: The Elements of Urban Form Through History* (London: Thames and Hudson, 1992).

Krier, Léon. *Architecture: Choice or Fate* (Windsor, UK: Andreas Papadakis Publisher, 1998). Wonderful examination of the impact of good urban design and architecture on the public realm, by a great contemporary architect. Krier designed the new town of Poundbury for Prince Charles, which project is also treated.

Krier, Rob. *Urban Space* (New York: Rizzoli, 1979, first published by Academy Editions, London, 1979). A visual encyclopedia of urban forms. Exhaustive, excellent conceptual framework.

Kunstler, James Howard. *The Geography of Nowhere: The Rise and Decline of America's Man-Made Landscape* (New York: Simon & Schuster, 1993). An often-hilarious discussion of the mess that Americans have made out of their everyday environment. Clearly articulates what many Americans are struggling to understand about the terrible degradation of their urban landscapes and the resultant civic dislocation.

Kunstler, James Howard. *Home From Nowhere: Remaking Our Everyday World for the Twenty-First Century* (New York: Simon & Schuster, 1996). Continues the themes of *The Geography of Nowhere,* this time with an emphasis on remedies, particularly the restoration of traditional civic design. Includes entertaining cultural criticism and an assault on the US automobile mania.

Lawson, Alexander. *Anatomy of a Typeface* (London: Hamish Hamilton, 1990). The history of typefaces.

Lowe, Marcia D. "Alternatives to the Automobile: Transport for Livable Cities," Worldwatch Paper 98, October 1990 (Worldwatch Institute).

Page 16

Page 69

Page 58

Page 44

Lowe, Marcia D. "Shaping Cities: The Environmental and Human Dimensions," Worldwatch Paper 105, October 1991 (Worldwatch Institute).

Lowe, Marcia D. "Back on Track: The Global Rail Revival," Worldwatch Paper 118, April 1994 (Worldwatch Institute).

Lynch, Kevin and Gary Hack. *Site Planning* (Cambridge: MIT Press, third edition, 1984). The standard work on site planning. Large, comprehensive, and full of useful numbers. The sorely-needed companion work on urban planning is yet to be written.

McCamant, Kathryn and Charles Durrett. *Cohousing: A Contemporary Approach to Housing Ourselves* (Berkeley: Habitat Press, 1988). The best source book I know of on the subject of cohousing, an arrangement that lies between private dwellings and communal life. Each family has its own private space but the community has common spaces, usually including a kitchen and dining room where meals are taken together regularly. Not intrinsically carfree but amenable to greatly reduced car usage. Includes case examples and plans.

McShane, Clay. *Down the Asphalt Path: The Automobile and the American City* (New York: Columbia University Press, 1994). The automobile was initially rejected when it first appeared, but by 1910 the world was ready to accept it, warts and all. Explains how this happened. Complements Goddard's book.

Moe, Richard & Carter Wilkie. *Changing Places: Rebuilding Community in the Age of Sprawl* (New York: Henry Holt and Company, 1997). Considers why historic preservation has become such a hot issue, now that most great urban landscapes in the USA have been destroyed.

Newman, Peter and Jeffrey Kenworthy. *Sustainability and Cities: Overcoming Automobile Dependence* (Washington: Island Press, 1999). Dense source book, full of tables and graphs. Essential for serious students.

Pucher, John and Christian Lefèvre. *The Urban Transport Crisis in Europe and North America* (London: Macmillan, 1996). A largely statistical analysis of transport issues, especially with respect to cars. Dry but useful.

Rabinovitch, Jonas and Josef Leitman. "Urban Planning in Curitiba" in *Scientific American,* vol. 274 no. 3 (March 1996). An interesting article about a cheaper means of achieving some of the carfree design goals. The Curitiba approach has allowed urban buses to function quite well. The basic city structure is generally compatible with the proposals made here, although Curitiba is by no means carfree.

Register, Richard. *Ecocity Berkeley: Building Cities for a Healthy Future* (Berkeley: North Atlantic Books, 1987). Imaginative musings on approaches to building an ecologically-balanced pattern of habitation in Berkeley.

Reid, Richard. *The Book of Buildings: Ancient, Medieval, Renaissance & Modern Architecture of North America & Europe* (New York: Van Nostrand Reinhold Company, 1983). An excellent summary of the Occidental architectural heritage and a fine source of ideas.

Richards, Brian. *New Movement in Cities* (London: Studio Vista, second edition, 1969). I found Richards' book late in the writing of this book. Richards developed some ideas that point the way toward the carfree city, although it was not his intention that these ideas would lead to carfree cities.

Rogers, Richard. *Cities for a Small Planet* (London: Faber & Faber, 1997). While I do not myself usually like his architecture, Lord Rogers has a passionate affair with the city and understands the terrible harm that has been wrought by cars.

Safdie, Moshe with Wendy Kohn. *The City After the Automobile: An Architect's Vision* (Basic Books, 1997). Safdie's vision of cities of the future is technologically centered and does not seem very workable. The ideas are interesting, however.

Schaeffer, K.H. & Elliot Sclar. *Access for All: Transportation and Urban Growth* (New York: Columbia University Press, 1980). The evolution of cities under the influence of transport innovations. Focuses on Boston.

Scientific American, "Special Report: Preventing the Next Oil Crunch," March 1998.

Scientific American, "The Future of Transportation" (Special Issue), October 1997. Includes articles on the technical future of cars.

Sitte, Camillo. *City Planning According to Artistic Principles* (New York: Random House, 1965; first edition [German]: Vienna, 1889. Translated by George R. Collins and Christiane Crasemann Collins). Hard to find and expensive, but a gold mine. Full of drawings and fascinating explanations of why some urban areas are attractive and others are not. Most of the places that Sitte criticized little more than a century ago are today regarded as architectural treasures. It's not that these old areas have improved, it's that the newer areas are so much worse. Essential.

Page 233

Page 119

Page 170

Page 166

Southworth, Michael & Eran Ben-Joseph. *Streets and the Shaping of Towns and Cities* (New York: McGraw-Hill, 1997). Includes a historical review.

Taylor, John S. *Commonsense Architecture: A Cross-Cultural Survey of Practical Design Principles* (New York: W.W. Norton & Company, 1983). A handwritten and illustrated book depicting hundreds of traditional patterns of building that have met particular needs around the world. An excellent source of ideas.

Van der Ryn, Sim and Peter Calthorpe. *Sustainable Communities: A New Design Synthesis for Cities, Suburbs, and Towns* (San Francisco: Sierra Club Books, 1986). An early work in the sustainable development effort.

Venice (New York: Alfred A. Knopf, Inc., frequently revised). Probably the best modern guide to Venice.

Venice & the Veneto (London: Dorling Kindersley, frequently revised). A worthwhile adjunct to the Knopf guide.

Vermeer, Bram. "Zachtjes sporen," *NRC Handelsblad,* 20 December 1997. Reports on the application of a thin layer of cobalt to train wheels. The cobalt apparently preserves the perfect roundness of the wheels and greatly reduces train noise.

Warren, Roxanne, *The Urban Oasis: Guideways and Greenways in the Human Environment* (New York: McGraw-Hill, 1998). Discusses the application of Personal Rapid Transit to urban areas and the implications this technology has for urban development. Like many recent hardcover books from McGraw-Hill, this one is not properly bound and does not fully open.

Whyte, William H. *City: Rediscovering the Center* (New York: Anchor Books, 1988). Whyte, a long-time observer of New York life, offers a rich lode.

Williams, Heathcote. *Autogeddon* (New York: Arcade Publishing, [n.d., probably 1991]). Excellent and appalling look at the ravages of cars.

Wolfe, Tom. *From Bauhaus to Our House* (New York: Farrar Straus Giroux, 1981). Tom Wolfe at his best as he deftly skewers Modern architecture in just 143 pages.

Zielinski, Sue & Gordon Laird, eds. *Beyond the Car: Essays on the Auto Culture* (Toronto: Steel Rail Publishing/Transportation Options, 1995).

Zuckermann, Wolfgang. *End of the Road* (Post Mills, Vermont: Chelsea Green Publishing Company, 1991). Thorough review of techniques for taming cars; considers unintended side effects.

Internet Resources

It is still risky to cite sources on the Internet because they may disappear or be relocated. URLs were current at press time. Carfree.com maintains a list of about 300 links, sorted by category.

http://www.vtpi.org/	Victoria Transport Policy Institute, an independent research organization
http://www.rudi.net/	RUDI (Resource for Urban Design Information.)
http://www.pps.org/	Project for Public Spaces
http://www.eyfa.org/	European Youth for Action works to reduce the burden of traffic in Europe.
http://www.intbau.org/	International Network for Traditional Building, Architecture & Urbanism
http://www.terrain.org/	Terrain: A Journal of the Built & Natural Environments
http://fcn.state.fl.us/fdi/	E-Design on-line provides information on sustainable development.
http://www.carfree.com/	Carfree.com
http://www.flora.org/afo/	Auto-Free Ottawa works to tame the urban automobile in Ottawa
http://www.ecoplan.org/	EcoPlan International hosts The Commons, a sustainability workgroup
http://www.transact.org/	Transportation Action Network publishes the Mean Streets report annually
http://www.kunstler.com/	James Howard Kunstler writes extensively about the New Urbanism
http://www.cyburbia.org/	Cyburbia: The Planning and Architecture Internet Resource Center
http://www.clix.to/katarxis/	Katarxis: On Contemporary Traditional Architecture and Urbanism
http://www.living-room.org/	The Living Room includes sprawl- and environment-related sections
http://www.worldwatch.org/	Worldwatch Institute is concerned about the global ecology
http://www.jhcrawford.com/	The home page of author J.H. Crawford
http://www.web.net/~detour/	Detour is a site established by pro-bike, anti-car organizations in Toronto.
http://www.newcolonist.com/	The New Colonist
http://www.preservenet.com/	The Preservation Institute works to stop sprawl and build ecological cities
http://www.xs4all.nl/~rigolett/	The Car-Free Society
http://www.fhwa.dot.gov/tcsp/	Transportation and Community and System Preservation Pilot Program
http://www.plannersweb.com/	Planning Commissioners Journal
http://www.carbusters.ecn.cz/	Car Busters
http://wwwistp.murdoch.edu.au/	The Institute for Science and Technology Policy (ISTP)
http://www.sierraclub.org/sprawl/	Highway and Sprawlbusters at the Sierra Club
http://www.access-eurocities.org/	Eurocities for a new mobility culture
http://www.railway-technology.com/	Railway Technology offers extensive data on railroading

ILLUSTRATIONS

Drawings

Arin Verner executed my crude sketches in Adobe Illustrator 8.0. I drew the reference topology myself, a task requiring no great skill with Illustrator but considerable patience. This drawing should repay study with a magnifying glass.

All drawings ©1996-2000 J. Crawford except as otherwise noted.

Pg.   Drawing

36   Floor Area Ratio (FAR)
55   Walking city, schematic
56   Railroad suburbs, schematic
57   Streetcar suburb, schematic
60   Auto-centric suburb, schematic
80   Hubbert curve
110   Tamarack   ©1997 Ken Avidor
130   Reference topology
131   Detail of the downtown area
132   Topology superimposed on Amsterdam
135   Topology unaffected by deformation
136   Alternative lobe design
137   City of 400,000
137   City of 4,000,000
137   Topology for a mega-city
138   Agglomeration of 6,000,000
138   Denser topology
139   Topology with spacing
142   Reference district
143   Detail of reference district
144   District with wrinkled edges
145   Radial district
146   Amsterdam, New York, Venice & Carfree compared
148   District with organic streets
149   Smaller district
150   Larger district
150   Denser district
151   Francesco di Giorgio Martini district
152   Reference block
153   Small neighborhood square
156   Arab-style family compounds
160   Street cross-sections
171   House plots
172   Boulevard cross-sections
173   Rail station & metro lines
176   Boulevard arrangement
176   Divided boulevard for trams

181   Four-track metro lines in downtown
182   Metro platform arrangement
191   Connections to external rail & highway network
194   Metro-freight arrangement
195   Detail of metro-freighter
200   Building profiles, downtown
201   Metro-freight right-of-way
214   Utility area
219   Road and rail connections
251   Ecocity Berkeley   ©1993 Richard Register
261   Carfree Two Harbors, Calif.   ©2000 Michael E. Arth
264   Peripheral parking
266   Satellite districts
268   Lyon, France, redeveloped as a carfree city
270   Amsterdam redeveloped as a carfree city
272   Midtown Manhattan redeveloped as a carfree city
274   Part of Los Angeles redeveloped as a carfree city
276   Mid-street infill housing for auto-centric cities
280   EuroCity in the Markermeer, Netherlands
292   The bicycle city
294   The auto-centric carfree city
Back cover: reference topology

Historical Photographs

The historical photographs were scanned from postcards and similar materials printed around 1900. The quality of some of these images is breathtaking, and the reproduction is exceptional by any standard. In no case is the photographer known. Damage to postcards was usually repaired. In some cases, spotting was de-emphasized by color filtration. Some of these images are slightly cropped for various reasons of convenience.

Photographs have been retouched almost from the beginning of photography, and many of the postcards were extensively re-touched when they were produced. In those days, it was difficult to photograph clouds, and skies were often added artificially, even painted in. It was also not terribly unusual to add figures to a scene, and I have even seen a small ship added to a scene. Some of this retouching is so artless that it is blatantly obvious even to casual observation.

Contemporary Photographs

The photographs of Venice were all taken during the week of Carnival, between 8 and 15 February 1997. With few exceptions, my photographs are reproduced from the entire full-frame scan.

Richard Risemberg and his son Jack, natives of Los Angeles, photographed their home town in the summer of 1999. Richard used a digital Olympus C2000Z, while Jack shot with a Canon Tele-Wide and Fuji Superia 200 film. My thanks to them and others who contributed photographs.

We have exercised restraint in retouching images. A total of three cars in two of my images were removed from places they did not normally belong. Carnival involves the liberal use of confetti, which has generally been removed from the photographs of Venice, along with litter in other places that are usually tidy. The raw scans from which the more extensively retouched images were derived are printed in the margins of the Bibliography. No other images were retouched as much as these examples. Arin Verner executed the seamless retouching in Photoshop 4 and 5. With a few slight exceptions, we respected the original croppings of other photographers.

Technical Notes

Two Nikon F3HP cameras and four wide-angle Nikkor lenses were used: 35mm $f2$, 28mm $f2$, 24mm $f2.8$, and 20mm $f2.8$. The 20mm was used for the lion's share of the work, especially after 1997. These lenses exhibit the slight barrel distortion characteristic of retrofocus wide-angle lenses designed for SLRs. This equipment has served me faithfully since 1986.

I used Kodak color negative film until I learned that expensive drum scanning is required for some 35mm color negatives. I have had no further trouble since switching to Kodak Ektachrome.

Pg.	Title	Copyright
2	Venice, Italy	©1997 J. Crawford
16	Venice	©1997 J. Crawford
17	Venice from the Campanile	©1997 J. Crawford
18	Village near Avignon	1965 J. Crawford
18	Campo, Siena, Italy	©1998 J. Crawford
19	Besakih Temple, Bali	©1985 J. Crawford
20	Certaldo Alto, Italy	©1998 J. Crawford
20	Summer, Amsterdam	©1998 J. Crawford
21	Piazza San Marco, Venice	©1997 J. Crawford
22	Hanging out, Amsterdam	©1999 J. Crawford
23	Human scale, Siena	©1999 J. Crawford
24	Zermatt, Switzerland	©1998 J. Crawford
25	Suburban neighborhd, LA	©1999 Richard Risemberg
26	Venice at night	©1997 J. Crawford
28	Smoggy Los Angeles	©1999 Richard Risemberg
29	Strip mall, LA	©1999 Richard Risemberg
30	Rialto market, Venice	©1997 J. Crawford
31	The Rokin then, Amsterdam	c.1900 anon
31	The Rokin now, A'dam	©1999 J. Crawford
32	Begijnhof, A'dam	©1997 J. Crawford
33	Brig, Switzerland	©1998 J. Crawford
34	Boat boys, Venice	©1997 J. Crawford
35	Supermarket parking, LA	©1999 Richard Risemberg
37	Bronze yardsticks	©1997 J. Crawford
37	Fine public amenities	©1998 J. Crawford
38	Near the Torre dell'Orologio	©1997 J. Crawford
38	Strip mall, LA	©1999 Richard Risemberg
42	No place to play, LA	©1999 Richard Risemberg
42	C. Santa Maria Formosa	©1997 J. Crawford
43	The Beverly Center, LA	©1999 Richard Risemberg
43	Street musician, Venice	©1997 J. Crawford
44	Strip mall sign, LA	©1999 Richard Risemberg
44	C. Santa Maria Formosa	©1997 J. Crawford
45	Somewhere, LA	©1999 Richard Risemberg
45	Rialto sunset, Venice	©1997 J. Crawford
46	Double jam, LA	©1999 Richard Risemberg
46	Accelerata, Venice	©1997 J. Crawford
47	Trucks, LA	©1999 Richard Risemberg
47	Freight at Rialto	©1997 J. Crawford
48	City Hall, LA	©1999 Jack Risemberg
48	Doge's Palace, Venice	©1997 J. Crawford
49	Oriental Mission Church, LA	©1999 Richard Risemberg
49	Church, Venice	©1997 J. Crawford
50	Apartment garages & cars	©1999 Richard Risemberg
50	Housing, Venice	©1997 J. Crawford
51	Bulk food store, LA	©1999 Richard Risemberg
51	Grocer & newsagent, Venice	©1997 J. Crawford
53	Smart, A'dam	©1999 J. Crawford
53	Montmartre, Paris	c.1900 anon
54	Amsterdam Stock Exchange	c.1900 anon
54	San Francisco, California	c.1900 anon
56	Old Nancy, France	©1997 J. Crawford
57	Brill Bullet triple, 4 Nov. 1977	©1977 Mike Szilagyi
58	New York skyscrapers	©1999 J. Crawford
60	Smog over Phoenix	©1983 Jean-Paul Bardou
61	Snout house, LA	©1999 Richard Risemberg
63	Strip mall, LA	©1999 Richard Risemberg
63	Miniature gated community	©1999 Richard Risemberg
64	Big box store	©1999 Richard Risemberg
65	Cars in Bologna, Italy	©1998 J. Crawford
69	Mating SUVs	©1998 J. Crawford
70	Canal District, Amsterdam	©1999 J. Crawford
72	Bald street, Bologna	©1998 J. Crawford
72	Café in Siena	©1998 J. Crawford
74	Nancy, France	©1997 J. Crawford
75	Freeway interchange, LA	©1999 Richard Risemberg
76	Parking garage, LA	©1999 Jack Risemberg
84	Depressed freeway, LA	©1999 Jack Risemberg
85	New metro line, Lisbon	©1999 J. Crawford
93	Grade separation, Venice	©1997 J. Crawford
93	The El in the Bronx	©1999 J. Crawford
95	EuroTram, Strasbourg	©1997 J. Crawford

97 Steamboat, Stockholm ©1985 J. Crawford
97 EuroTram, Strasbourg ©1997 J. Crawford
98 Tiled metro station, Lisbon ©1999 J. Crawford
100 Double-deckers of the NS ©1998 J. Crawford
102 People mover, Newark, NJ ©1999 J. Crawford
103 Urban room, Strasbourg ©1997 J. Crawford
106 Freight scows, Venice ©1997 J. Crawford
106 NJ Transit PCC streetcar ©1999 J. Crawford
108 Manarola, Italy ©1998 J. Crawford
109 Leiden, NL ©1998 J. Crawford
114 Old & new windmills ©1997 J. Crawford
119 Sunset, Siena ©1998 J. Crawford
121 Lago di Como-Bellagio c.1900 anon
122 Campo San Bartolomeo ©1997 J. Crawford
124 Zeitglockenthurm, Bern c.1900 anon
125 Wharf & business, Venice ©1997 J. Crawford
126 Gondolas, San Marco ©1997 J. Crawford
126 Family bakery, Manhattan ©1999 J. Crawford
127 Urban park, Nancy, France ©1997 J. Crawford
128 Freight handling, Venice ©1997 J. Crawford
129 Frankfurt am Main, Germany c.1900 anon
133 Park, Siena ©1998 J. Crawford
139 Duplex house, Montréal ©1999 Louis-Luc Le Guerrier
141 Grote Markt, Groningen c.1900 anon
148 Mixed-use street, Venice ©1997 J. Crawford
155 Carfree street, A'dam ©1999 J. Crawford
155 City Museum, A'dam ©1998 J. Crawford
157 Burano, Venice ©1997 J. Crawford
157 Mixed uses, Venice ©1997 J. Crawford
158 Residential street, Parma ©1998 J. Crawford
158 Ramo San Zulian, Venice ©1997 J. Crawford
158 Tiny courtyard, Bologna ©1998 J. Crawford
159 Sottoportego, Venice ©1997 J. Crawford
159 Main street, Siena ©1998 J. Crawford
161 Freiburg, Germany ©1998 J. Crawford
162 Commerzbank, A'dam ©1999 J. Crawford
163 Bijlmer district, A'dam ©1999 J. Crawford
164 Closer living, Burano ©1997 J. Crawford
165 4-Story buildings, A'dam ©1999 J. Crawford
166 Connected buildings, Nancy ©1997 J. Crawford
168 Major street, Siena ©1998 J. Crawford
168 Stores, Venice ©1997 J. Crawford
169 Rooftop balconies, Bologna ©1998 J. Crawford
170 Narrow buildings, A'dam ©1999 J. Crawford
175 Bikes, A'dam Central Station ©1999 J. Crawford
179 IRT subway entrance, NYC ©1999 J. Crawford
183 Fast tram, A'dam ©1999 J. Crawford
184 Tram platforms, Strasbourg ©1997 J. Crawford
189 Electric taxi, Zermatt, Switz. ©1998 J. Crawford
193 Parking garage, A'dam ©1999 J. Crawford
196 Freight delivery, Venice ©1997 J. Crawford
197 Container port, Vancouver ©1999 John Madden
206 Electric postal wagon, Brig ©1998 J. Crawford
208 Freight bicycles, A'dam ©1999 J. Crawford
209 Postal pushcart, Brig, Switz. ©1998 J. Crawford
210 Electric utility vehicle ©1999 J. Crawford
213 Garbage scow, Venice ©1997 J. Crawford
221 Prague c.1900 anon
222 Campo San Vitale, Venice ©1997 J. Crawford
224 San Marco, Venice ©1997 J. Crawford
225 Carfree area, Freiburg ©1998 J. Crawford
226 Yosemite Valley, California c.1987 J. Crawford
227 Bairro Alto, Lisbon ©1999 J. Crawford
231 Package express boat ©1999 J. Crawford
233 Grote Markt, Groningen, NL ©1997 J. Crawford
234 Westerpark project, A'dam ©1998 J. Crawford
234 Kärnthnerring, Vienna c.1900 anon
236 Iriya District, Tokyo ©1998 R.W. Hollier
238 Parking lot, Houten, NL ©1997 J. Crawford
242 Montezuma Hills, California c.1988 J. Crawford
246 Schuhgasse, Hildesheim c.1900 anon
247 Prototype maquette ©1997 J. Crawford
248 Arcosanti in New Mexico ©1989 J. Crawford
249 High-rise, Bijlmer, A'dam ©1999 J. Crawford
250 Early morning, Siena ©1998 J. Crawford
253 Four-story buildings, A'dam ©1999 J. Crawford
255 Central square, Houten, NL ©1998 J. Crawford
255 Arcades, Bologna ©1998 J. Crawford
260 Giudecca, Venice ©1997 J. Crawford
262 Square in Venice ©1997 J. Crawford
263 Hand truck delivery, Venice ©1997 J. Crawford
267 Square with Cars, Bologna ©1998 J. Crawford
269 Premier arrondisement, Lyon 1999 Randy Ghent
271 Leidseplein, A'dam ©1999 J. Crawford
273 Washington Square North ©1999 J. Crawford
275 Downtown LA in smog ©1999 Richard Risemberg
278 Chiesa di S. Pietro, Genoa c.1900 anon
279 Cloaked horde, Venice ©1997 J. Crawford
286 Untere Bahnhofstrasse, Zür. c.1900 anon
287 Sundown, Parma, Italy ©1998 J. Crawford
288 Riva degli Schiavoni, Venice c.1900 anon
289 Bridge of Sighs, Venice c.1900 anon
290 Freiburg, Germany ©1998 J. Crawford
296 Nancy, France ©1997 J. Crawford
297 and following: see first appearance for copyright data
308 Florence, Italy c.1900 anon
322 Zadelstraat, Utrecht c.1900 anon
Front cover: Sundown, Parma ©1998 J. Crawford

Florence, c.1900

INDEX

A

Acceleration
  limitations on 177
  need for high rates of 94
Access
  emergency, in carfree cities 150
  for persons with disabilities 46
Access, handicapped 174
Activism
  carfree 232
  effectiveness of 232
Administration, democratic 261
Agee, James 57
Agriculture 12
  locations for 110
  use of energy in 117
Airport 192
Alexander, Christopher 19, 32, 168,
      250–251, 253, 255–258
  connected buildings 167
  four-story buildings 165
Amenity, public 38, 49
American Renaissance 7
Amsterdam 15, 20, 74, 271
  as the Venice of the North 70
  cars in 66
  downtown 271
  increase in geographic extent of 271
  metro 271
  moving house in 212
  problems with public transport in 96,
      105, 280
  small houses in 231
  trams 92, 271
  use of hoisting beams in 170
  Westerpark carfree development 234
Animal, draft 56, 59
Appleyard, Donald 72
Apprentice system, disappearance of 163
Arcade 255
Architecture
  domestic, effects of transport on 50
  effects of cars on 51
  modern 259
  monumental 48
  rich detail in 49
  throwaway 7
Arcology 248
Arcosanti 248

Area
  carfree
    attraction of 225
    design of 251
    merchant resistance to 233
    prototypes 234
    success of existing 233
  floor
    per-capita requirements 248
  gross floor
    defined 154
  land
    consumed by transport 39
    of carfree cities 133
  open
    See Park
  rural 19
    proximity to carfree cities 229
  urban
    converting to open space uses 275
    evolution of 250
Arizona 244
Arth, Michael E. 261
Artisan, importance of 163
Atlanta 78
Auction, countdown, described 190
Australia 65
Automobile
  See Car
Automobility
  costs of 227
  failure of for urban transport 28, 75
Autophilia 227
Avidor, Ken & Roberta 110

B

Baby strollers 184
Baggage 218
Bakfiets, illustrated 208
Bali 288
Bangkok 64, 89
Barge 273
BART 56, 89, 98, 177
  and land use 56
Basement, delivery of freight into 199
Battle of Seattle 23
Beauty 28, 48, 127
  absence of in auto-centric cities 40, 44

  importance of 20, 288
Behavior, effects of driving on 71
Beijing 255
Berkeley 56
Berkeley, California 31
Bicycle
  aboard trams 184
  and danger from cars 42
  craze 59
  delivery 208
  design priority for 174
  free 217
  freight 208
    use of to move house 212
  in carfree cities 135
  problems associated with 175
  space provided for 140
  speed restrictions on 175
  use of central boulevard by 176
Bicycling
  problems associated with 109
Bicycling, and the Dutch 271
Bicyclist
  reckless behavior by 176
Biomass, conversion of to energy 114
Block
  based on grid pattern 153
  in carfree cities 153
    limiting size of 156
    small 156
  number of in carfree districts 154
  reference 154
  size of 154
Block, advantage of short 155
Boarding, roll-on 209
Bologna, Italy, squares in 267
Bonds, municipal, value of in sprawl
      townships 277
Boston 22, 55, 58, 106, 263
  Central Artery project 39
  irregular streets in 153
  MBTA 92
Boulevard 147
  central 158
    bicycle traffic signals 176
    separation of 260
    split if trams used 260
Braking, regenerative 107
Brasília 238, 240
Bridge 46–47

Brig, Switzerland 206
Brill Bullets 57
Bronx, New York City 59
Brooklyn 59
Brownfield site, redevelopment of 276
Brussels 280
Building
    admitting light into 168
    attractiveness of old 288
    classical style 161
    connected 166
        and reference design 256
    depth of
        limitations on 167
    depths of 161, 168
    design of in carfree cities 161
    design requirements for 165
    economical design & construction 162
    enclosures created by 159
    energy consumption of
        effects of shared walls 118
    facade 44
    featureless 51
    four-story 165
        and elevators 166
    free-standing 167
    height
        limitations on 32, 161
    height of 38, 161
    joined 162
    low-rise
        replacement of with four-story 276
    mass-produced 162
    mid-rise 253
    multifamily 169
    multistory 118
    narrow frontage of 161, 169
    need for deeper 168
    postwar
        monotony of 163–164
    reference design
        absence of explained 165
    small 51, 169, 255
        advantages of 161
    styles of
        homogeneity 150
    tall 32, 58
        effects of on mental health 165
    unique 163
        importance of 161
        production of 164
    use of several by larger businesses 162

    variations on standard 170
    vernacular style of 162
Building footprint 144
    of reference block 155
    See also Plot ratio
Burano 27
    FAR of 157
Bus 46
    application of in carfree cities 179, 185
    as principal public transport mode in
            Los Angeles 275
    capacity of 186
    crosstown lines
        in New York City 273
    diesel-powered 185
    disadvantages of in carfree cities 185
    electric trolley
        advantages of 185
    improvements to 101
    intercity
        in carfree cities 192
    limitations of 105
    low quality of service by 100
    operating costs of 186
    pollution from 185
    speed of 185
    trolley 185, 188
    urban
        unprofitability of 88
    weather-related delays of 181
Business, streetfront 45

                              C

Calcutta 236
California, wind energy production in 114
Canada 65
Canal 47, 50, 271
    barge 54
Canberra 238–239
Capacity
    effects of reduction on congestion 77
    highway
        costs of expanding 295
Car
    accommodation of in cities 8
    as cause of social isolation 45
    as democratic instrument 14
    as means of urban mobility 39
    as symbol of success 227
    automated 83

    city 53
    computer guided 83
    cost of operating 81, 284
    damage to communities 72
    danger to pedestrians from 71
    death and injury caused by 40, 70
    demands of on commerce 44
    disposal of when scrapped 79
    driver behavior 71
    early adoption of 87
    effect of on cities 24, 64
    effect of on quality of public spaces 25
    effect of on social systems 72
    effect of on street life 43
    effect of on urban mobility 18
    insurance 40
    intrusion of 59
    loading personal freight into 219
    need for in rural areas 70
    parking for in carfree cities 193
    police 175
    power imbalance 71
    problems caused by 18
    problems with early models 75
    raw materials consumed in construction
            of 79
    requirements of 53
    size of world fleet 80
    space required by 24, 56, 65
    steam-powered 59
    subsidy of 14
    technical improvements to 29
    urban
        defined 69
Carbon dioxide
    effects of biomass combustion on
            atmospheric levels of 115
    emission of 110
    emission of by cars 79
Carfree Two Harbors project 261
Cargo
    bulk 47, 217
    handling of bulk 198
    See also Freight
Carjacking 98
Car-sharing 193
Cart 218
    design of 209
    electric 210
    use of aboard trains 100
Catalina Island, California 261
Cathedral 48

Center, of a community 57
Century Freeway, Los Angeles 77
Chandigarh 238–240
Change, inevitability of 10
Charette
  design 245
Charette, defined 245
Charleston, South Carolina 171
Chicago 64
Children
  freedom of to explore 40
  mobility of by bicycle 42
China
  adoption of cars in 66
  levels of car use in 285
  shortage of arable land in 237
  urban migration in 237
Church 49
  as organizational force 44
City
  as cradle of civilization 21
  as host for community 23
  as host for culture 21
  as setting for economic activity 21
  auto-centric
    buildings in 64
    compared to carfree 41
    comparison of to carfree 248
    contemporary form of 53
    contraction of 275
    conversion of to carfree 244, 247
    defined 22
    dispersed form of 55
    Los Angeles as archetype 275
    public buildings in 49
    redevelopment of as carfree 31, 279
    sustainability of 109
  carfree
    and links to external transport 219
    auto-centric 295
    bicycle-centric 293
    broad-based planning of 244
    building support for 225
    compromise with 32, 295
    data collection for conversion to 245
    demonstrating livability of 262
    design details to be addressed 247
    development of in southern and
      southwestern USA 282
    development of preliminary concept
      for 245
    difficulty of redeveloping auto-centric

  cities as 275
  economic base for 284
  economic efficiency of 284–285
  existing city-centers in Europe 233
  feasibility of 125
  funding of research and
    development for 244
  human density of 31, 138, 229
  importance of good planning in 227
  land speculation in 243
  large 137
  locations for new 279
  locations for prototypes 263
  lower density 139
  need for broad support 227
  need for early action in West 227
  need for early development of 279
  need for enabling legislation 242
  need for full-scale prototype 280
  need for local autonomy 242
  opposition to 32, 226
  planning of 247
  planning techniques for 251
  policy support for 242
  practicality of 226
  progress towards 232
  prototype 247, 261, 280
  prototype district with peripheral
    parking 263
  prototype districts connected to
    existing city center 264
  prototype districts with trams 264
  prototype lobe 265
  redevelopment of existing 267
  redevelopment of existing cities 279
  reference design 32
  regulation of traffic in 242
  rejection of by some 226
  separation of uses in 229
  sites for full-scale prototype 265
  size of prototype neighborhood 263
  size of site required for 265
  small 137
  sources of funding for 279
  sponsors for 279
  sudden emergence of need for 279
  sustainability of 119
  trucks in 196
  very low density 139
centers
  roads through 8
compact

  and lower energy consumption 118
  cultural institutions in 120
  demolition of existing 267
  energy consumption in 109, 117
  evacuation of 189
  existing, redevelopment of as carfree
    267, 279
  exodus from 9
  in colonial times 55
  land-grant, in USA 282–283
  medieval 53
  new
    economic basis for 241
    importance of being true city 241
    need for 238
    possible locations for 241
    precedents for 238
  overcrowding of 228
  polycentric 257
  resources consumed by 109
  Roman 248
  social resources in 120
  sustainable 18, 109
  taxes 61
  traditional, mixed uses in 149
  USA, contemporary 63
  walkable 55
City Beautiful 7–9, 239
City Hall 48
Citysteader 283
Cleveland 11, 55
Climate change
  anthropogenic 110
  See also Global warming
Cohousing, defined 156
Community 17
  abandonment of 63
  development of 10
  gated 63
  healthy, signs of 73
  identifiable boundaries of 144
  small 253
    governance of 253
Community land trust 243, 284
Computer simulation of travel patterns 177
Concrete, delivery of 212
Congestion
  effects of motorized transport on 228
  effects of on public transport 86
  highway 77
  traffic
    effects of trucks on 47

in auto-centric cities 64, 285, 295
in pre-automobile cities 56
psychological effects of 13
urban 9
Construction, cost of 127
Container
standardized shipping 25, 47
advantages of 197, 231
and overland transport 198
automated handling of 197
empties 213
global standards for 198
objections to use of 231
storage of 213
use of as warehouse 216
Copenhagen 74
Corbusier, Le 30
and Chandigarh 239
and FAR 249
and mechanistic urban design 250
and underestimate of space required by
cars 240
attitudes towards public by 249
deliberate segregation of populations
by 240
demolition of cities proposed by 249
demolition of urban projects based on
thinking of 250
disregard for climatic conditions by 240
errors by in estimating garage
requirements 249
influence of on Bijlmer district 249
Cost
capital, of rail 81
car
borne by drivers 81
operating 81
external
defined 40
of energy production 114
externalized 105, 111
of cars 81
infrastructure 61
non-monetary, accounting for 111
operating, of rail 81
Courtyard
interior 50, 150, 158, 276
allocation of space in 159
size of 154
Crane 212
yard 216
and intermodal terminals 215

automation of 216
Crime, increases in street 99
Crisis
banking 276
environmental, and carfree cities 226
Critical Mass 232
Cuba 233
reduction of petroleum imports in 235
Cul-de-sac 61
Curitiba, Brazil 101, 173, 185, 209
Curtains, for privacy 262

D

Demolition of cities 55
Denmark 97, 280
Density
calculation of 248
gradient 159
in carfree cities 266
human 13, 53, 56, 149
achieving increases in 276
advantages of higher 140
carfree cities with lower 266
challenges of increasing 164
declines in 64
favorable effects of high levels on
social life 282
high 26, 262, 282
in Los Angeles 45
in Lyon, France 269
in reference design 229
need for increase in 275
reduced energy consumption 117
suburban 61
of construction 136
Depot
district freight 199
rental of carts at 209
Design
goal 126
parameter 125
reference
alterations to 125
and positive outdoor space 256
and small communities 253
compromises with 247, 265
defined 27, 123
deviation from 123
effects of geography on 136
standards for 126

Design, urban
See Planning, urban
Detail, importance of in buildings 288
Detroit 11
Developer, real estate, subsidy of 88
Development
linear 57
mixed use 60
sustainable 280
Diaspora, human 120
Dilemma, moral 284
Disincentive, establishment of to reduce
resource consumption and
pollution 111
Dislocation, economic 276
Disney, Walt 288
Distance
walking 53, 55, 57
District
advantages of distinct 32, 144
circular 144
diameter of 136, 147
distinct character of each 154, 261
graduated density of 144
granularity of 150
importance of individual character 144
in carfree cities 143
number of in carfree city 134
number of residents in 145
number of workplaces in 145
outer, increased diameter of 136
population density of 147
provision of basic services in 144
radial street pattern in 144
reasons for radial design of 145
reference 144–145
compared to other urban forms 147
variations on 149
Doge's Palace 48
Donkey, electric 293
Door
garage 50
speed of opening 95
Downtown 56
commercial center 62
demolition of in Europe 65
Driver, isolation of 73
Dwell time
defined 94
minimizing 94
Dwelling, demolition of 275

E

Earth's ecosystem 53
Ecology, global crisis affecting 279
Economics
    Keynesian
        and economic stability 111
        limitations of 111
Economy
    sustainable 10
Economy, diverse, requirements to
        achieve 126
Ecosystem 17
Elderly, dangers of continuing to drive 281
Electricity, stationary generation of 84
Elevator
    and disabled people 46
    and freight handling 209
    effect of on social fabric 58
    effect on building heights 56
    effect on urban form 58
Emergency
    personal 189
    public 189
Emergency vehicle, speed of 175
Energy
    cogeneration 116
    continuing supply of 295
    efficiency, by mode 105
    efficient use of
        and competitive position 277
        requirements for 126
    from nuclear fusion 109
    from solar sources 109
    geothermal 115
    hydrogen
        economies based on 116
        in sustainable economies 117
    rationing of 117
    renewable 109
    storage of 113
    sustainable 113, 280
    wind 114
Engine, internal combustion 106
England 54
Enterprise, small 51
Environment, damage to 18
EuroCity 280
Europe
    acceptance of cars in 65
    ambivalence toward cars 65
    car usage in 89

closing of tram lines in 88
differences between northern and
        southern 66
    Eastern 66
    effects of railroads on 54
    electrified rail lines in 106
    introduction of cars in 59
    irregular streets in 153
    northern 280
    preservation of urban qualities in 10
    public safety in 99
    road networks in 87
European Union, government installations
        of 280
European Youth for Action 232
EuroTram 95, 97
Exercise 42

F

Falsework, defined 180
Family, low-income, advantages of carfree
        cities for 284
FAR
    and buildings 161
    and carfree city 255
    and connected buildings 166
    and reference design 260
    calculations relating to 248
    defined 36
    limited by low-rise buildings 162
    need for high 149, 157
    need to achieve specified level 251
    of carfree blocks 159
    of reference block 155–156
    of reference district 144
    of San Marco district 262
    of suburban development 63
    of US suburbs 157
    of various types of development 156
Fare
    cost of collection of 99
    delays caused by collection of 99
    exact change, cause of exasperation 99
    on public transport, need for elimination
        of 99
Fare recovery ratio 99
Florida 244, 281
Food
    distribution of 217
    transport of 110

bulk products 111
Ford, Henry 8, 87
Form
    urban 37, 53–54
        effect of on travel time 38
        history of 55
Forum Vauban 234
France 66, 89, 280
Freiburg, Germany 27, 233
    carfree development in 234
Freight
    air, containers used for 198
    alternatives to metro-freight 203
    and bar codes 218
    and need for service vehicles 210
    and street space required 196
    between adjacent districts 207
    between districts in carfree cities 207
    break-bulk, defined 197
    building materials 211
    classes of 196
    concrete, delivery of 212
    consolidation of 218
    costs of excessive handling 195
    dedicated system
        costs of 196
    delivery
        consumers as freight forwarders 13
        in cities 25
    delivery by bicycle 208
    delivery by boat 47
    delivery in a carfree New York 273
    delivery of by water 269, 271
    delivery of full containers 205
        off metro-freight line 206
    delivery of in prototype districts 263
    delivery of over tram tracks 203
    delivery of packages 206
    delivery of to narrow streets 206
    delivery of using carts 195
    delivery over metro tracks 203
    delivery within districts 208
    district depots 199
    electric vans for delivery of 195
    external 205
    heavy, within a district 209
    in bike-centric carfree city 293
    in carfree cities 195
    intermodal facilities and 199
    internal 206
    local delivery 13, 47
        by stores 210

moving house, use of standard shipping
    containers 212
overhead delivery of 204
package express 47
packages 218
    and use of district depots 218
personal 188, 209
    aboard trams and metros 218
    and compromises with convenience
        in carfree cities 219
    transshipment area 218
sidings for delivery of 264
sorting, and automation of 218
standards of service 199
tram 204
transshipment of 47, 293
trash 211
tube delivery systems 205
urgent 210
utility areas and 196
very low-speed delivery vehicles 195
warehousing of 216
waterborne 105–106, 220
Freight interchange facility 203
Fuel, fossil, supplies of 109
Funding, for development of carfree
        prototypes 279
Funds, Federal, influence of on
        development 60

G

Garage
    connections to highway system 193
    individual 266
    location of 56, 217
Garden Cities 148, 249
Garden, in carfree cities 140
Gas
    greenhouse 110, 279
    natural
        production of from wastes 115
        use during transition to sustainable
            economies 110
        use of to produce hydrogen 116
Gasoline, price of 60
Germany 280
    carfree areas in 233
Ghetto 61, 283
Giudecca district, Venice 260, 262

Global warming
    and Kyoto Accords 110
    as externalized cost 40
    as impetus for carfree development 276
    cars as cause of 79
    cataclysm caused by 11
    effects of energy efficiency on 105
    influence of on local economies 13
    trucks as cause of 47
Grade separation
    explained 93
    illustrated 93
    need for 91
    need for in automated systems 182
Gradient, intimacy 170
Granny flat 283
Gravity 36
Green
    accessible, and reference design 254
    and reference design 252
Green area
    See Park
Green Heart, of the Netherlands 241
Greenbelt
    regulation of 242
    uses of 242
Greenpeace 114
Grote Markt, Groningen, Netherlands 233
Growth, suburban 60

H

Hackney, Rod 250
Hall, Peter 239
Halt
    See Stop
Hamburg, Germany, Saarlandstraße 235
Hand cart
    See Cart
Hasselt, Belgium 99
Havana 235, 279
Hazard
    fire 229
    traffic 61
Headway, defined 92
Heating, solar 115
Highway
    capacity of traffic lanes 39
    cost of new 78
    effects of on cities 25

Interstate system of 8, 28, 88
    maintenance costs of 40
    relationship between speed and
        capacity 77
    underground 84
    US Interstate system 279
    See also Road
Hill, effects of on public transport
        operations 269
Hollywood Freeway, Los Angeles 84
Holtzclaw, John 81
Homeless 43
Hong Kong 27
Horse 55–56
    See also Animal, draft
Hotel, provision of access to 192
House
    side-porch 171
    single-family
        at higher density 139
        in carfree cities 170
    snout 61
Housing 50
    above retail stores 283
    affordable 283
    carfree, prototypes 233
    dearth of low-cost in USA 282
    decline in value of 276
    duplex 171
        advantages of 139
    inexpensive 283
    mother-in-law 276
    need for variety in 163
    owner-occupied 284
    public, general failure of 282
    suburban 8
    traditional Arab 156
Houston 78
Houten, the Netherlands 238, 255
Howard, Ebenezer 148, 249
Human needs 53
Human scale 10, 13, 28, 38, 56, 288
    illustrated 23, 38
    loss of in auto-centric cities 40
    need for 12
Human sounds 43
Human uses 50
Hydrogen
    production of 116
    use of in sustainable economies 110
Hydropower 113

I

Income, rising and demand for space 162
India, rate of car ownership in 240
Industry
cottage, limitations of 120
heavy, freight needs of 216
smokestack 148–149
Industry, heavy, locations for 134
Infrastructure 280
cost of 61
economies of in carfree cities 284
Inner city, damage to 61
Insulation, sound 74
Interchange
elevated, cost of constructing 295
space required by 76
Interests, road 62
Isolation
acoustic 230
of non-drivers 73
social 51
of elderly 281

J

Jacobs, Jane 21, 148, 155, 253
and mixed uses 148
and small blocks 155
Japan 280
rail service in 89
Jeanneret, Charles-Edouard
See Corbusier, Le
Jerk, limitations on 94

K

Keynes, John Maynard 111
Krier, Léon 7, 251, 258–259
Kunstler, James Howard 7, 62

L

Land
amount required 54
area required by metro 58
area required by suburbs 63
unbundling of rights in 243
Land grant 282

Lane
capacity of 76
travel, separation of 295
Le Corbusier
See Corbusier, Le
Leaders, isolation of 24
Leidseplein, Amsterdam 255
Lending, in downtown areas 60
Lerner, Jaime 101
Life
city, deterioration of 9
civic 72
importance of 15
in carfree cities 225
quality of 31, 127
in carfree cities 285
in Venice 52
street 38, 49, 57, 64
urban, deterioration of in the USA 11
Lift
See Elevator
Limit, four-story 165
and reference design 253
Lisbon 100
Living, standard of 8, 37
Load factor and energy efficiency 105
Loading dock 199
Lobe
alternative designs for 136
in carfree cities 133
London 12, 255
influence of canals on growth of 54
underground 58
Los Angeles 31, 41, 118, 263
area devoted to cars in 78
as auto-centric city 22, 64
contrasted with Tokyo 237
contrasted with Venice 37, 41, 52
public transport in 275
redeveloping as a carfree city 275
LRV
See Tram
Luggage, importance of handling 100
Luxembourg 280
Lyon Protocol 244–245
Lyon, France 93, 232, 244–245, 269

M

Macclesfield, England 250
Madrid 72

Magic 288
as shared civic responsibility 288
need for in human environments 287
Main street 10
Mall
shopping, suburban 62–63
strip 12, 63, 277
absence of in carfree cities 162
transit 27
reasons for failure of some 233
Manhattan 27
See also New York City
Maquette 257
depicting prototype carfree district 259
errors in 260
illustrated 247
scale of 259
Marin County, California 243
Markermeer, the Netherlands 280
Martini, Franceso di Giorgi 151
Measurement
of quality of life 37
units of 36
Megacity
problems with 236
Tokyo as 236
Metro 46
absence of weather-related delays 181
access to by disabled 182
Amsterdam 271
application of in carfree cities 179
automated 182
capacity of 19
capacity of in carfree cities 177, 181
close-loop arrangement of 134
construction of 182
construction of in Los Angeles 275
costs of 105
construction 180
elevated 93
experience with 179
first development of 58
in carfree cities 173
interlocking signal systems and 184
mezzanine levels in 181–182
Moscow 66
multiple entrances to 181
New York, additional lines needed 273
personal freight aboard 218
platform arrangement in 182
security in 182
speed of 94, 179

Stockholm 232
storage of extra trains 220
strikes affecting 182
various names for 58
Metro-freight 269, 271
alternatives to 203
amount of direct access to 201
and compatibility with standardized
shipping containers 200
and use of roller frames with 202
arrangement of routes 199
capacity of 200
container interchange facilities 200
cost advantages of 231
costs of 200
defined 196
energy consumed by 200
externalized costs of 200
freight interchange facilities and 203
in a carfree Los Angeles 275
introduction to 196
land required for 200
location of heavy shippers near 199
operation of 201
one-way 201
package express service 219
propulsion of 202
right-of-way 200
dimensions of 201
service to downtown areas 201
specialized rail vehicles for 199
storage of extra trains 220
testing concept 264
trains 202
unloading of 202
use of to move small vehicles 211
Mexico City 236, 285
metro 89
Milton Keynes, United Kingdom 238
Mobility, excessive rates of 11
Mode of transport 54
Model, spreadsheet 247
Modernism 27
Montezuma Hills, California 241
Montréal 139
Moscow 96, 98
Motorcade, replacement for 190
Motorcycle 75
Movement, anti-car 232
Moving
and shipping containers 231
in carfree cities 170, 212

N

Nashville, Tennessee 11
National automobile slum 9, 15
Nations
developed, need to lead in developing
carfree cities 284
developing 66
Neighborhood
demolition of for roads 64
lilong 27
prototype carfree, population of 263
See also Community
See also District
Netherlands 280
freedom from geographic constraints in
136
wind energy production in 114
Network, compact 95
New Delhi 238, 241
New Urbanism 15, 169, 227, 242, 283, 285
New York City 12, 22, 58
block size in 155
crime in 99
early suburbs of 56
grid layout of 153
high density in 263
Manhattan as carfree city 273
metro, influence of on population 59
personal safety in 98
rail systems in 64
separation of uses in 137
skyscrapers in 58
streetcars in 88
suburbs of 59
tenements in 228
use of hand carts in 209
NIMBY 75
Noise
absence of from underground rail lines
106
adverse effects of 67
and acoustic insulation 230
and isolation of buildings 165, 230
as externalized cost 40
caused by cars 9, 43, 66, 72
caused by dogs 230
caused by highways 75
control of 230
control of in carfree cities 229
effects of on livability 30, 74
from buses 185

problem of amplified music 230
transmission of between floors 164, 231
North America
cities during colonial times 55
effects of railroads on development in
54
low density habitation of 118
urban renaissance in 285
Not in my back yard 75
Nuclear fission 113
Nuclear fusion 113

O

Oakland, California 56, 73, 287
Office, provision of space for small 169
Oil
See Petroleum
Open space
See Park
Opinion, public 232
Overcrowding, and disease 228

P

Package
consolidation facility for 218, 264
delivery of 218
express delivery of 218, 231
See also Freight
Paris 288
and Corbusier, Le 30
density of central city 147
early level of car usage in 240
first-class metro cars in 190
human density of, compared 229
quality of public transport in 90
suburbs of 66
Park
around districts 144
in Venice 42
locations for 110
need for nearby 38, 127, 252, 254
regulation of open space 261
reversion of urban areas to 275
walking times to 140
Parking
as insoluble problem 48
as ugly feature 49, 62
at edge of carfree cities 217, 226

costs of 82
demolition to provide additional 271
free 9
integration of into buildings 43
land required by 45, 50, 54, 63
multilevel garages 76
not allowed in district centers 267
number of spaces required 76
peripheral 266
shortage of 50
underground 271
PATH 98
Pathway, redundant 156
Pattern language 251
  applicability of to carfree cities 252
  supposed shortcomings of 252
PCC streetcar 94, 106
Pedestrian
  in carfree cities, rights of 175
  intimidation of 40
  priority for 38
Pedicab 189
People mover 101–102, 265
  See also PRT
People Pods 187
Personal rapid transit 103, 187
Perugia, Italy 11
Petroleum
  effects of price increases on global
        economy 12
  exhaustion of supplies 14, 80–81, 279
  price increase 81
  rate of new discoveries 81
  rising demand for 80
Philadelphia 55, 58, 263
Phoenix 64, 118, 237, 275, 281
Photovoltaic cell 113
Piazza San Marco 21, 44, 254
Place
  need for high 166
  sense of 57
Platform
  advantages of dual 182
  importance of level-loading 95
  level-loading 184
Plot ratio, defined 36
Polder 123
Policy support 242
Pollution 78
  air
    and quality of life 38, 67
    as externalized cost 40

by mode 79
caused by cars 69, 78–79
caused by trucks 47, 79
in auto-centric cities 64
in carfree auto-centric cities 295
in Europe 66
in Los Angeles 46
in Mexico City 285
relation of to energy consumption
        106
of land and water
  by cars 79
urban 280
Population
  decline of in auto-centric cities 55
  density of 55
  of reference design 132
Porch 56, 171
Port Elizabeth 273
Port Newark 273
Positive outdoor space 159
Poundbury, United Kingdom 258
Power
  motive 84
  overhead 202
Preservation, historic 30, 277
Prince of Wales 258
Privacy, use of curtains to assure 262
Procession, Sunday 49
Project, demonstration 226
PRT
  and direct routing 187
  application of in carfree cities 179, 187
  See also People mover
Pruitt-Igoe housing project, demolition of
        250
Pumped storage 113
Pushcart, use of aboard trains 100

Q

Queens, New York City 59

R

Radburn, New Jersey 56
Rail
  adequacy of for carfree cities 173
  as urban transport system 64
  capacity of 54

connection of carfree cities to national
        network 219
durability of infrastructure 89
electrification of, effects on air pollution
        106
energy consumption of 118
freight 47
high-speed systems 191
improvements in, 1850–1935 25
route network of 60
Rail system
  advantages of 90
    land use 90
  and human density 90
  competition of cars with 87
  cost of 104
    strikes 104
  energy consumed by 91
  improving speed of 93
  limitations of 90
    avoiding 91
  need for priority over cars 93
  needed improvements 107
  new attitudes needed 92
  profitability of 85
  quality of service of 90
  route inflexibility of 91
  speed of 91
  underground 90
Railroad
  and monopolies 86
  as herald of industrialism 8
  decline of 87
  invention of 54
  regulation of 86
  safety of 70
  transcontinental 282
  unpopularity of 86
Rapid Transit
  See Transport, public
Rationing of resource and pollution 112
Real estate, suburban, falling value 283
Recycling 109
Red Cars 46
Redevelopment
  contrasted to demolition 250
  denser 277
Redundancy, in public transport 96
Register, Richard 251
Rehabilitation, of urban areas 250
Reliability, of public transport, importance
        of improving 96

Research & development, need for early
    beginning 226
Research, environmental 280
Resistance, rolling 105
Resistance, wind 105
Resources
    consumption of 80
    efficient use of 126
Restaurant 43, 45
    odor problems of 229
    space requirements of 169
Retirees 281
Rickshaw, bicycle 189
Ridership, declines in 88
Right-of-way
    need for grade separation of 93
    underground 84
Risemberg, Richard 41
Riva degli Schiavone, Venice 48
Road
    capacity of 54
    connection of carfree cities to 219
    construction of in Europe 65
    poor condition of 87
    See also Highway
Road Gang, the 87, 100
    suppression of trams by 88
Road rage 71, 98
Roller frame
    defined 202
    loading of onto metro-freighter 202
    speed of 202
Rome 167
Roof, use of 169

S

Sacramento 184
Safety
    enforcement of 83
    of driving 98
    of transport, by mode 70
    personal, in public spaces 98
San Diego 184
San Francisco 7, 22, 56, 97–98, 106, 243,
    257, 287
San Marco district
    FAR of 262
    width of streets in 262
São Paulo 236, 285
Savannah, Georgia 62

School, need to decentralize 12
Scooter, motor 75
Sewage, treatment of 217
Shanghai 27, 236
Shopping 51
    effects of on travel patterns 11
Shopping center 8, 12, 43, 277
Siding, freight 264
Sign 7, 38, 44, 261
Simulation, 3-D 259
Simulation, computer 247
Singapore 280
Site, building, sale of 277
Siting, of various uses 217
Sitte, Camillo 167
Skyscraper 27, 32, 58
    See also Building, tall
Social conditions, decay of 63
Social encounter, casual 55
Society, sustainable, plans for 110
Soleri, Paolo 248
Sottoportego 256
    defined 159
Sounds, harmonious in cities 288
Soviet Bloc, use of trams in 66
Soviet Union 89
Space
    allocation of in carfree cities 157
    bicycling, provision of adequate for 140
    ground-floor commercial 168
    negative 257
    positive 256
    public 7, 54
    required by cars & trucks 76, 118, 271
    requirements of cars
        in auto-centric cities 78
    rooftop 169
Speed
    maintaining high average 177
    of vehicles, in carfree cities 94, 175
Sprawl 76
    declining acceptance of 285
    economic drag of 276
    environmental consequences of 281
    stopping continued development of 276
    suburban 22, 30, 61
        as topic of discussion 29
        defined 39
Square
    central 150
        access to 158
        in each district 148

excessively large 260
    need for many small 158
    public 44
    small 254
        and reference design 254
        in districts 155
St. Louis 11, 250
Station, train, in carfree cities 192
Stockholm 232
Stop
    importance of having few 95
    interval between 57
    metro, increased density near 269
Storage, long-term 218
Store
    big box 66
    in carfree cities 168
Strada Nuova, Venice 151, 262
Strasbourg 97
Street
    city 57
    cross 273
    curved 260
    freight delivery and traffic congestion
        effects 13
    in basements 267
    in carfree, cities
        width of 157
    medieval, width of 158
    narrow 26, 49, 150, 255, 271
        capacity of in carfree cities 175
    pedestrian 255
        and reference design 255
    radial 251
        use of for deliveries 212
    radial plan for 144
    reductions in width of 275
    safety on 43
    social function of 29, 49
    tapered 260
    transport priorities on 174
    underground 267
    very narrow 157, 262
    wide
        advantages of 158
        division of 275
    width of 56
        and emergency access 157
        in cities of antiquity 151
    See also Boulevard
Streetcar
    See Tram

Strip, commercial 57
Strøget, Copenhagen 233
Style, architectural 261
Subsidy, of cars 82, 86
Suburb
    as urban form 22
    auto-centric 60, 63
        flight to 62
    depopulation of 276–277
    in Asia 66
    in Europe, density of 66
    outer, special problems with 277
    railroad 9, 56, 139
    streetcar 57
Subway
    See Metro
Sweden 280
Switzerland 225, 280
    carfree areas in 233
Sydney 65, 89

                        T

Tamarack 110
Tax
    income, treatment of home owners 60
    occupancy 199
    resource-added 112
        effects of on economy 112
    value-added 112
Taxi, slow 189
    for carfree cities 174
Technology
    advanced, need for in sustainable
        societies 120
    effects of improvements in 83
    effects of on cars and cities 69
    transport 53–54
    unfettered application of 18
Terminal
    freight 273
    intermodal 215
Tienanmen Square, Beijing 255
Tivoli Gardens, Copenhagen 288
Tokyo 232
    as megacity 137, 236
    effective 90
    rail transport in 89, 237
    use of public transport in 236
Topology
    defined 131

effects of deformation on 135
effects of geography on 136
effects of on transport efficiency 131
effects of on urban life 131
of carfree city 131
of reference design 131–132
    variations on 135
    problems caused if incorrect 134
Toronto 65
Toulouse, France 11
Town
    carfree 19
    livable 258
    new 255
    shanty, conditions in 236
Town of Mount Royal, Quebec 139
Traction, animal, problems of 59
Trade, international, declines in 120
Tradesman 211
    freight needs of 210
Trafalger Square, London 255
Traffic
    calming of 30, 82–83
    danger for children 42
    foot 255
    street, in New York City 273
    truck, in carfree cities 293
Train
    acceleration of 94
    freight, advanced design 198
    intercity 191
    noise 198
    private 190
    station, capacity of in carfree cities 192
    See also Rail, Rail system, Railroad
Tram 46, 57
    acceleration of 184
    Amsterdam 271
    application of in carfree cities 179, 183
    capacity of 183–184
    crosstown service in New York City 273
    dangers associated with 183
    demolition of 65
    effect on real estate development 57
    fast 183
    freight 204, 271, 273
        with off-rail capabilities 264
    greater frequency of service by 183
    horse-drawn 58
    improving safety of 183
    in carfree cities 173
    interurban 57

Brill Bullets 58
    speed of 58
level-loading of low-floor 184
low-quality 107
modified, as testbed for metro-freight
    development 264
PCC 106, 180
replacement of by buses 62
signaling systems and 184
speed of 183
various names for 57
weather-related delays 181
Transfer
    between tram and metro 273
    need to minimize number of 91
    single, in reference topology 132
Transit
    See Transport, public
Transport
    between cities 191
    between districts 176, 179
    bicycle
        effects of weather on 174
        in carfree cities 173
    crisis in cities 30
    direct costs of 39
    duration of waiting times 92
    effects of on quality of life 17, 37
    effects of technology on 55
    energy consumed by 78, 109
    externalized costs of 40
    for people with disabilities 174
    freight line 148
    freight, in carfree cities 128
    in carfree cities
        duration of trips 135
        on foot 135
    influence of on urban form 37, 54
    measuring effectiveness of 38
    on foot 46, 51
    passenger 46
        in a carfree Los Angeles 275
        in a carfree Manhattan 273
        in carfree cities 127, 173
    posh 97
    public 280
        and special circumstances 188
        by ferryboat 46
        capacity of in carfree cities 173
        controlling costs of 178
        deterioration of 62, 65
        difficulties in suburbs 281

direct costs of 104
disdain for 85, 228
dwell times 178
effects of cars on availability of 40
effects of no-fare systems on 178
energy efficiency of 179
exurban commuters 191
faster 91
first-class space 189
four modes compared in carfree
    cities 187
importance of convenient 96
importance of short walking
    distances to 145
improvement, difficulty of 98
improvements to 85
intensive use of 132
maintenance-related outages 178
maximum speed of 177
nearby service 95, 143
need for 24/7 service 177
need for adequate seating 100
need for excellence 173
need for personal safety 96
need for redundancy in 178
no-fare systems 181
pleasant 96
required capacity of 176
segmentation of by use 97
tolerable acceleration on 177
use of in Europe 65
use of metro in carfree cities 179
radial routes 132
rail 293
rail network 134
road network 134
road-based 64
simulation of systems 248
speed of, rail vs driving 91
stops, proximity to 217
sustainable 118, 293
tangential routes 132
types of journeys 174
urban 51
    history of 85
within districts 174
Trash 211, 213
    and recycling facilities 213
Travel, possibility for declines in 11
Trip, length of 55
Trolley
    See Tram

Truck
    damage done to roads by 88
    in Los Angeles 47
    intrusion of on city streets 196
    space required by 56
    use of in carfree cities 93, 196, 204
Trucking
    inefficiency of 88
    long-haul, prospects for continued 13

U

Underground
    See Metro
Urban planning
    approaches to 256
    as incremental process 250, 257
    coherent 256
    controls needed for effective 261
    effect of zoning regulations on 242
    failure of modern 258
    history of 248
    influence of noxious industries on 249
    of carfree cities 251, 275
    problems with 248
    rapid 258
    redevelopment of Lyon, France 269
    speed of process 257
    traditional 251
    traditional methods 258
    unique to site 256
    utility of maquettes for 259
Urbanization
    continuing 235
    coping with continuing 237
USA
    auto-centric cities in 275
    auto-centric development in 55
        economic effects of 113
    breakdown of social systems in 23, 72
    carfree districts in 233
    carfree malls in 233
    contrasted with Europe 66
    contrasted with rest of world 88
    cost of driving in 81
    decline of railroads in 86
    demographic changes in 285
    devastation of inner cities in 73
    diesel-powered trains in 106
    displacement of trains in 87
    homelessness in 283

introduction of cars in 59
loss of community in 64
mixed use development in 229
need for carfree cities in 281
political sentiments in 277
problems caused by pervasive
    suburban sprawl in 277
prohibition of mixed uses in 169
public safety in 99
quality of public transport in 97
rail systems in, profitability of 85
regulation of railroads in 86
resource consumption in 113
road deaths in 98
safety of driving in 70
shopping malls in 62
social isolation in of non-drivers 74
subsidy of highways in 104
suburban development, and gated
    communities 63
tracts of open land in 283
urban planning in 103
urban renaissance in 285
Uses
    mixed 143, 229, 252, 255
        and reference design 252
        importance of 148, 249
        prohibition of in USA 169
    noxious 229
    separation of 60, 149
    siting of in carfree cities 135
Utility area 196, 293
    and metro-freight system 215
    and parking requirements 215
    and personal freight 219
    defined 215
    demands placed on 215
    location for in prototype lobe 264
    number of in carfree cities 134, 215
    siting of 134
Utopia, automobile 7

V

Vacation and energy consumption 119
Van Popta, T. 204
Van, moving 212
Vapor, toxic 230
Variety, need for 154
Vehicle
    electric service 210

speed of 210
    taxes on 210
high-capacity 100
See also Car, Bus, Metro, PRT, Train,
    Tram
Venice 29, 33, 41
    as proof of workability of carfree cities
        26, 262
    attractiveness of 225
    building heights 262
    canals, use of for freight delivery 195
    contrasted with Los Angeles 37, 41, 52
    economy of 126
    freight in 195
    high places in 166
    human density of 228
    industry in 26
    package express companies in 231
    problems in 26
    quality of life in 17–18, 66, 287
    quaysides 261
    quiet in 74
    shutters in 262
    sottoportego in 159

squares in 254
    streets in 260, 262
    waterborne transport in 54
    width of streets in 151
Vibration 40
Vienna, Green Party and carfree
        development 234
Ville contemporaine, la 249
Ville radiuse, la 249
Virtual reality, effect of on cities 22

W

Walking speed 36
Wall, demising, defined 164
Walls, shared common 118
Warehouse, huge stores in USA seen as 13
Warren, Roxanne 103
Washington, D.C. 238–239
Water
    importance of having open 288
    treatment of 217
Wellhead 44

Wheelchair 46
Whitelegg, John 111
Wire, overhead 45
Woonerf 31
Work, scattered 252

Y

Yard
    container handling 198
    marshalling 220
    storage 215
        use of as warehouse 216
Yard crane 201
    automation of 197
    defined 197
Yosemite Valley, California 226

Z

Zermatt, Switzerland 24, 215, 225, 233
Zürich, public transport in 228

Zadelstraat, Utrecht, c.1900

Meters	Feet		Kilometers	Miles		Hectares	Acres
1	3.3		1	0.62		1	2.5
2	6.6		2	1.24		2	4.9
3	9.8		3	1.86		5	12.4
4	13.1		4	2.49		10	24.7
5	16.4		5	3.11		20	49.4
6	19.7		6	3.73		30	74.1
7	23.0		7	4.35		40	98.8
8	26.2		8	4.97		45	112
9	29.5		9	5.59		50	124
10	32.8		10	6.21		60	148
11	36.1		11	6.84			
12	39.4		12	7.46			
13	42.7		13	8.08		Kilograms	Pounds
14	45.9		14	8.70			
15	49.2		15	9.32		1	2.2
20	65.6		16	9.94		2	4.4
25	82.0					5	11
30	98.4					10	22
35	115		Square	Square		20	44
40	131		Meters	Feet		50	110
50	164					100	220
60	197		1	10.8			
70	230		5	53.8			
80	262		10	108			
90	295		20	215			
100	328		50	538			
150	492		100	1076			
200	656		200	2152			
300	984						
380	1247						
760	2494						

THE AUTHOR

J.H. Crawford was born and raised in North America. From the age of seven he lived within the orbit of New York City, except for two spells in the Town of Mount Royal, a railroad suburb of Montréal. As a youth, he traveled by train and bicycle through a Europe still relatively free of cars. He later traveled widely in North America, Asia, and Europe. He eventually settled in Amsterdam, where he makes his home today.

His university education was in the liberal arts, although he delved into science, architecture, and engineering as a youth. After taking a few years off to sail and to photograph George McGovern's 1972 run for the presidency, he went back to school for a masters in social work. For three years in the late 1970s, he provided child welfare services to families and children. During those years, he learned much about the lives of the poor and downtrodden. The grim reality of their lives made a lasting impression on him.

In 1979, as public transport ombudsman for the New Jersey Department of Transportation, a statewide bus and rail operator, he learned about most aspects of public transport operation during the investigation of customer complaints.

In the early 1980s, he consulted with resorts in coastal South Carolina. Typical of these resorts is Sea Pines, on Hilton Head Island. This planned beachfront golfing community includes a mix of houses, apartment buildings, restaurants, stores, activities, and Harbour Town, a small, dense community built around a circular boat basin dredged into the island. A quayside promenade, free of cars, surrounds the harbor. The harbor is fronted by multistory condominiums that are some of the most desirable housing on the island. In season and out, many people converge there, despite an entrance fee for nonresidents.

While working in South Carolina, he discovered Christopher Alexander's *A Pattern Language,* a work that provided the theoretical basis for understanding the popularity of partially carfree communities such as Harbour Town. He began thinking about the urban form in the context of Alexander's patterns and soon realized that high-quality urban life was impossible while cars still ruled the streets and occupied so much land.

Between 1983 and 1985, he managed projects for a robotics systems developer that specialized in the automated handling of standardized shipping containers. He saw that the universal adoption of a single standard for these containers offered an ideal method for shipping and storing freight.

Since 1985 he has taken assignments as a software developer, designer, photographer, editor, and writer.

Ordering information for *Carfree Cities* can be found on the Internet at: http://www.carfree.com/book/